eBay®
Top 100
3rd Edition

Simplified®

TIPS & TRICKS

by Julia Wilkinson

D1412510

Visual

WILEY

eBay®: Top 100 Simplified® Tips & Tricks, 3rd Edition

Published by
Wiley Publishing, Inc.
111 River Street
Hoboken, NJ 07030-5774

Published simultaneously in Canada

Copyright © 2006 by Wiley Publishing, Inc., Indianapolis, Indiana

Library of Congress Control Number: 2006922517

ISBN-13: 978-0-471-93382-3
ISBN-10: 0-471-93382-1

Manufactured in the United States of America

10 9 8 7 6 5 4 3 2 1

3K/RX/QV/QW/IN

Trademark Acknowledgments

Contact Us

For general information on our other products and services contact our Customer Care Department within the U.S. at 800-762-2974, outside the U.S. at 317-572-3993, or fax 317-572-4002.

For technical support please visit www.wiley.com/techsupport.

WILEY

Wiley Publishing, Inc.

Sales

Contact Wiley at (800) 762-2974 or fax (317) 572-4002.

PRAISE FOR VISUAL BOOKS

"I have to praise you and your company on the fine products you turn out. I have twelve Visual books in my house. They were instrumental in helping me pass a difficult computer course. Thank you for creating books that are easy to follow. Keep turning out those quality books."
Gordon Justin (Brielle, NJ)

"What fantastic teaching books you have produced! Congratulations to you and your staff. You deserve the Nobel prize in Education. Thanks for helping me understand computers."
Bruno Tonon (Melbourne, Australia)

"A Picture Is Worth A Thousand Words! If your learning method is by observing or hands-on training, this is the book for you!"
Lorri Pegan-Durastante (Wickliffe, OH)

"Over time, I have bought a number of your 'Read Less - Learn More' books. For me, they are THE way to learn anything easily. I learn easiest using your method of teaching."
José A. Mazón (Cuba, NY)

"You've got a fan for life!! Thanks so much!!"
Kevin P. Quinn (Oakland, CA)

"I have several books from the Visual series and have always found them to be valuable resources."
Stephen P. Miller (Ballston Spa, NY)

"I have several of your Visual books and they are the best I have ever used."
Stanley Clark (Crawfordville, FL)

"Like a lot of other people, I understand things best when I see them visually. Your books really make learning easy and life more fun."
John T. Frey (Cadillac, MI)

"I have quite a few of your Visual books and have been very pleased with all of them. I love the way the lessons are presented!"
Mary Jane Newman (Yorba Linda, CA)

"Thank you, thank you, thank you...for making it so easy for me to break into this high-tech world."
Gay O'Donnell (Calgary, Alberta, Canada)

"I write to extend my thanks and appreciation for your books. They are clear, easy to follow, and straight to the point. Keep up the good work! I bought several of your books and they are just right! No regrets! I will always buy your books because they are the best."
Seward Kollie (Dakar, Senegal)

"I would like to take this time to thank you and your company for producing great and easy-to-learn products. I bought two of your books from a local bookstore, and it was the best investment I've ever made! Thank you for thinking of us ordinary people."
Jeff Eastman (West Des Moines, IA)

"Compliments to the chef!! Your books are extraordinary! Or, simply put, extra-ordinary, meaning way above the rest! THANKYOU THANKYOU THANKYOU! I buy them for friends, family, and colleagues."
Christine J. Manfrin (Castle Rock, CO)

CREDITS

Project Editor
Leslie Joseph

Acquisitions Editor
Jody Lefevere

Product Development Supervisor
Courtney Allen

Copy Editor
Marylouise Wiack

Technical Editor
Kerwin McKenzie

Editorial Manager
Robyn Siesky

Business Manager
Amy Knies

Special Help
Sarah Hellert
Barb Moore

Manufacturing
Allan Conley
Linda Cook
Paul Gilchrist
Jennifer Guynn

Indexer
Sherry Massey

Book Design
Kathie Rickard

Production Coordinators
Adrienne Martinez
Jennifer Theriot

Layout
Elizabeth Brooks
Jennifer Click
Amanda Spagnuolo

Screen Artist
Jill A. Proll

Illustrators
Ronda David-Burroughs
Cheryl Grubbs

Proofreader
Sossity R. Smith

Quality Control
John Greenough
Joe Niesen
Brian H. Walls

**Vice President and Executive
Group Publisher**
Richard Swadley

Vice President and Publisher
Barry Pruett

Composition Director
Debbie Stailey

ACKNOWLEDGMENTS

Thanks to my husband, Nick Gallagher, for his support; and to my kids, Lindsay and Kyle, for understanding why I didn't help as much with homework during this book. I'd also like to thank the folks at Wiley: Project Editor Leslie Joseph, for her friendly and helpful expertise; Editor Sarah Hellert, for her guidance; Acquisitions Editor Jody Lefevere, for her continued faith in me; Copy Editor Marylouise Wiack, for her thoroughness, as always; and Technical Editor Kerwin McKenzie, who never misses a beat and is nice, to boot. A big thanks, also, to Ina Steiner for her continued help and support, and David Steiner for putting up with all my questions. I'd also like to express my appreciation to Thom Downing and Rebecca Thomas for helping out in a pinch.

How To Use This Book

eBay®: Top 100 Simplified® Tips & Tricks, 3rd Edition includes 120 tasks that reveal cool secrets, teach timesaving tricks, and explain great tips guaranteed to make you more productive with eBay. The easy-to-use layout lets you work through all the tasks from beginning to end or jump in at random.

Who is this book for?

You already know eBay basics. Now you'd like to go beyond, with shortcuts, tricks and tips that let you work smarter and faster. And because you learn more easily when someone *shows* you how, this is the book for you.

Conventions Used In This Book

❶ Steps

This book uses step-by-step instructions to guide you easily through each task. Numbered callouts on every screen shot show you exactly how to perform each task, step by step.

❷ Tips

Practical tips provide insights to save you time and trouble, caution you about hazards to avoid, and reveal how to do things in eBay that you never thought possible!

❸ Task Numbers

Task numbers from 1 to 120 indicate which lesson you are working on.

❹ Difficulty Levels

For quick reference, these symbols mark the difficulty level of each task.

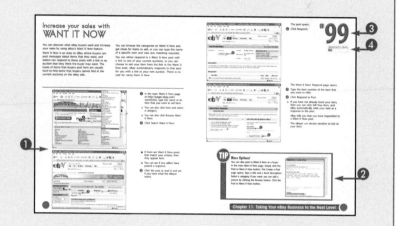

DIFFICULTY LEVEL — Demonstrates a new spin on a common task

DIFFICULTY LEVEL — Introduces a new skill or a new task

DIFFICULTY LEVEL — Combines multiple skills requiring in-depth knowledge

DIFFICULTY LEVEL — Requires extensive skill and may involve other technologies

Table of Contents

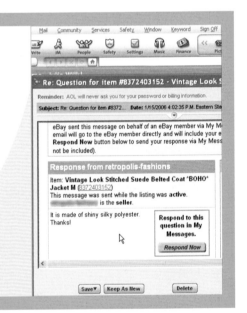

3 Improving Your Bidding and Buying Strategies

4 Paying for Items Painlessly

Table of Contents

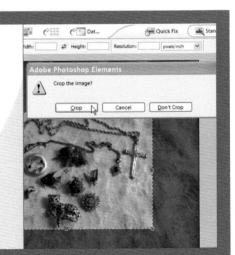

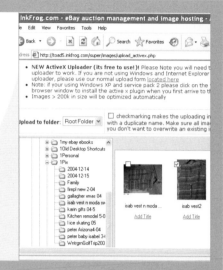

Table of Contents

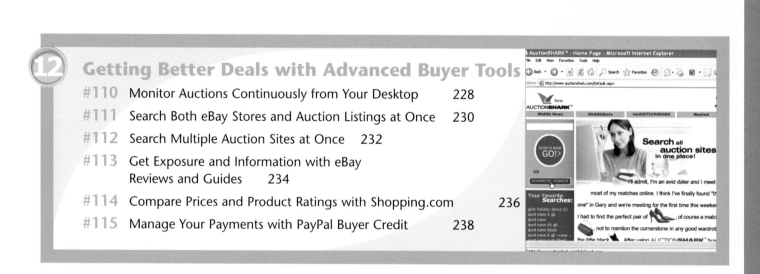

Table of Contents

Smart Searching on eBay

With millions of items for sale on eBay, and more appearing every day, finding what you want can be very time-consuming. Good search skills can help you to find bargains and save time.

Although you can sort through listings using the eBay Browse feature, the huge number of items in many categories can be overwhelming. Because of this, many people prefer to use searches rather than to browse on eBay.

You can use some tips and tricks to make your searches more effective. The eBay search pages feature different parameters that narrow down your hunt for a specific type of item, and you can even combine browsing and searching as a search strategy.

In addition to eBay's search features, you can use third-party tools such as timeBLASTER, to save time and more easily narrow down the items that you seek among the millions of eBay listings. For information about using timeBLASTER to search both eBay Stores and regular auction listings at once, see Task #111.

You can benefit from eBay's search features as both a buyer and a seller. As a buyer, you can use search tricks, such as searching for listings with typos and transpositions, to find items that other buyers may overlook. As a seller, you can use parameters, such as Completed Items only, to research items that are similar to those that you sell. Because eBay shoppers expect good deals, it is critical to know what kind of sales prices you can expect for your items. As a result, you know what you can afford to spend on inventory and still make a reasonable profit.

Top 100

Expand your
SEARCH DEPTH

You can increase the number of search hits that you receive by looking for items by both title and description. The Search title and description option on the eBay Basic Search tab allows you to retrieve items that contain keywords in both the item description and the item title.

If you search using titles only, then you may miss a large percentage of the available items. For example, in one search for blue Wedgwood — a popular type of collectible china — with the title and description option activated, the search results produced 50

items. A similar search using the titles-only option resulted in only 19 items, missing more than half of the available items.

You may miss items when you use the titles-only search because sellers do not always include the keywords that you expect in their titles. This occurs when sellers do not have enough space to fully describe their item in the title, do not choose the most appropriate words, or have several ways to describe the item.

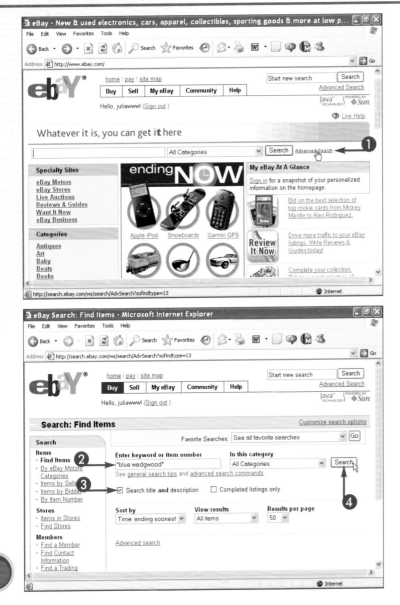

① In the main eBay home page, click the Advanced Search link.

The Search page appears.

② Type the keywords that describe the item you want, leaving spaces between each keyword, and placing quotation marks around all of the words.

③ Click to select the Search title and description option.

④ Click Search.

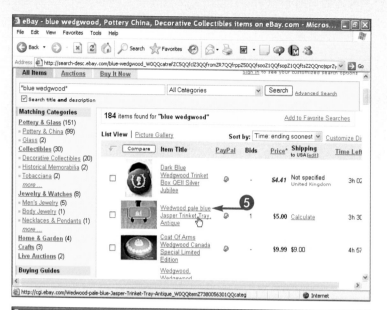

eBay retrieves and displays all items with titles or item descriptions that contain your keywords.

⑤ Click a listing.

DIFFICULTY LEVEL

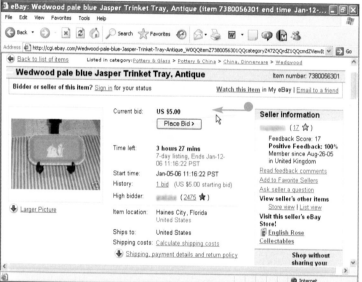

The details page appears for the listing.

● The page contains information that includes the item's current bid, the time left in the auction, how many bids the item has received, and the identity of the current high bidder.

TIPS

Buyer Beware!

Carefully read the descriptions of items on which you intend to bid. Although your keywords may appear in an item description, you may not want the item. For example, the parameters "blue Wedgwood" may return an ottoman of blue Wedgwood color, as well as blue Wedgwood china.

Did You Know?

You can also access the Advanced Search page by clicking the Advanced Search link on the upper right of the eBay home page, below and to the right of the Start new search field. If you want to perform only a simple title search, then you can type your search words into the text box on the main eBay home page, to the left of the All Categories drop-down box; or into the text box above the Advanced Search link.

Perform an
ADVANCED SEARCH

You can perform a more powerful search by using eBay's Advanced Search feature, which contains many parameters that you can use to narrow down your search.

Although you can combine some of these parameters to optimize your search, using too many of them together may severely limit your search results. For this reason, it is important to understand how each option can benefit you.

The Exclude these words text box allows you to eliminate certain keywords from the search. For example, if you know that you want metal and not wooden toy trains, then you can type **wooden** in this text box.

The Show only Buy It Now Items option displays items for immediate purchase, and is especially useful if you see a bargain. For more on this feature, see Tasks #9 and #43.

The Show only Gift Items option yields listings that the sellers designate as gifts. In some cases, the seller may even offer gift wrapping and shipping to the gift recipient.

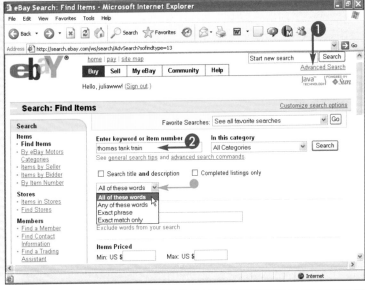

① In the eBay home page, click the Advanced Search link.

The Advanced Search page appears.

② Type the word or phrase for the item that you want to find.

● You can click here and select a search option.

③ Type the word or words that you want to exclude.

● You can type a minimum and a maximum price.

● You can select a From Sellers option.

● You can select a Location option.

You may need to scroll your screen to view all of the options.

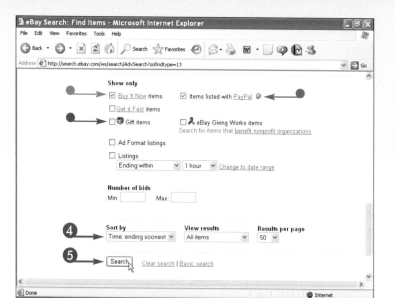

2

DIFFICULTY LEVEL

● You can select the Show only Buy It Now items option to show items for immediate purchase.

● You can click the Show only Gift items option.

● You can select the Show only Items listed with PayPal option.

④ Select a Sort by option.

You may need to scroll your screen.

⑤ Click Search.

The search results appear.

This example lists all Buy It Now, non-wooden Thomas Tank train items that are payable by PayPal, with auctions that end first at the top of the list.

More Options!

When you select the Completed listings only option, you receive hits for auctions that have ended. This is useful when you want to research how past items have sold. For more information on this option, see Task #3.

More Options!

In the Sort by list, you can select these options: the Time: ending soonest option lists auctions that are about to end first; the Time: newly listed option displays auctions that have just gone live first, followed by those that are about to end; the Price: lowest first option shows items from the cheapest to the most expensive; the Price: highest first option shows items from the most expensive to the cheapest. You can also choose an option to sort by distance and payment type.

FIND MARKET PRICES
for completed items

You can use the Completed listings only option in the Advanced Search page to research the final selling prices for different types of items from the last two weeks. As a buyer, this information gives you an idea of what to expect as a final bid. As a seller, this information allows you to estimate what market prices you can expect for your own, similar items. Knowing an item's recent market price helps you to avoid buying inventory at a price that is too high to yield a profit.

To see what has sold for the most and least money, you can use the Sort by menu to select either the Price: highest first or Price: lowest first option. Viewing the highest prices shows you the items that can make you the most money; viewing the lowest prices shows you what items to avoid selling.

Keep in mind that items that do not meet their reserve, or asking prices, are not necessarily good reflections of a particular item's market value, nor should you use them for research purposes.

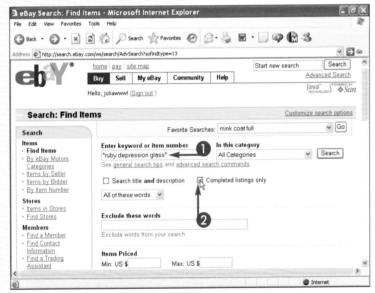

① In the Advanced Search page, type a keyword or phrase.

   Note: See Task #2 for more information on the Advanced Search page.

② Click to select the Completed listings only option.

③ Click here and select the Price: highest first option.

   You may have to scroll to see this option.

④ Click Search.

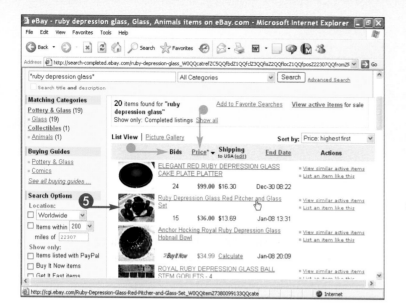

The search results appear.

● You can scan the Price column to see which items resulted in the highest prices.

● You can scan the Bids column for the highest number of bids, which indicates a popular item.

⑤ Click a listing.

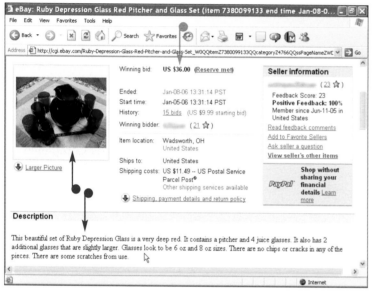

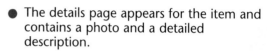

● The details page appears for the item and contains a photo and a detailed description.

You should review the listing carefully to learn why the item sold for such a high price or had the highest number of bids.

● This example shows an item that met its reserve price.

Items that do not meet the reserve price are not necessarily accurate reflections of a market price.

TIPS

Savvy eBaying!
For a thorough search, try different word combinations for items. For example, consider using the words antique glass as well as Depression glass, as different sellers may select different names or descriptions for their items.

Buyer Beware!
Various factors can influence the final sales price of an item, including condition, age, color, and season.

Buyer Beware!
Look at a variety of hits in the search returns, because the highest and lowest prices may not reflect the average sales price of a certain type of item. The Bids column on the results page shows the number of bids that the item received and indicates the level of interest in it. Lower numbers in this column usually indicate lower interest.

View what
OTHERS HAVE BOUGHT

You can use the Items by Bidder feature in the eBay search page to view what other users bid on and buy. The Items by Bidder option allows you to benefit from other people's shopping skills, because they may find a great item that you would otherwise miss. If you often bid against certain users in key categories, then you can use their user IDs in an Items by Bidder search.

On the Items by Bidder page, when you type the bidder's eBay ID, a list of the items on which that person is bidding appears. This information includes

an item number, a start and end date and time, price, title, current high bidder, and seller.

You can choose not to include completed items if you only want to see the items on which a user is currently bidding. You can also select the As high bidder only option to eliminate auctions that the user has lost. Finally, you can specify how many results display on each page: 5, 10, 25, 50, 75, 100, or 200.

1 In the eBay Search page, click the Items by Bidder link.

The Items by Bidder page appears.

2 Type the bidder's user ID.

3 Click to select whether you want to include or exclude completed listings.

● You can select either the Even if not the high bidder or As high bidder only options.

● You can click here and select the number of results that you want to see on each page.

4 Click Search.

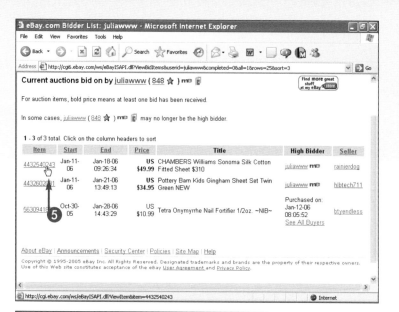

The titles appear for auctions on which the user has bid.

⑤ If eBay lists any item on which you want to bid, then click that item number.

DIFFICULTY LEVEL

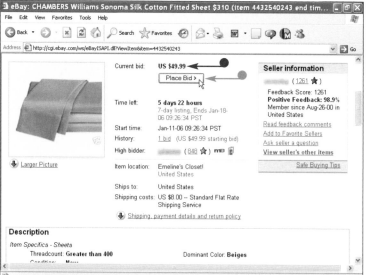

● You can view an item on which the bidder is presently bidding.

● You can click Place Bid to begin bidding.

Savvy Selling!

You can use the Items by Bidder page to learn what your customers want. For example, if you sell bubble wrap, and you see your repeat customers bidding on tape and envelopes, then you should consider adding those items to your inventory.

Did You Know?

Have you received e-mails from an eBay member who does not specify their user ID? If you have completed previous transactions with this member, then you can look up their user ID. In the Items by Bidder page, click the Find a Member link, and then type the e-mail address in the Enter User ID or email address of member text box. eBay prompts you through a security screen, where you can click Search to retrieve the user's ID.

BROWSE
to supplement your searches

You can increase your chances of finding items if you supplement your searches by browsing in the appropriate eBay category. This is because some sellers use titles or descriptions that you may not find when you perform a search.

Some eBay treasure-hunters actively use this search method to find listings where a seller has an item whose true value they do not realize. For example, one eBay browser bought an old manuscript written by a famous author, although the seller did not know that the writer of the manuscript was famous. The buyer found this manuscript by looking for clues to its origin from the seller's description.

Because eBay offers a steadily growing number of category choices, you must check similar categories to obtain a thorough search. For example, under the Jewelry and Watches category, some items make sense in both the subcategories of Loose Beads and Loose Diamonds & Gemstones. Although some sellers list items in a second category, not all sellers do. Sellers sometimes even have items that can belong in more than two categories.

1 In the eBay home page, click a main category of your choice under the Categories heading.

The list of categories appears.

2 Click a subcategory.

Because eBay can have long category lists, you may need to scroll down through the page.

You may need to click through several layers of subcategories to find the subcategory of your choice.

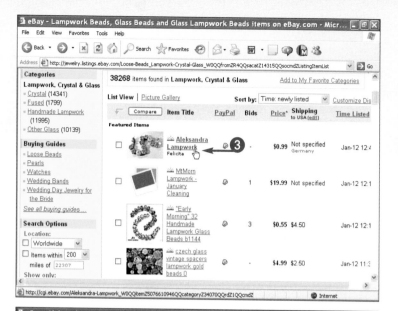

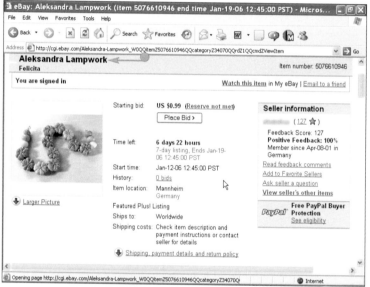

The results list appears, displaying all of the items in the category that you selected.

Review the different types of auctions that are available.

3 Click a listing.

The details page appears for the listing.

You may find an unusual item that you may otherwise not find when you do a search.

● In this example, the listing title does not contain the word bead, but is instead for lampwork, a type of bead.

More Options!

To get a quick overview of eBay's categories, click the All Categories link, located beneath the Everything Else link on the eBay home page. The All Categories link allows you to see all of the first- and second-level eBay categories on one page, which can quickly help to familiarize you with the various category options as they currently stand.

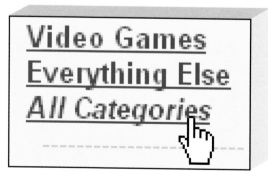

Use categories to
REFINE YOUR SEARCH

You can combine browsing and searching to narrow down your search. This technique allows you to take advantage of eBay's large category hierarchy by moving through the many category layers — sometimes referred to as *drilling down* — to access the items that you want. You may need to drill down into several subcategories before you find your item.

Combining the Search and Browse features is especially useful when you want to browse for a specific item, but do not know in which category that

item belongs. You may also find this technique useful if the item falls into several different categories. For more information on browsing, see Task #5.

You can combine the Browse and Search features by using the Matching Categories list, which appears on the left side of the page after you do a search. eBay often lists more than one category here, and presents you with a list of matching categories.

When you perform a search and then enter a matching category, eBay's search continues to filter out items according to your search words.

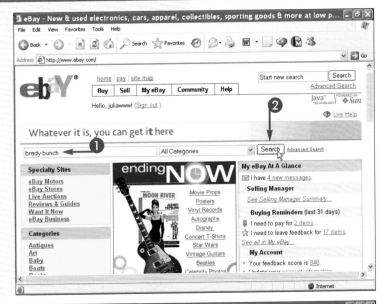

① Type a search word or phrase into an eBay Search text box.

② Click Search.

The search results appear.

● The Matching Categories pane appears on the left side of the page.

These categories vary, depending on the search words that you typed.

③ Click the category that you want.

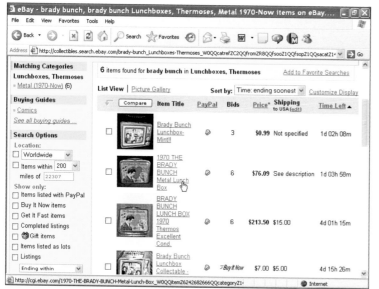

The search results appear.

eBay narrows down the Matching Categories list to smaller categories.

④ Click another category under Matching Categories.

eBay displays the search results, further narrowing down the items.

TIPS

More Options!

You can perform a search within any given category. In the eBay home page, click a top-level category. Once you drill down into a category with auction listings on the right, you can type search words into the Search text box on the upper left, and then select an option from the category drop-down list next to it.

Did You Know?

You can get information about keywords that eBay buyers and sellers use most often in the Common Keywords page, located at http://keyword-index.ebay.com/a-1.html. From there, you can browse a list of keywords, and sort them Alphabetically, by Products Only, By Category, or by Stores. If you click a link, then a list of popular keywords displays, sorted by the option of your choice.

Find
HOT ITEMS

You can read the Hot Items by Category document, located in Seller Central, to determine which items have sold well recently. eBay staff creates a list of items that are hot sellers in each category. eBay defines *hot items* as recent items whose bidding growth significantly outpaces new listings growth, or where the bid-to-item ratios are higher than other products in the same parent category.

As a seller, you can read the Hot Items by Category list to get ideas for things that you can sell to make the most money. You can put the hot items

information to work and experiment with new types of products, and see what sells.

Because the hot items list changes regularly, it is a good idea to check it frequently to get the best idea of what sells well in a particular category.

As an alternative to the steps in this task, you can also use a pay service that does the tedious work of searching for hot items for you. One service is Andale's What's Hot. To use Andale's service, go to www.andale.com.

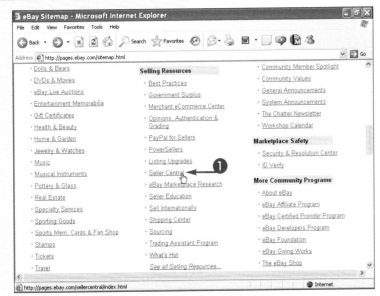

① In the eBay Site Map page, located at pages.ebay.com/sitemap.html, click the Seller Central link under Selling Resources.

The Seller Central page appears.

② Click the What's Hot link.

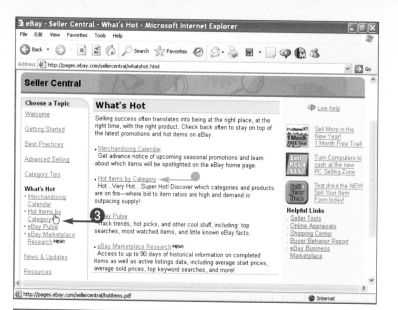

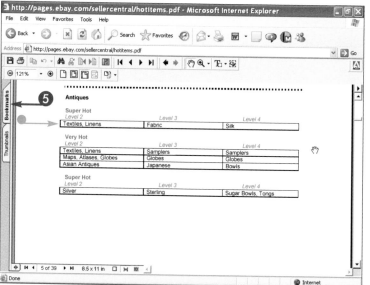

The What's Hot page appears.

③ Click the Hot Items by Category link.

You may need to scroll down to access this link.

● You can also click the Hot Items by Category link here.

The Hot Categories Report opens as an Adobe Acrobat PDF file.

If you do not already have the Adobe Acrobat Reader, then eBay may prompt you to download it.

⑤ Click the Bookmarks tab to view the report.

● You can view the Hot Products by category.

More Options!

You can get more information about what's selling well on eBay, including up to 90 days of completed items data, information on average sale prices, and charts, by using eBay's Marketplace Research feature. Prices range from a one-time, two-day usage fee of $2.99 to a Pro subscription fee of $24.99 each month.

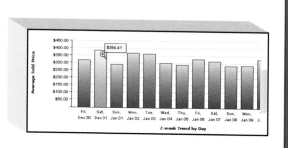

Search
WHILE YOU SLEEP

You can use eBay's My Favorite Search feature to have the system regularly scan for a certain type of item. This is a convenient and timesaving way to locate a particular item without having to perform multiple manual searches. This technique is especially useful when you are not in a hurry, and can take your time to find an item over days, weeks, or even months.

You can give the search a name. For example, if your search is for a medium-sized, black cardigan, then you can name the search black cardigan M. You can

also designate for how long you want eBay to e-mail you the daily results of the search, with options ranging from 7 days to 12 months.

You can specify whether eBay e-mails your search results using the E-mail me daily whenever there are new items option. You can also check the saved search anytime in the My Favorite Searches area located in My eBay's Favorites tab.

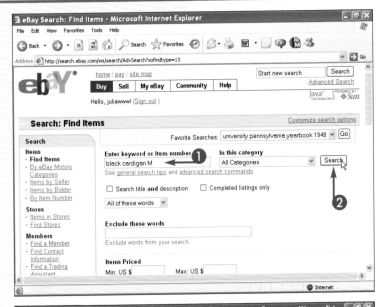

① In the eBay Search page, type a search word or phrase.

② Click Search.

The search results appear.

③ Click the Add to Favorite Searches link.

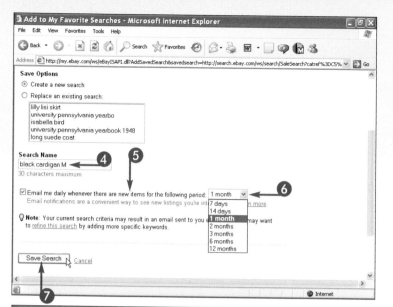

The Add to My Favorite Searches page appears.

④ Type a name for your search.

⑤ Click to select the Email me daily whenever there are new items option.

⑥ Click here and select a time frame for the search.

⑦ Click Save Search.

8

DIFFICULTY LEVEL

eBay e-mails your Favorite Search results to you.

You must sign on to your e-mail service to check your Favorite Search e-mails.

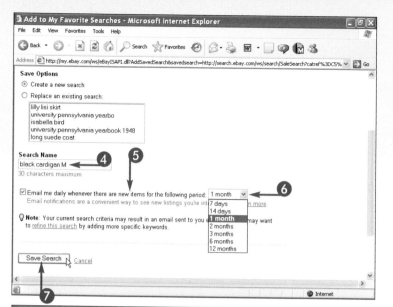

TIPS

Did You Know?

When you find the item that you want, you can delete its Favorite Search to make room for new searches. Click My eBay in the eBay home page, or any eBay page, and then click the Searches link under All Favorites. Click the option next to the name of the search, and then click Delete. You can save up to 100 searches.

More Options!

If you want to quickly and easily view new items from a preferred seller or store, then you can save them as favorites. In the My eBay page, click the Sellers link under All Favorites. Click Add new Seller or Store, and type the seller's user ID or store name. Click Continue, and then click Add to Favorites.

Find eBay's
HIDDEN GEMS

You can find great items that other eBay users may miss by searching for alternate spellings and typographic variations of words. Because many searchers overlook alternate spellings, fewer people view and bid on these listings, thus allowing you to find wonderful bargains.

For example, if you look for Lilly Pulitzer brand clothing, which tends to sell very well on eBay, then you may want to search under the spelling Lily Pulitzer, as this is a common misspelling of the brand name. Another common error that sellers make is transposing two letters. You can almost always find items with this mistake. For example, try DNKY instead of DKNY, or Evlis instead of Elvis.

As an example, a recent search on DNKY brought up 45 listings, only six of which had bids. These listings without bids give you an opportunity to find bargains. Compare that to the correct spelling, DKNY, which brought up 6,695 listings, where out of the first 50 items, 19 had bids.

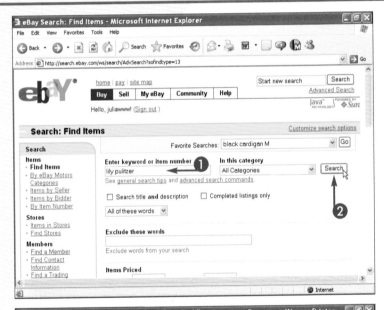

1 In the eBay Search page, type a misspelled word or phrase.

2 Click Search.

Search results appear with misspelled listings.

● eBay prompts you with alternate spellings.

3 Search through the Bids and Price columns for auctions that still have low bids and prices.

● You can click these items to investigate further and to bid.

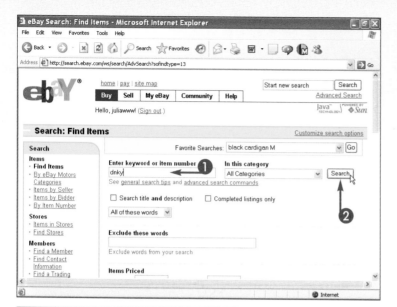

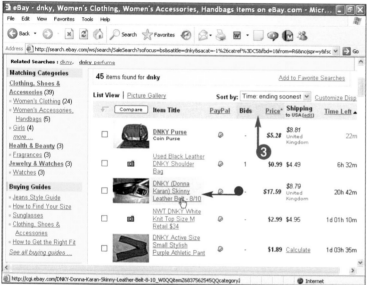

1. In the eBay Search page, type a word or acronym with transposed letters.

2. Click Search.

DIFFICULTY LEVEL

The search results appear.

3. Search through the Bids and Price columns for auctions that still have low bids and prices.

● You can click these items to investigate further and to bid.

TIPS

eBay Savvy!

A misspelled item with a Buy It Now option is great, because you can buy it immediately at a low price and prevent other typo-hunters from finding it. For more information on the Buy It Now option, see Tasks #2 and #43.

eBay Savvy!

Try searching for both newly listed and Buy It Now items to increase your chances of finding a bargain, because the good deals go quickly. For example, when you browse, look for the New Today items.

Did You Know?

When you deliberately search for items with incorrect spellings, you can ignore the eBay search engine's prompt near the top of the page that suggests alternate spellings.

CREATE PHOTO ALBUMS
of search results

Have you ever scrolled through numerous eBay listings of similar items, clicking into each listing to find the specific one that you want? You can reduce the time that you spend finding items by using a tool called timeBLASTER, which was invented by an avid stamp collector who spent long hours on eBay. With timeBLASTER, you can reduce searches that take 20 hours a week to an hour a week. timeBLASTER is also great for sellers. For example, one sports trading card dealer uses a standing timeBLASTER search to monitor market prices.

timeBLASTER automatically searches eBay, downloads the item descriptions and photos, and creates photo albums of the results by neatly lining up rows of photos and item information. Instead of scrolling through many pages of listings and clicking each auction to see photos, you can view the search results in a compact, easy-to-view format. You can also easily bid on or watch an item directly from the Photo Album page.

Before you can use timeBLASTER, you must first download and install the timeBLASTER software from the Web site, www.timeblaster.com/tbeindex.shtml.

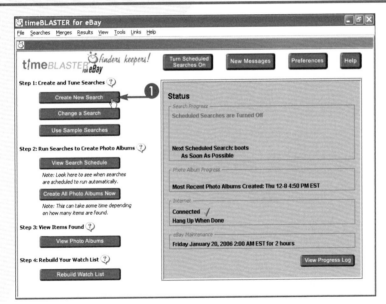

1 In the timeBLASTER main page, click Create New Search.

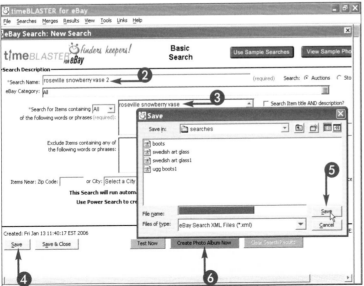

A Search Description window appears.

2 Type a name for your search.

3 Type the items for which you are searching.

4 Click Save.

5 In the Save dialog box that appears, click Save.

6 Click Create Photo Album Now.

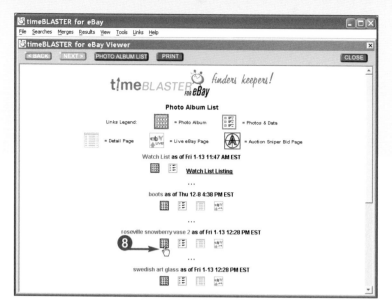

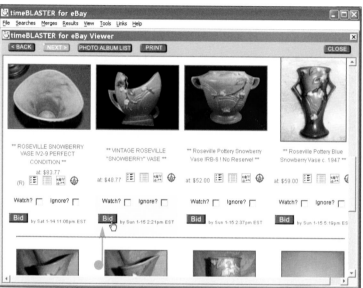

The timeBLASTER main page reappears, showing the status of the newly created search.

⑦ Click View Photo Albums.

The Photo Album List appears.

⑧ Click an icon of a photo album that you want to view.

The Photo Album appears, displaying photos and titles of multiple items on one page.

● You can click the options to watch, bid on, or ignore an item.

TIPS

Did You Know?

The timeBLASTER software for eBay is only available for Windows. You can view a free animated demonstration of how the software works on the timeBLASTER Web site. The example in the demonstration is of a search for Roseville vases, a popular collector's item. timeBLASTER offers a 30-day free trial. A one-year subscription to the service costs $39.95, and timeBLASTER pays you $4 for every friend that you refer who buys a one-year subscription.

eBay Savvy!

You can run searches automatically by clicking Turn Scheduled Searches On from the main timeBLASTER page. You can run scheduled searches at night, or at any time that is most convenient for you, so that you can do other things while the search runs.

Find it fast with eBay's
SITE MAP

An easy way to find a particular section of the eBay site is to use the site map. Because eBay can be many layers deep in some areas, the site map acts as a valuable guide, displaying the broad array of features, services, and information that are available on the eBay site, and enabling you to navigate to a particular link. The site map can save you time and frustration in trying to find a specific part of eBay, because it compactly organizes all of the eBay links on one page.

You can access the eBay site map from any eBay page through the link that appears at the top of every page.

The site map is organized as a series of links under headings that describe every area on eBay, such as Buy, Sell, Help, My eBay, and Community. In some cases, if there are many links under one section, then you can click the See all link to view links to all of the features under that section, such as See all Selling Resources under the Selling Resources heading.

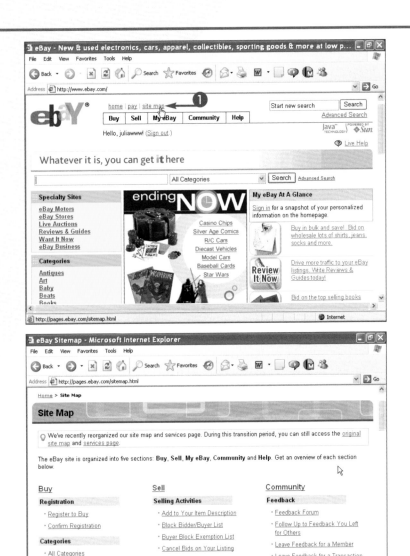

1 In the eBay home page, click the site map link.

The eBay Site Map page appears.

Links to all eBay areas appear in the lists on this page.

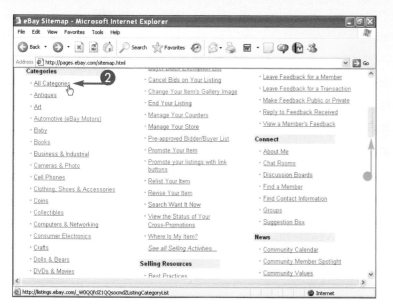

● You can scroll down to see the entire site map.

② Click a link that interests you.

This example uses the All Categories link.

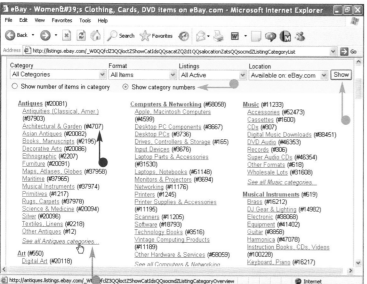

The All Categories page appears, allowing you to find an eBay area that you may not otherwise notice.

● You can click the Show category numbers option to view the category numbers, and then click Show.

● You can use the numbers in the Sell Your Item form to specify the category in which to list your item.

● You can click a See all categories link for a particular category to view all of the subcategories below it.

More Options!

If you cannot find what you need on eBay's site map, then you can search eBay's Help section. Click the Help tab, which is the top-right tab that appears in most eBay pages. You can search the help database by typing your search words in the text box at the top of the Help window, and then clicking Search Help. You can also browse a complete alphabetical list of help topics by clicking the A-Z index link in the eBay Help page window.

Did You Know?

If you still cannot find what you need using the site map or the eBay Help Center, then you can use the Contact Us link, under eBay Glossary at the upper left of the Help search page.

Chapter 2

Smart Shopping on eBay

With so much competition from other buyers and sellers on eBay, it helps to know some tricks to buy the items you want at the right time and for the right price.

You can use the Watch this item option to mark an item that you may want to buy, but do not think you can find later in the huge selection of eBay items. You can also use tools like the eBay Toolbar Alert to set up an alarm on your computer so that you know when your auctions are about to end.

To ensure that you have all of the important details that you need about an item, you can use the Ask seller a question link.

Checking a seller's feedback rating is critical to your success as a buyer. You can save time finding negative or neutral feedback with tools such as Toolhaus's Negative/Neutral Feedback checker.

To find good deals, you can look for auctions that are about to end and that have few to no bids, or you can use the Buy It Now feature when the price is right. You can also shop for items in other countries, for which you may have less competition.

Other things that you can do to save money include buying items within your own geographical area, and buying several things from the same seller to save on shipping. Remembering hidden costs such as shipping, handling, and insurance also helps you to spend your money wisely.

Top 100

WATCH AN ITEM
you want to buy

You can track items that interest you by using the Watch this item feature. When you browse through many pages of listings, you may find it confusing to go back to an earlier page and find an item that interests you. The Watch this item feature makes it very easy to keep track of all of the items that you may want to buy, because you can mark an item on which you may want to bid, and then continue to browse for similar items before you decide to bid on one of them.

You can view a complete list of all of the items that you are watching in My eBay, under the Items I'm Watching heading. The list shows you the item numbers, titles, current prices, number of bids, time left in each auction, and the sellers' user IDs. You can even bid on the item directly from the Items I'm Watching list.

Once the auctions end for the items that you are watching, you can delete them to make room for more items.

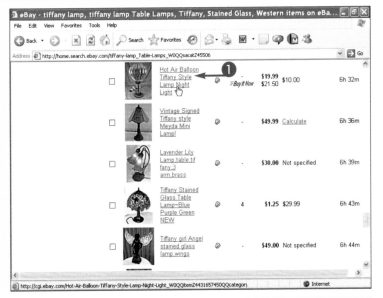

ADD AN ITEM TO YOUR WATCH LIST

❶ In a browsing or searching list, click a listing.

In this example, the item is a Tiffany-style lamp.

Note: For more on searching and browsing, see Chapter 1.

The details page appears for the listing.

● The photo and price of the item display.

● You may need to scroll down to view the item description.

❷ Click the Watch this item link.

eBay tracks the item.

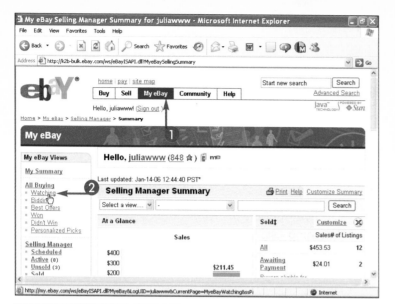

#12

DIFFICULTY LEVEL

1 From any eBay page, click My eBay.

The My eBay page opens.

2 Click the Watching link.

You can also access your My eBay watch list from the My eBay link in the listing that you add to your watch list, after you click Watch this item.

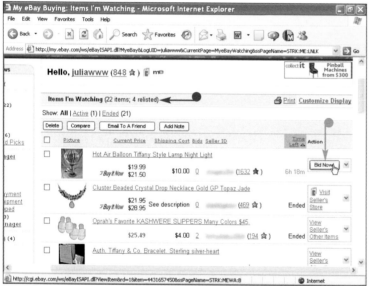

The Items I'm Watching page appears.

● You can view the items under the Items I'm Watching heading.

● You can bid on the item directly by clicking the Bid Now button.

TIPS

More Options!

For a quick, easy way to review items you want, you can use the My Recently Viewed Items or My Recent Searches features, which eBay displays at the bottom of search results and listings. Both features list the last three items you viewed or your last three searches.

Did You Know?

You can watch up to 100 items. As a reminder, eBay e-mails you a daily list of auctions that you are watching that end within 36 hours. If you do not want to receive this e-mail list, then you can go to My eBay, click the Preferences link, located beneath the My Account heading, click Edit beneath Notification Preferences, and then deselect the Watched item daily list emails option.

Ask a
SELLER A QUESTION

You can get more information about an item before you buy it by using the Ask seller a question link. Because of privacy concerns, eBay does not publish a user's e-mail address, name, address, or phone number. Therefore, this link is the only way that you can communicate directly with a seller, unless an auction is over and you win an item, at which point eBay sends your e-mail address directly to the seller.

If the seller does not include all relevant details in the auction's description, such as the measurements of an item of clothing, an item's age, or the shipping cost to your location, then this option allows you to do further research. Getting detailed and complete information on an item helps you to avoid buying something that you do not want.

eBay sends your question to the seller's e-mail address. The seller can then e-mail you back with the answer to your question. You can specify if you want to receive a copy, or cc, of the e-mail for your records.

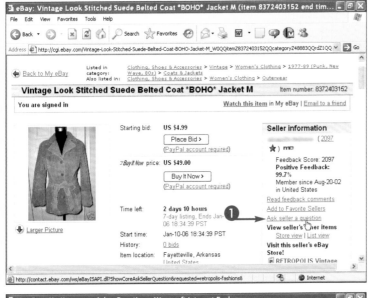

1 In an item listing, click the Ask seller a question link.

The Ask a Question page appears.

2 Type a question for the seller.

● You can select this option if you want to receive a copy of the e-mail.

3 Click Send.

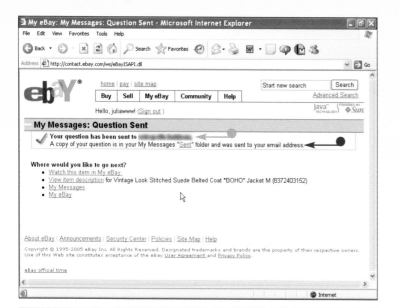

- eBay confirms that your e-mail has been sent to the seller.

- If you selected the Send a copy to my email address option on the Ask a Question screen, then eBay tells you that it was sent to your e-mail address.

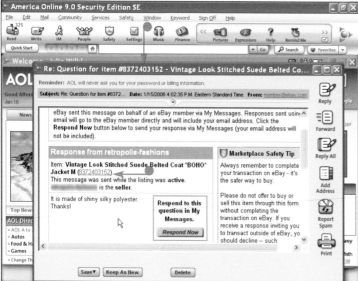

④ Launch your e-mail application and check your e-mail.

⑤ Open the e-mail from the seller.

- The item number appears in the e-mail and subject heading.

    The seller's response helps you to make a more informed decision about whether to purchase the item.

Did You Know?

You can request an eBay member's contact information during an active transaction, and in a successful closed transaction, winning bidders and sellers can request each other's contact information. Click the Advanced Search link, and then click the Find Contact Information link. Type the member's User ID and the item number of the item that you are trading with that member. Click Search. eBay tells you that it has processed your request, and e-mails you the contact information.

Caution!

It is against eBay's rules to ask a seller to sell you an item outside of eBay. Also, external transactions do not offer the same protections that eBay offers, such as buyer protection, dispute resolution, mediation, and feedback.

Save time with
FEEDBACK TOOLS

Before you bid on an item, it is critical to perform a thorough check of a seller's feedback rating to determine the seller's integrity. Located next to the seller's eBay ID, their *feedback rating* tells you how many transactions they have completed, as well as what percentage of these transactions resulted in positive comments from buyers. eBay also allows you to read a seller's feedback comments.

To save time scrolling through hundreds of feedback comments, you can download the free feedback tool at www.Toolhaus.org and view only the negative and neutral comments together on one page. You can also use the tool directly from the www.Toolhaus.org Web site. With this Negative/Neutral feedback tool, you can also see information about the auction that a comment references.

Preferably, the seller's percentage of positive feedback comments should be very high — 100 percent, or close to it. Keep in mind that even the best sellers have a few neutral or negative comments, especially if they complete numerous transactions. This is why it is important to read what those comments say.

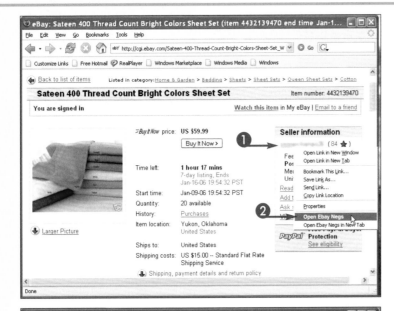

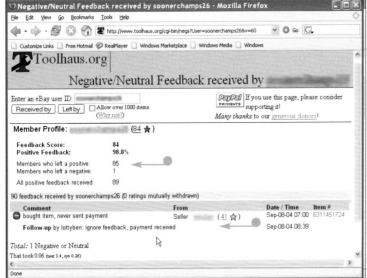

USE THE NEGATIVE/NEUTRAL FEEDBACK TOOL ON EBAY

① In an item listing, right-click the seller's feedback rating number or eBay ID.

② Click Open Ebay Negs.

Note: The steps in this section assume that you have Toolhaus's Negative/Neutral feedback tool installed.

The Toolhaus software opens.

● You can see how many positive, negative, and neutral comments the seller has.

● A list of the comment or comments appears.

This example shows a seller with a Positive feedback rating of greater than 98 percent.

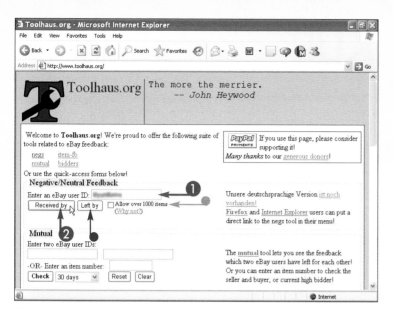

❶ In the www.toolhaus.org main page, type the eBay user ID that you want to check.

❷ Click Received by.

● You can also click Left by.

● You can choose to allow over 1,000 items.

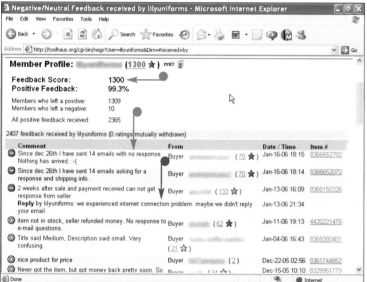

● The eBay member's feedback score appears, along with any negative or neutral comments.

● The seller's follow-up comment also appears, if applicable.

More Options!

Toolhaus offers three other ways to look up member feedback: Mutual, Item-FB, and Bidders. Mutual allows you to view the feedback that two eBayers have left for each other. Item-FB shows a member's recent feedback, as well as the items' titles. Bidders allows you to type an item number, and view the bidders for that item.

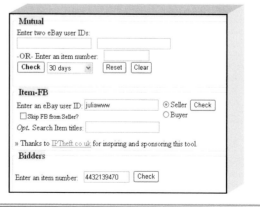

USE LOCAL PICKUP
to save shipping fees

You can save a lot of money on the shipping of heavy items if you find an eBay item that is located near where you live. You can use eBay's Location menu on the Advanced Search page to select the closest city to where you live and then perform a search. If you win the item, then you can reduce the shipping cost, or you can simply drive to the seller's location and pick up the item.

For example, if you want a bicycle and you live near the Washington, D.C., area, then you can select that city in the Items near me menu and perform a

search. If you can drive to other nearby cities to pick up an item, then you can also perform additional searches for these cities.

You should check the item's description to find out if the seller permits you to pick it up in person. If this information is not in the description, then you can use the Ask seller a question link. For more information on the Ask seller a question feature, see Task #13.

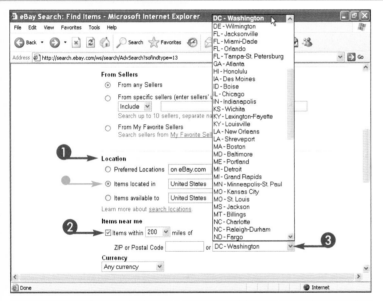

① From the eBay Advanced Search page, select a Location option.

Note: If you are accessing Advanced Search for the first time, you need to click the Advanced Search link on eBay's Advanced Search page.

● You can also select a country option here.

② Click an items within...miles option.

You can select from between 10 and 200 miles.

③ Click here and type a ZIP code or select a city.

④ Scroll the screen up to the search text box and type your search word or phrase.

● You can select a category option.

⑤ Click Search.

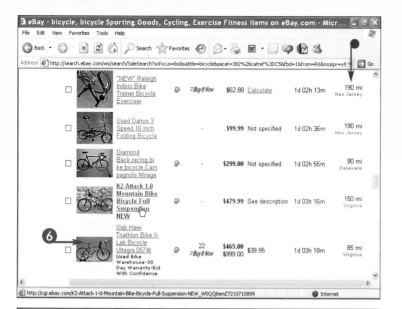

The search results appear, with a list of items located in the region that you specified.

● You can view the location of each item and how far away it is in the Distance column.

⑥ Click the item that you want to view.

A description and photo of the item appear.

● The location of the item displays.

Note: The item may actually be located in a town near the major center that you specified in your search.

You can scroll to view the Shipping and handling costs, as well as specific details about pickup and delivery.

TIPS

Buyer Beware!

Although buying a heavy item regionally on eBay often makes sense, if an item is valuable or fragile and shipping is a fraction of its cost, then sometimes you are better off searching the whole country or the world on eBay and paying for the shipping. You can use a special shipping service such as Craters and Freighters. For more about shipping large, valuable, or fragile items, see Task #87.

More Options!

If you live near more than one city, then you can perform more than one regional search in case the item you want is located in another city nearby. For example, if you live in northern Virginia, then you can search in Baltimore, Md., as well as in Washington, D.C.

Buy multiple items to
SAVE ON SHIPPING

You can save money on shipping costs by buying several items from the same seller. Because it is usually cheaper to mail two items in one envelope or box than it is to ship them separately, sellers usually offer to pass the savings to you.

Sellers often try to get you to buy more from them by offering to combine shipping costs. If you need those other items anyway, then it makes sense to buy them from the same seller and save money on postage. For example, if you need both bubble wrap and padded mailers, and the seller offers both, then

it makes sense to buy both at the same time and save money on shipping fees.

You can use the View seller's other items links under the Seller information heading to view the other items that the seller offers.

You can also search using the words "combine shipping," with the Search title and description option selected, to find auctions where sellers offer savings on shipping.

For more information on using the title and description option, see Task #2.

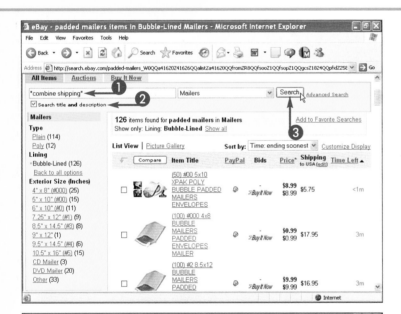

① After selecting an eBay category, type "**combine shipping**".

② Click to select the Search title and description option.

③ Click Search.

A list appears with items for which the sellers offer to combine shipping in their auction descriptions.

④ Click a listing.

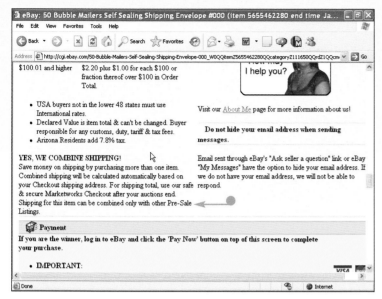

A details page appears for the listing.

● Scroll down through the auction description to confirm that the seller will combine shipping.

● You can click the View seller's other items links under the Ask seller a question link to see if the seller offers other items that you want to buy.

In this example, the seller allows you to buy multiple items to save money on shipping costs.

TIPS

eBay Savvy!

Look for opportunities to combine shipping, even on items that you do not buy regularly. Consider buying other, similar items that you need from sellers that you use regularly. If a seller does not specify whether they combine shipping, then you can use the Ask seller a question link, described in Task #13.

Did You Know?

When you buy multiple items regularly from a seller, you can add that seller as a Favorite Seller in your My eBay page to save on shipping. In the eBay home page, click My eBay, click the Sellers link, located beneath the All Favorites link, and then click Add new Seller or Store. Type the seller's user ID in the appropriate box, click Continue, then click Add to Favorites.

Find unique items in
OTHER COUNTRIES

You can shop for items from around the world by using the Location options in the eBay Advanced Search page. This is a great way to find unique items that are hard to locate in your own country.

For example, you can search for authentic Celtic jewelry by using the Items located in option under the Location heading to find items in Ireland.

If the seller does not state in the auction description that they ship to your country, then you can use the Ask seller a question link to find out if they do. For more information on the Ask seller a question feature, see Task #13.

You can also use the Items available to option to search for items that sellers ship to your country, although this usually brings up a mixture of both local and international items.

Another way to find unique items is to select All Countries/Regions from the Items available to option. However, to confirm that sellers ship their items to your country, you should check the item description for shipping details.

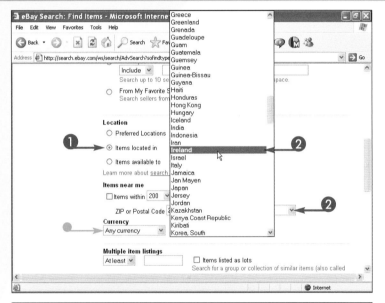

① In the eBay Advanced Search page, click to select the Items located in option.

Note: If you are accessing Advanced Search for the first time, you need to click the Advanced Search link on eBay's Advanced Search page.

You may need to scroll down the page.

② Click here and select a country.

● You can select a currency here.

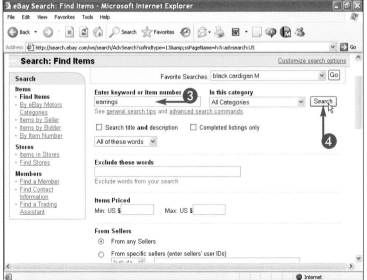

③ Type your search word or phrase.

④ Click Search.

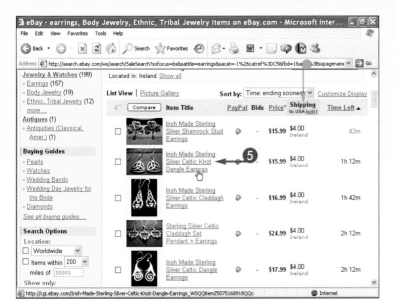

The search results appear for the list of items that are located in the country you specified.

- You can view items that will ship to the USA in this column, if it is available.

⑤ Click the item that you want to view.

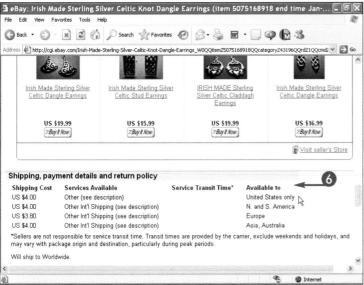

The details page appears for the listing.

⑥ View the shipping and payment details section to confirm that the seller ships to your country.

You may need to scroll down to see the shipping and payment details.

TIPS

More Options!

Another way to search for items in different countries is to go directly to the international eBay site of a particular country, using that country's domain name. For example, to look for items in Germany, you can go to www.ebay.de. For a list of eBay's worldwide sites, with links to each, scroll to the bottom of the eBay home page and look for the links to other countries' sites. However, remember that these sites appear in their respective country's native language.

Buyer Beware!

When you buy internationally on eBay, you must pay with whatever currency the seller specifies. You can view a currency converter at http://pages. ebay.com/services/buyandsell/currencyconverter. html. For more about international buying, go to http://pages.ebay.com/internationaltrading/ findingitems.html.

RECEIVE BUYING ALERTS
with the eBay Toolbar

You can use the eBay Toolbar to receive a notice on your desktop, reminding you to bid on an auction on which you have already bid, and which is about to end. These notices are called *buying alerts,* and they are especially helpful when you bid on numerous items and want to spend less time keeping track of when these auctions end.

Although the eBay Toolbar is free, you must download it from http://pages.ebay.com/ebay_toolbar/ and install it before you can perform the steps in this

task. Once installed, you can specify how many minutes before the auction ends that you want to receive your buying alert.

You do not have to be online or have your browser window open to see the buying alert. The alert appears on your desktop and links you to the item's auction page on eBay.

If you win the auction, then the item appears in My eBay, and you can access it through the Won link beneath the All Buying heading.

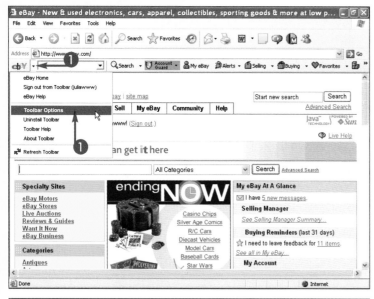

SET BID ALERT PREFERENCES

① Click here and select Toolbar Options.

The eBay Toolbar Options dialog box appears.

② Click here and select when you want eBay to send you a buying alert.

● You can click here and select an option to dismiss the notification.

● You can click here to select the option to play sound when displaying the alert.

③ Click OK to accept your new settings.

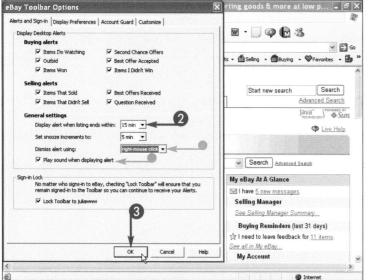

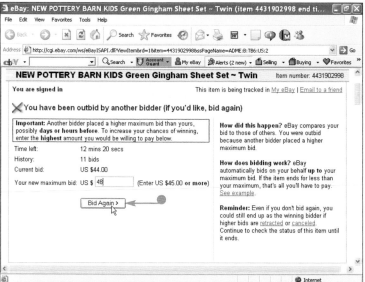

DIFFICULTY LEVEL

● At the time that you specified before the end of the auction, the buying alert appears in the lower-right corner of your desktop.

If you have the default Play sound when displaying alert option selected in your eBay Toolbar preferences, then you hear a noise.

① Click Bid Now!

Your browser opens, and the item's auction page appears.

● eBay allows you to bid on the item before the auction ends.

TIPS

More Options!

You can also receive alerts as a seller. Click the eBay Toolbar menu, and then select the options that you want under the Selling alerts heading. You can select any or all of the options to receive notices for items that sold, items that did not sell, best offers received, and questions received.

Did You Know?

You can access a complete list of your alerts, as well as a list of items that you are selling and buying, directly from the icons on the eBay Toolbar. From the eBay Toolbar, simply click the appropriate icon for Alerts, Selling, or Buying. You can also click the icons for Account Guard, My eBay, and Favorites.

Shop for
LAST-MINUTE BARGAINS

You can take advantage of great deals by bidding on soon-to-end auctions with few or no bids. Because of a poor title or misspelled name, you can find a nice, low-priced item that many eBay buyers overlook. For more on running a search for these items, see Task #9.

When you browse categories, you can select the Time: ending soonest option in the Sort by drop-down menu to find appealing items with few or no bids. You can also sort listings by Time: ending

today, which shows you auctions that will be closing today. You can also use the Time: ending soonest and Time: ending today parameters in the Sort by menu in the eBay search page.

Although you can find some great bargains with the ending soonest feature, there may be a good reason why some items have no bids. For example, the item may have a flaw or be outdated. Always read the auction description carefully to ensure that you do not bid on something you do not want.

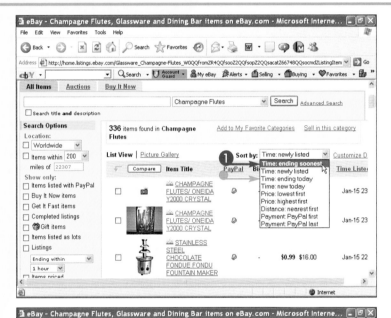

BROWSE FOR ITEMS ENDING SOONEST

① In a browsing or searching list, select the Time: ending soonest option from the Sort by menu.

● You can select the Time: ending today option for auctions that end today.

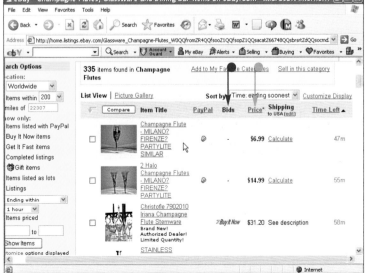

eBay sorts the list by the auctions that end soonest.

You can view the list of auctions for items that you want to buy.

● The Price column allows you to quickly find items that have a low price.

● The Bids column allows you to see if any items have no bids or only a few bids.

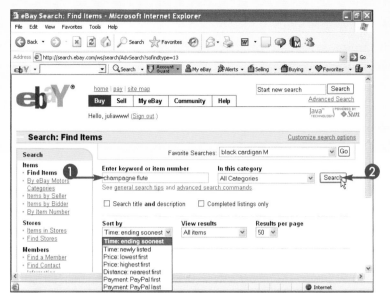

 # 19

DIFFICULTY LEVEL

① In the eBay Search page, type your search word or phrase.

The default Sort by setting for the search is Time: ending soonest.

② Click Search.

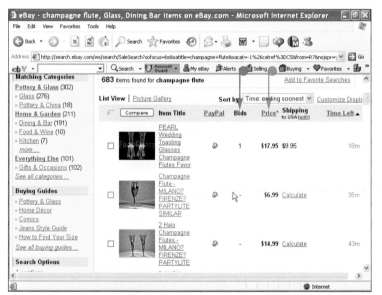

A list of auctions appears, sorted by the auctions that are ending soonest.

You can view the list of auctions for items that you want to buy.

● The Price column allows you to quickly find items that have a low price.

● The Bids column allows you to see if any items have no bids or only a few bids.

TIPS

More Options!

While browsing, you can sort items using the new today link, on the top of a browsing list, which shows listings that just started today. Sorting by new today is useful when you want to find good items that have just gone live, thus decreasing the possibility that other eBay buyers may view the same bargain.

eBay Savvy!

You can check for items whose auctions are about to end and that have a Buy It Now icon. When the Buy It Now icon appears next to an item that you want, you can buy it right away and not worry about losing the item to another bidder. For more information on using the Buy It Now feature, see Tasks #2, #9, and #43.

Use Picture Gallery
TO QUICKLY SHOP

Have you ever been in a situation where you need to find a gift quickly? You can combine two options on eBay, the Picture Gallery view and the Buy It Now feature, to expedite your shopping.

When you combine the Picture Gallery view option with the Buy It Now feature, you can find what you want more quickly, and then purchase it right away.

The Picture Gallery view option allows you to view the items in a list of search results as neatly aligned

rows of photos. You can then efficiently scan the pictures to see if there are any items that you want.

To find Buy It Now items, you can use the Buy It Now option in the Advanced Search page, or on the left side of the page under Search options in a search or browse results list. eBay also displays a Buy It Now icon in the Bids column of a results list. For information about finding bargains with Buy It Now, see Tasks #2, #9, and #43.

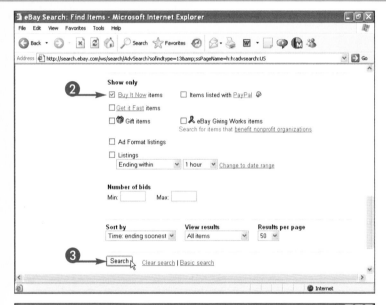

① In the eBay Advanced Search page, type your search word or phrase.

② Click to select the Buy It Now items option.

You may need to scroll down the page.

③ Click Search.

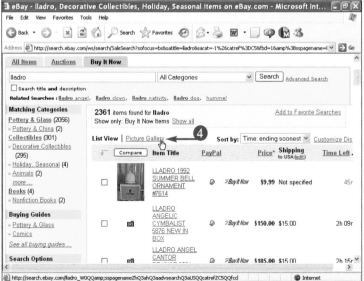

The search results appear, with a list of Buy It Now items.

④ Click the Picture Gallery link, located to the right of List View on the left side of the page.

The items display in Picture Gallery format, with the item photos horizontally aligned.

⑤ Click the item that you want to view.

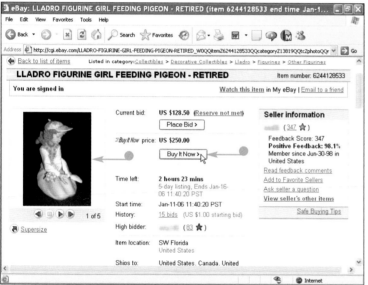

The details page appears for the listing.

● You can view a larger photo of the item.

● You can click Buy It Now and purchase the item right away.

More Options!

Another way to quickly view photos of items is to use the timeBLASTER tool, which downloads photos of eBay items for offline viewing in a Photo Album format. For more information, see Task #10.

Did You Know?

Items can either have a Buy It Now price in addition to a starting bid price, or they can have only a Buy It Now price, with no option to bid — this is known as a *fixed-price listing*.

Did You Know?

The Buy It Now option disappears after a buyer places a bid, unless the auction has a reserve price, in which case the Buy It Now option remains until someone bids at or above the reserve price.

Factor in
HIDDEN COSTS

Although you can find many great deals on eBay, you should factor in hidden costs to determine if you really have a bargain. To do this, you can add up the less obvious fees associated with buying through an online auction, such as shipping, handling, and insurance.

On eBay, the buyer usually pays for the shipping costs. Some sellers also charge a handling fee, which is a value that they place on their time to wrap, package, and send the item to you. Some sellers may offer insurance, although this is usually optional for buyers.

It is a good idea to read an item's description carefully to ensure that you understand all of the fees that the seller charges. For example, if you win an auction for a pair of shoes for twelve dollars, shipping and handling fees may bring the total cost to acquire those shoes up to twenty dollars. If you can buy the same shoes at a store for eighteen dollars, then you may be better off doing so.

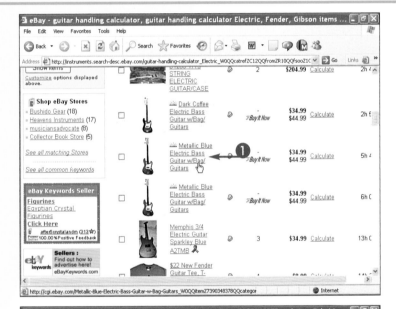

1 In a browsing or searching list, click an item that you want to buy.

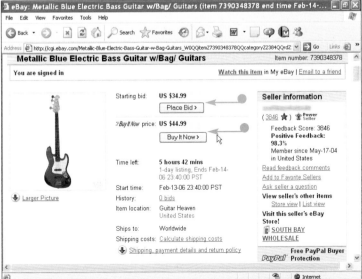

The details page appears for the listing.

● You can see the current bid price.

● You can see the Buy it Now price, if applicable.

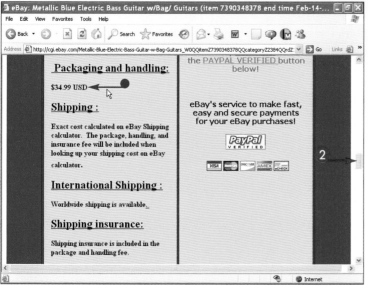

② Scroll down to view the shipping details.

● You can see if the seller charges a handling fee.

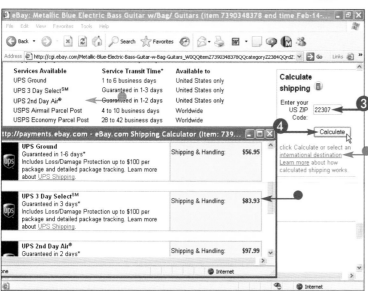

● You can see the seller's shipping methods.

③ Click here and type your ZIP code.

● You can click the international destination link if you are not in the U.S.

④ Click Calculate.

Not all listings have a shipping calculator.

● The shipping calculator displays your total shipping cost or cost options.

⑤ Add any handling and insurance costs, if applicable.

You can now make an informed decision about the total cost of buying the item and having it shipped.

eBay Savvy!

You can estimate shipping fees by using the United States Postal Service Web site, at www.usps.com; the Federal Express Web site at www.fedex.com; or the UPS Web site, at www.ups.com. To calculate these fees, you need both your ZIP code and the seller's ZIP code (or other location information, if you are not located in the U.S.) which is usually included in the end-of-auction e-mail. This is only an estimate, because sellers determine and set the shipping fees in different ways. For more about shipping, see Chapter 9.

Buyer Beware!

Be sure to find out the shipping charges before you bid, as some sellers inflate their shipping charges. If the seller does not state the shipping charges in the listing, then you can use the Ask seller a question feature, as discussed in Task #13.

Improving Your Bidding and Buying Strategies

Whether you intend to buy items at low cost through a Dutch Auction, or big-ticket items such as a house or car, the advanced bidding strategies in this chapter show you how to beat the competition.

Sniping techniques can mean the difference between winning and losing an auction. You can either snipe manually, or use a sniping service to snipe automatically. You can also set up bid groups that snipe similar types of items until you win. Another useful technique is to bid odd numbers to limit your chances of being outbid. You can also increase your chances of getting a low price by bidding on items in a Dutch Auction.

Not sure if a seller is offering you an item at a fair price? You have several options to research a particular item's price before bidding.

You can take advantage of the big-ticket items, such as cars and real estate, on eBay. eBay Motors offers an attractive alternative to the daunting negotiations that accompany buying a car at a dealership. You can use Blue Book pricing to educate yourself about your car deal and to find a lower price. eBay Real Estate listings can help you find that dream home or timeshare vacation deal.

The eBay Giving Works charity section and the Live Auctions offer some of the most exciting auction items — including celebrity-signed merchandise and unique opportunities, such as a walk-on part on a television show — while allowing you to help a worthy cause.

Top 100

USE PROXY BIDDING
to your advantage

You can avoid paying too much for an item by simply taking advantage of the eBay default bidding system, known as proxy bidding.

With *proxy bidding,* you set a price that is the most that you want to pay for an item. The eBay software places a bid that is only high enough to outbid the current bidder by the auction's bid increment, and no higher. If another bidder outbids you, then eBay places another bid that is only as high as it needs to be to outbid that bidder, given that your maximum

bid is high enough. eBay continues placing proxy bids until you are the high bidder or another bidder outbids your maximum bid.

eBay determines the bid increment by the current price of the auction. This means that you do not have to pay the most that you may be willing to pay for an item, as long as another bidder does not bid as much as your maximum bid. For more information about advanced bidding strategies, see Tasks #23, #24, and #25.

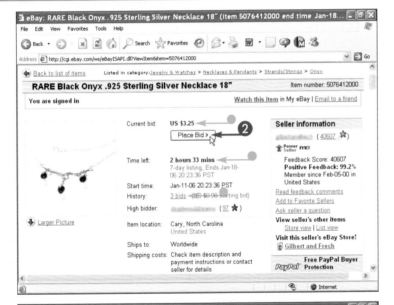

① Click an item to view its details page.

Note: For more on accessing the details page for an item, see Tasks #1 and #2.

● You can view the current bid price, the time left in the auction, and the number of bids, if any.

② Click Place Bid.

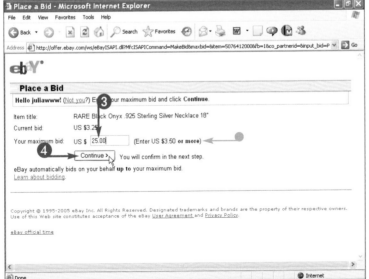

The Place a Bid page opens.

eBay displays the current bid.

● eBay displays the minimum amount that you need to bid.

③ Type the maximum amount that you want to bid.

④ Click Continue.

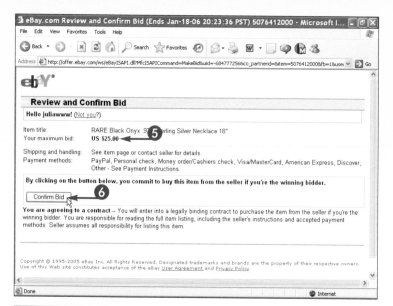

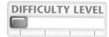

The Review and Confirm Bid page opens.

5 Review your bid to ensure that it is correct.

6 Click Confirm Bid.

 # 22

DIFFICULTY LEVEL

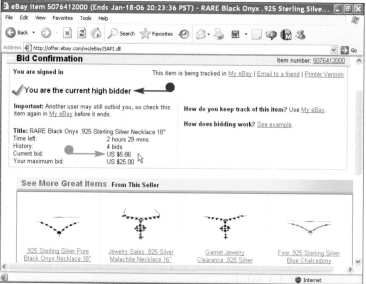

● eBay tells you if you are the current high bidder.

● eBay places a proxy bid that is just high enough to make you the high bidder.

TIP

Did You Know?

eBay's bid increments vary, depending on the current price of an item. This table shows the bid increments for various prices. However, if the winning bidder's maximum bid beats the second-highest maximum bid by an amount that is less than the full bid increment, then you can be outbid by less than a full bid increment.

Current Price	Bid Increment
$0.01 – $0.99	$0.05
$1.00 – $4.99	$0.25
$5.00 – $24.99	$0.50
$25.00 – $99.99	$1.00
$100.00 – $249.99	$2.50
$250.00 – $499.99	$5.00
$500.00 – $999.99	$10.00
$1000.00 – $2499.99	$25.00
$2500.00 – $4999.99	$50.00
$5000.00 and up	$100.00

Snipe with
LAST-SECOND BIDDING

You can increase your chances of winning an item by bidding in the last seconds of the auction, a strategy known as sniping.

To snipe an item on eBay manually, you need to take note of the exact end time of the auction so that you can have your browser window open and ready to bid.

The speed of your Internet connection determines how many seconds before the end of an auction you need to place your bid in order to successfully snipe. Some bidders with fast connections wait until only

five seconds before the end of an auction to place a bid. Others prefer more time and may wait until 20 seconds or more remain.

One strategy, shown in this task, is to open two browser windows and place them side by side to keep track of the time. You need to refresh one of the windows regularly. Then with the other window, you can quickly place your bid.

You can also use sniping software to place a snipe automatically. For more information on sniping software, see Tasks #24 and #25.

① In the details page that opens for an eBay listing that is about to end, click File.

② Click New.

③ Click Window.

You can also press Ctrl+N.

You may want to begin the sniping process at least a few minutes before the listing ends, to allow yourself enough time to arrange the windows.

A second browser window opens.

④ Arrange the windows side by side by clicking and dragging the title bars, making sure that you can see the current bid, time left, and the Place Bid button in each window.

● You can resize each window by dragging the bottom-right corner.

⑤ A minute or two before the auction ends, click Place Bid in one of the windows.

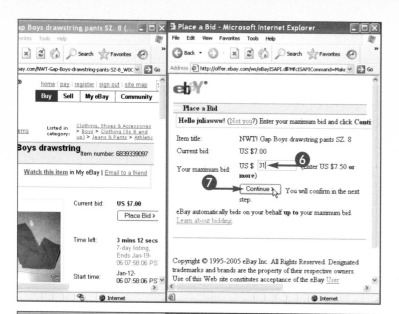

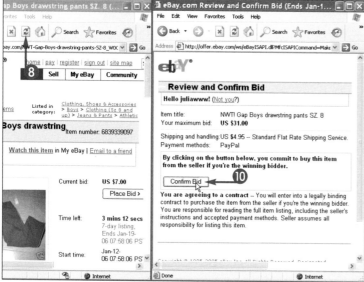

The Place a Bid page opens.

⑥ Type the maximum amount that you want to bid.

⑦ Click Continue.

The Review and Confirm Bid page opens.

⑧ Click the Reload button to refresh the other browser window.

⑨ Repeat step **8** to continue refreshing the item details page so that you can see how much time remains.

⑩ When you are ready to snipe, click Confirm Bid.

If your maximum bid is high enough, you win the auction.

TIPS

eBay Savvy!

To estimate the minimum time that it takes your connection to snipe, refresh your browser and then note the time left for the auction, which is in minutes and seconds. Refresh your browser again, and note the new remaining time. The difference in seconds between the two numbers is the time that it takes your connection to place a snipe.

Caution!

It may happen that both you and another bidder snipe the same auction. In that case, the winner is the bidder who places the highest maximum bid. It is also possible that the hidden maximum bid of an earlier bidder is higher than your maximum bid. If two snipers place the same bid, then the winner is whoever places the bid first.

SNIPE
while you sleep

You can snipe an item automatically with sniping software, such as Auction Sniper, which does the waiting for you. This prevents human error and allows you to do other things besides watching the auction.

To use Auction Sniper, you must first set up an account at www.auctionsniper.com/register.aspx. To place a snipe, you specify the item number of the eBay auction that you want to snipe, and the maximum that you want to spend on that item. You can also enter a *lead-time* — the amount of time

before the auction ends — in seconds, that you want Auction Sniper to place your bid.

One sniping strategy involves placing a snipe with your sniping software, but not bidding on the item first; if you place a bid and then place a snipe, you drive up the bid price by that much more.

Auction Sniper displays a status report message that you have won. You can also receive an e-mail message informing you of your win, or see all of your wins by clicking the Wins tab.

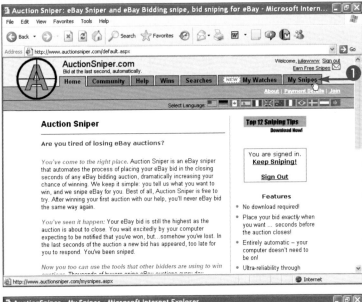

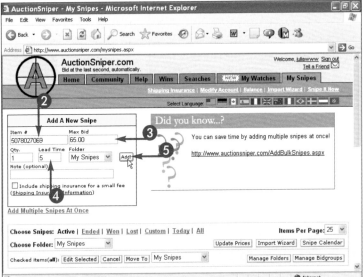

① In the Auction Sniper home page, click the My Snipes tab.

Note: You must first Sign In to Auction Sniper.

The My Snipes tab opens.

② Type the number of the eBay item that you want to snipe.

③ Type the maximum amount that you want to bid.

④ Type the lead time.

The default is 5 seconds.

⑤ Click Add!

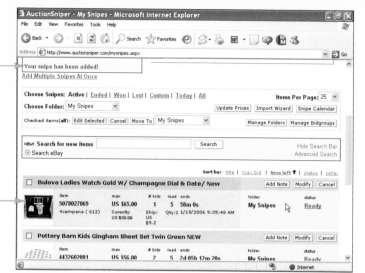

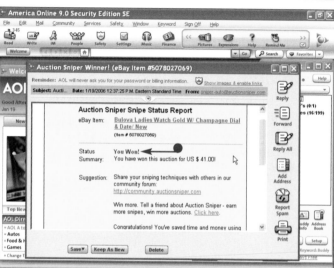

● Auction Sniper places your snipe and displays a message that confirms that your snipe has been added.

● Your snipe appears at the bottom of the page.

⑥ Launch your e-mail application and open the e-mail from Auction Sniper.

● Auction Sniper sends you an e-mail that tells you if you won the item.

Note: You may see a different screen, depending on your e-mail application.

To view your wins, you can also click the Wins tab, located at the Auction Sniper home page.

TIPS

More Options!
You can use other sniping services, including Bidnapper, Bidslammer, eSnipe, EZsniper, Hammersnipe, Justsnipe, Powersnipe, and Snipeville. For a comparison of 11 different sniping services, including their pricing, see AuctionBytes at www.auctionbytes.com/cab/pages/sniping.

More Options!
You can keep track of your payments and feedback using the Auction Sniper Wins Tracker, by signing in to Auction Sniper and clicking the Wins tab.

Did You Know?
Although Auction Sniper offers a free trial, once the trial is up, they do charge for this service. For more information about the cost of the service, go to www.auctionsniper.com/payment.aspx. You pay only for auctions that you win.

OUT-SNIPE SNIPERS
with advanced techniques

Rather than spend time sniping several auctions that you may lose, you can set up multiple bids at once. You can increase your odds of winning a certain type of item with Auction Sniper bid groups, which you can use to bid on multiple similar items that are available simultaneously on eBay. This technique is not for a unique item, but rather for items with a lot of competition, such as a popular laptop computer. You can find out more about the bid groups feature at www.auctionsniper.com.

When numerous people bid on an item, they may try to snipe the item. Likewise, they may have a higher maximum bid that is set by eBay's proxy bidding system and is unknown to you until the auction's end. For more on proxy bidding, see Task #22. For more on sniping techniques, see Tasks #23 and #24.

You can set up the software to bid until you win only one of that type of item; Auction Sniper then cancels the other snipes so that you do not buy items that you do not want.

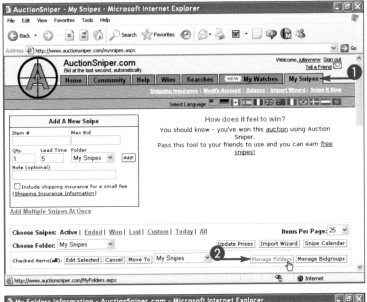

① In the Auction Sniper home page, click the My Snipes tab.

Note: You must first Sign In to Auction Sniper.

The My Snipes page opens.

② Click Manage Folders.

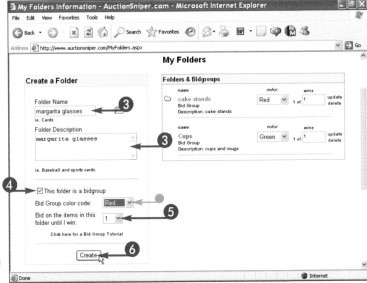

The My Folders page opens.

③ Type a folder name and description.

④ Click to select the This folder is a bidgroup option.

● To help distinguish your bid groups, you can color code them by clicking here and selecting a color.

⑤ Type the number of items that you want to win in this bid group.

⑥ Click Create.

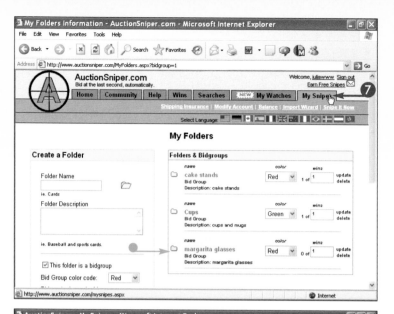

● Auction Sniper Bid Groups creates the folder.

⑦ Click the My Snipes tab.

You can see the list of items that you are sniping.

⑧ Click to select the items that you want to move into the bid group folder.

⑨ Click here and select the bid group folder into which you want to move the items to snipe as a bid group.

⑩ Click Move To.

Auction Sniper moves your items into the bid group folder that you specify and places snipes until you win an item.

TIPS

More Options!

You can toggle between the Auction Sniper and eBay interfaces and place snipes with a single mouse-click by using Auction Sniper's browser. For more information, see www.auctionsniper. com/sniperbrowser.aspx.

More Options!

Bid groups are also available at www.bidslammer.com and www.esnipe.com. BidSlammer allows you three free snipes, after which you pay $0.25 for every item that you win under $10.00, and 1 percent of the closing price (capped at $5) for items over $10.00. See www.bidslammer.com/help/?s=pricing for more information. eSnipe is free for 14 days, after which it costs $0.25 for items that you won up to $24.99, 1 percent of the winning amount for items from $25.00 to $1,000.00 — rounded down to the nearest penny — and a maximum of $10.00 thereafter.

MAKE ODD NUMBERS
work for you

If you bid odd amounts, then you can increase your chances of winning auctions. Many buyers bid in simple, round, whole-dollar amounts, without cents. Others try to outsmart the system by adding one penny to their bids. If you regularly bid odd numbers, such as $13.39 or $23.17, then you increase your chances of outbidding others who bid amounts such as $13.01 or $23.00.

Because other bidders' maximum bids are hidden until the auction closes, you must make educated guesses as to what they are bidding in order to try

to outbid them. For example, if the current bid of an item with one bid is $28.99, then you may guess a bidder's obvious maximum bid, such as $30.00 or $30.01, and place a bid such as $31.05.

DIFFICULTY LEVEL

Of course, these strategies do not guarantee a win. If you prefer to keep your bid amount secret until the last few seconds of an auction, then you can try sniping. For more information on sniping, see Tasks #23, #24, and #25.

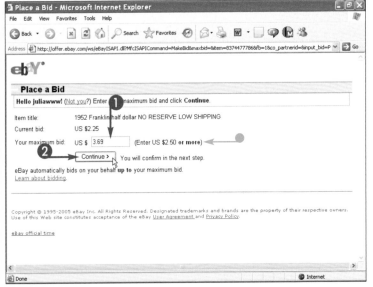

① In the Place a Bid screen for a listing, type an odd number for your maximum bid amount.

Note: See Task #4 to access this screen.

● eBay bases the minimum bid that you must make on the current bid.

② Click Continue.

The Review and Confirm Bid page opens.

③ Click Confirm Bid.

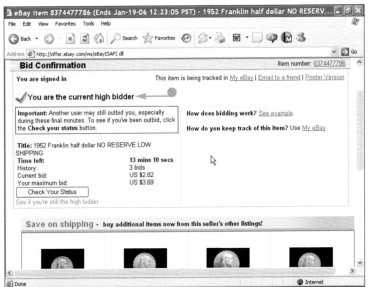

● eBay displays a message that you are the high bidder.

If no one outbids your odd number bid, then you win the auction.

If you are outbid, then you can place another odd number bid by following steps **1** to **3**.

CHECK PRICES
of common items

You can ensure that you do not pay too much for an item on eBay by using a price comparison Web site such as Froogle.com. Froogle searches the Web to find products for sale online and presents you with the results in an easy-to-read format. You can go directly from Froogle's search results to a merchant's Web site to buy an item.

Froogle is owned by Internet search company Google, and uses Google's powerful search technology to find items from a wide range of online retailers.

You can find prices for items by browsing Froogle's search. You can also search within a certain category, or search the whole Froogle site.

When you check prices by combining both your Froogle results and eBay's Completed items options in the Advanced Search, you have a powerful tool for educating yourself about the best deals you can find for a particular item.

For more information on using the Completed items option in eBay's Advanced Search, see Task #3.

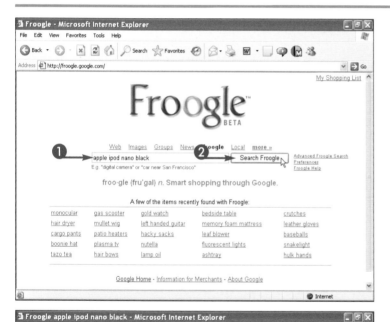

① In the Froogle home page, type your search phrase into the text box.

② Click Search Froogle.

The search results appear.

● You can see photos and sale prices of items.

● The Sponsored Links on the right are ads.

● You can click an item link to go to the retailer's Web site and buy the item.

Get a low price with
DUTCH AUCTIONS

You can take advantage of the *Dutch Auction,* or *multiple item auction,* format to find a low price on an item. This is because in a Dutch Auction, all winning bidders pay the same amount: the lowest successful bid. In a Dutch Auction, the seller offers multiple identical items. For example, if a seller has 100 party favors, then they may list a Dutch Auction of ten lots of ten party favors each.

If you have more bids than available items in a Dutch Auction, then the bidders who offer the highest total bid price — which is the bid price times the number of items bid on — win the auction. Earlier successful bids beat later ones. However, you often find more available items than bids for a Dutch Auction, which means that all bidders pay the starting, and therefore the lower, price.

To identify a Dutch Auction, you look for a number in the Quantity field in the item description that is 2 or greater.

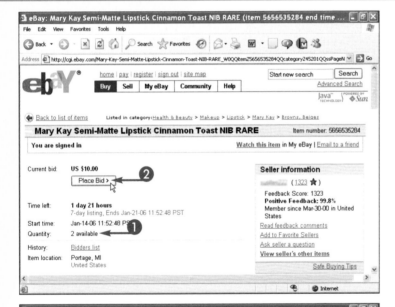

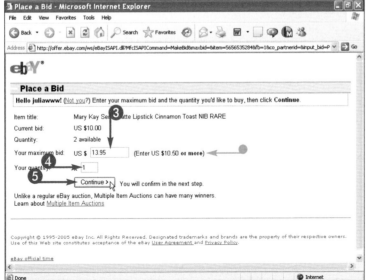

① In an eBay listing, look for a number of 2 or greater in the Quantity field, which indicates that this is a Dutch Auction.

You can also use the Advanced Search tab's Multiple item listings option to find Dutch Auction items.

Note: For more information about Advanced Search, see Task #2.

② Click Place Bid.

The Place a Bid page opens.

③ Type the maximum amount that you want to bid.

● eBay displays the minimum bid that you must make.

④ Type the quantity of items that you want.

⑤ Click Continue.

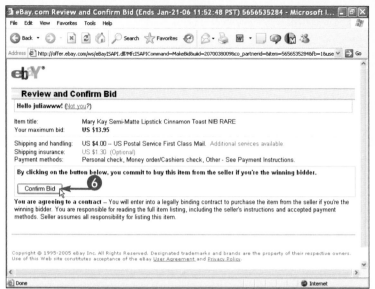

The Review and Confirm Bid page opens.

⑥ Click Confirm Bid.

 # 28

DIFFICULTY LEVEL

● eBay tells you how many items you are bidding on and how many you are winning.

In this example, you win the item for the minimum bid price as long as no more than two other bidders bid on this auction.

● You can click the Learn more link to find out more information about Dutch Auctions.

Did You Know?

Besides Dutch Auctions, eBay offers other auction formats, including the following: regular auctions; reserve price auctions, where the seller designates a hidden minimum price; Buy It Now auctions; Ads, as in the Real Estate area; and Private Auctions, where bidders' user IDs do not display on the listing. For more on the various auction formats, go to http://pages.ebay.com/help/buy/formats-ov.html.

Did You Know?

If the seller offers you a partial quantity at the auction's end — or fewer items than the number on which you bid — then you can refuse all of the items.

Did You Know?

You can see all of the item's bids — including unsuccessful bids — at the end of the auction by clicking the Winning bidders list link in the item listing.

Buy a car with
EBAY MOTORS

You can get a great deal on a car and avoid the stressful negotiation process of traditional car dealerships by buying a car on eBay Motors.

You can buy a car either with the traditional auction format or the fixed-price Buy It Now format.

You should look carefully at the car's description, and assume that the vehicle is being sold as is. Because of the higher dollar amount involved compared to most auctions, it is especially critical to check a seller's feedback. For more information on checking feedback, see Task #14.

You should consider using an escrow service, such as the one at www.escrow.com, to protect yourself from fraud. However, be aware that there are fake escrow sites targeting online auto buyers.

If you bid on any automobiles over $15,000, then you need to provide background and credit verification. This means that you must have your credit card on file with eBay. eBay notifies you when you place a bid, so you should allow yourself extra time for credit verification if you bid near the end time of an auction.

① In the eBay Motors home page, click here and select a vehicle make.

② Click here and select a vehicle model.

● You can also browse the categories.

● You can type search words here.

③ Click Search.

The search results appear.

④ Click a listing.

Note: For more on searching and accessing listings, see Tasks #1 and #2.

● In the listing of a vehicle that you want, you can click the Read feedback comments link to check the seller's reputation.

● eBay displays the current bid, which is where your bidding must start.

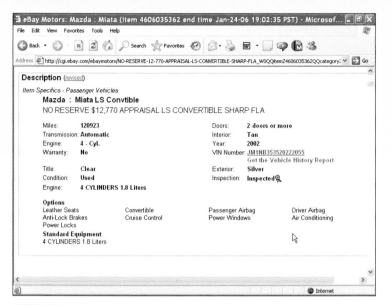

⑤ Scroll down to see a description of the vehicle.

The seller should include information such as the transmission type and mileage, as well as vehicle options.

Make sure that you read the entire description to find out if the car has ever been in an accident or had bodywork done.

⑥ Scroll down to see if the seller included a report from the Kelley Blue Book.

You can go to www.kbb.com and verify the report yourself.

eBay Savvy!

If you are unable to pick up the vehicle, then you can use a delivery service, such as Dependable Auto Shippers, or DAS. DAS offers free shipping quotes at http://pages.ebay.com/ebaymotors/services/das-shipping.html.

eBay Savvy!

You can obtain a vehicle history report on any used car to find out information such as the accident history, or if the car has been in a flood. To obtain a report, click the VIN link on the vehicle description page. For eBay Motors users, a single Vehicle History Report costs $7.99, or you can receive ten reports for $14.99. You can view a sample vehicle history report at http://pages.ebay.com/ebaymotors/services/vehicle_history_report.html.

Find
REAL ESTATE BARGAINS

You can shop for a property anywhere in the world with eBay Real Estate. If you do your research and understand the listing details, then you may find a good deal.

Different from the rest of the site, many eBay Real Estate listings are in an Ad format. With the Ad format, you provide your name, contact information, and any questions through the listing's Contact the Seller form to inform the seller of your interest.

In addition to residential homes, the other types of property for sale on eBay include land parcels and

commercial real estate. You can also find timeshares and vacation rentals.

You can narrow your search by state or province, and by sale type, such as a foreclosed home or a new home. You can also select a number of bedrooms or bathrooms, and a price range.

Please note that eBay strongly recommends that you seek your attorney's advice before entering into any binding real estate transaction. For more information, see eBay's disclaimer page at http://pages.ebay.com/help/community/re_agreement.html.

① Open the eBay Real Estate page by clicking the Real Estate link under Categories in the eBay home page.

② Click the Residential Homes subcategory link.

eBay also lists other types of real estate, including timeshares, land, and commercial real estate.

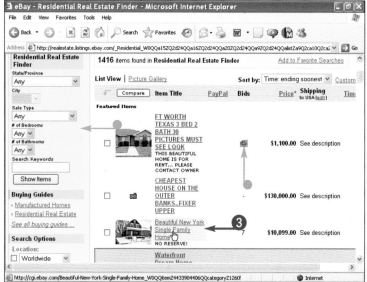

The Residential Real Estate listings appear.

● This icon shows that a listing is an ad, not an auction.

● You can select a city, state, number of rooms, and sale type, then click Show Items to narrow your search.

③ Click a listing that interests you.

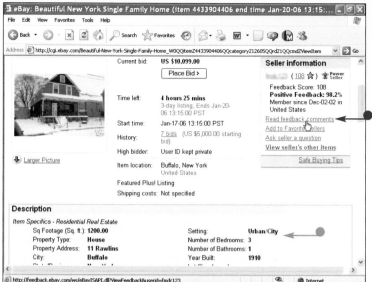

The details page opens for the listing.

● You can view the property description.

● You can click this link to read the seller's feedback comments.

DIFFICULTY LEVEL

④ Scroll down to the Ready to bid? section.

⑤ Type your bid.

⑥ Click Place Bid.

eBay prompts you to confirm your bid.

When you bid on the property, you commit that you will follow through with the transaction in good faith.

Did You Know?

eBay displays real estate listings in both an Auction format and an Ad format. A listing is in Auction format if it shows a number of bids in the Bids column — instead of the Ad icon — in the search or browse results list.

eBay Real Estate Auctions offer either non-binding or binding bids. A note at the bottom of the listing tells you if the auction is binding or non-binding. With non-binding auctions, you can view properties in the familiar, auction-style format without committing to the seller to complete the transaction. Binding auctions are more likely to result in a sale, because the buyer is expected to complete the purchase in good faith, or else risks negative feedback.

Support a
GOOD CAUSE

You can buy items on eBay and support a charity of your choice at the same time by shopping at Giving Works, eBay's charity section. Giving Works offers many wonderful items, as well as services, and even some unique experiences, such as a golf trip with Redskin Super Bowl great Ricky Sanders, or a VIP package for the Grammy Awards.

You can also find many items signed by celebrities, such as a guitar signed by the Rolling Stones and a signed CD from Trisha Yearwood.

You can search the eBay Giving Works section for items at http://pages.ebay.com/givingworks.

You can also search for items benefiting a specific nonprofit organization by name, keyword, mission area, and geography, or browse the categories from that page.

You can bid on eBay Giving Works items the same way that you bid on any other eBay items. Simply find an item that you like, sign in with your eBay account, and place a bid.

In the item description, you can see the percentage of the item's final price that the seller donates to the benefiting nonprofit organization.

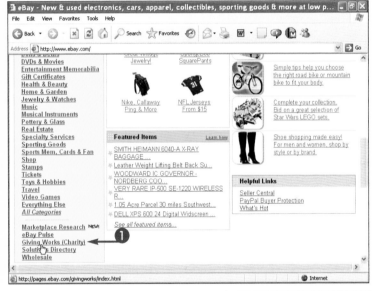

1 In the eBay home page, click the Giving Works (Charity) link.

The eBay Giving Works page opens.

eBay displays a list of nonprofit organizations and charity auctions.

2 Click the charity icon of your choice.

● You can also browse the links alphabetically to find a charity.

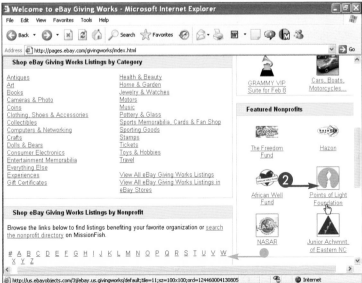

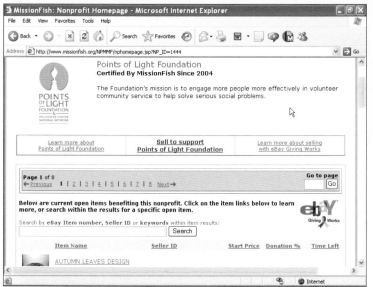

The charity-listing page opens.

You can read the description of the charity and whom it helps.

❸ Scroll down to see the actual item listings.

● You can click a listing that interests you and bid on it, thus donating money to the charity.

TIPS

eBay Savvy!

As an eBay seller, you can donate your auction's proceeds to a designated charity. eBay works with MissionFish, a third-party nonprofit organization, to facilitate transactions between charities and sellers. To list an eBay Giving Works item, you must first register with MissionFish and list your items using the MissionFish Giving Assistant. After an auction ends, MissionFish forwards the funds to the designated nonprofit organization. To register with MissionFish, go to www.missionfish.org and click the Start selling now or Register to benefit link.

Did You Know?

If you pay over fair market value for an item from a nonprofit organization, the amount you overpaid may be tax-deductible. However, fair market value or below is not tax-deductible. Consult your accountant or tax advisor for specific advice.

Join the elite fray of
LIVE AUCTION BIDDING

You can bid in real-time auctions in some of the world's most elite auction houses with eBay's Live Auctions.

In addition to offering exquisite and unique merchandise, Live Auction places you in contact with highly reputable and experienced sellers, to minimize your chances of having a bad transaction.

Before bidding in a live auction, you can prepare yourself by browsing live auctions either by the auction catalog or by categories. The catalog features all of the lots that are available in a particular live auction. You can search both live auction lots and

categories at http://pages.liveauctions.ebay.com/ search/items/search.html. Categories include Books and Manuscripts, Antiques and Decorative Arts, Arts, and Jewelry & Timepieces.

To participate in a live auction, you must first register, which you can do in the Browse tab at the top of any eBay Live Auctions page. Once you register, you can place absentee bids, or you can go to the live auction.

The Live Auction sellers each have their own terms and conditions of sale for each event, which usually include a satisfaction and authenticity guarantee.

① In the eBay home page, click the Live Auctions link under Specialty Sites.

The Live Auctions page opens.

② Scroll down to the Special Events and Upcoming Auctions sections.

③ Click View Live.

● You can also sign up for an upcoming auction by clicking Bid Now.

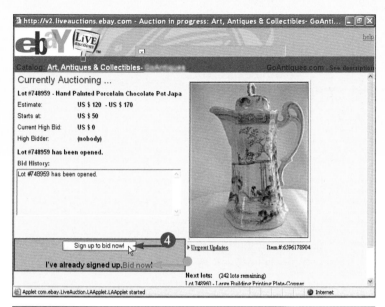

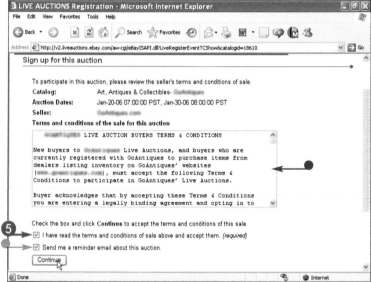

The Live Auction page opens.

④ Click Sign up to bid now!

● If you have signed up to bid, then you can click the Bid now! link to place a bid.

DIFFICULTY LEVEL

The Sign up for this auction page opens.

● You can read the seller's terms and conditions.

⑤ Select the option that you have read, and accept the terms and conditions.

● You can select the option to receive a reminder e-mail about this auction.

You are signed up to bid in a Live Auction.

In some cases, the seller may request that you contact them directly.

TIP

Did You Know?

When you sign up to bid in a live auction, eBay displays the seller's terms and conditions of sale. For example, the buyer may need to contact the seller within a certain number of business days, or the seller may have a disclaimer about the auction items, such as that items are all sold as is. Click Continue. eBay then informs you that you have successfully signed up to participate in the upcoming live auction, and displays the catalog name, auction dates, and seller name.

Paying for Items Painlessly

You can please both buyers and sellers on eBay by understanding how payment services work, and by correctly handling any problems that may arise. You can also protect yourself and your reputation by using features such as escrow services, and by regularly leaving and reviewing feedback, a critical component of eBay's community.

Many eBay buyers and sellers prefer eBay's integrated payment service, PayPal, for its ease of use and because it allows sellers to accept credit card payments. PayPal also allows you to transfer funds into and out of a designated bank account.

When making a large purchase, you can protect yourself with an escrow service, which holds your payment until you receive and inspect the item to ensure that it is not damaged.

Although most eBay transactions go smoothly, you should know what to do when you encounter a problem. For example, you should follow the recommended procedures if you receive a misrepresented item. It is very important to follow eBay's process, such as attempting to contact the seller before leaving negative feedback. Otherwise, you may receive negative feedback in return, if the seller perceives that you acted prematurely.

The SquareTrade service offers a valuable, impartial way to find a solution to a variety of transaction problems when the recommended procedures fail.

You can also build your own feedback rating by leaving feedback promptly after receiving items, to increase the likelihood that sellers will leave you feedback as well. A good feedback rating means that both sellers and buyers implicitly trust you.

Top 100

Set up a PAYPAL ACCOUNT

You can make it easier for yourself and your customers to pay for items on eBay by having a PayPal account. PayPal allows buyers to make online payments from their designated bank account or a credit card. PayPal is owned by eBay and is seamlessly integrated into the Web site as a payment option.

With a PayPal Premier or business account, you can accept credit card payments without paying the high overhead of a credit card merchant account. You can set up a PayPal account by going to their Web site at www.paypal.com and following the relatively simple steps to sign up for the account.

Once you have a PayPal account, you can pay for many auction items right away by simply using the Pay Now or PayPal link in the auction listing.

Not all sellers on eBay accept PayPal, and so you may need to pay by personal check or money order. However, many sellers realize the value in accepting eBay buyers' favorite payment method. For more information on PayPal, see Tasks #34 and #35.

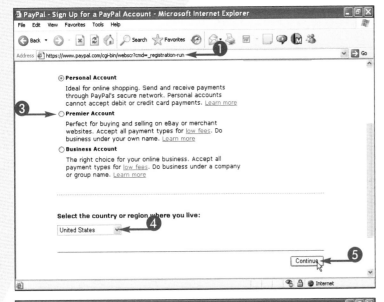

① Type **www.paypal.com** into your Web browser Address bar, and press Enter.

② In the PayPal home page, click the Sign Up link.

③ In the Sign Up for a PayPal Account page, click to select an account option.

④ Click here and select your country.

⑤ Click Continue.

The Account Sign Up page appears.

⑥ Type your personal information in the provided text boxes.

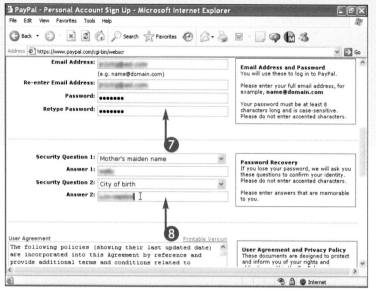

⑦ Type your e-mail address and password.

⑧ Select the security questions and type your answers.

⑨ Click Yes in the PayPal's User Agreement and Privacy Policy section.

⑩ In the section about understanding your rights regarding arbitration of claims, click to select the Yes option.

⑪ Type the security letters into the text box.

⑫ Click Sign Up at the bottom of the page.

A page appears, asking you to confirm your e-mail address.

⑬ To confirm your e-mail address, follow the steps.

⑭ Click Continue.

PayPal creates your account.

#33

DIFFICULTY LEVEL

TIPS

Did You Know?

Although personal accounts are free, your buyers cannot pay with a credit card. However, personal accounts can use PayPal's Winning Buyer Notification feature, which automatically sends payment requests to your auction winner. PayPal business and Premier accounts accept credit card payments, but they cost 2.9 percent plus $0.30 for each transaction to receive funds. If you qualify, then you may receive a reduced Merchant Rate of 2.2 percent plus $0.30 for each transaction.

eBay Savvy!

Premier PayPal accounts have access to PayPal's premium features, such as the ability to receive credit card payments. The cost is 2.9 percent plus $0.30. Sending payments is free. Sign in to PayPal and click the Profile tab to upgrade from a Personal to a Premier account.

Add
PAYPAL FUNDS

You can transfer money to your PayPal account from your bank account. You can also accept payments from other PayPal users to your PayPal account.

To transfer funds to your PayPal account, you must first add your account to PayPal and then verify your bank account. Electronically transferred funds become available in your PayPal account within three to four business days. PayPal sends you an e-mail confirming when you add funds to your account, as well as when eBay buyers pay you with PayPal for items that they purchase from you.

If you receive an e-mail notification that a payment has been made to your PayPal account but the transaction does not appear on your History page, then the sender may have typed an incorrect e-mail address. You should contact the sender and confirm that they have sent the payment to the correct address.

You should check your PayPal balance periodically to ensure that you have adequate funds to cover any eBay purchases. For more information on PayPal, see Tasks #33 and #35.

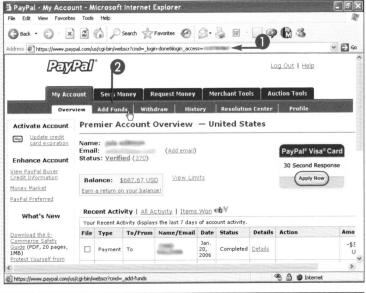

① Type **www.paypal.com** into your Web browser Address bar, and then press Enter.

Note: You need to log in to the PayPal site, if you have not already done so.

② In the main PayPal page, click the Add Funds tab.

The Add Funds tab appears.

③ Click the Transfer Funds From a Bank Account in the United States link.

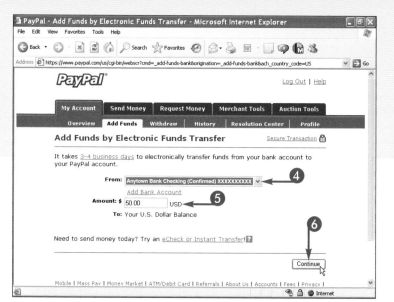

The Add Funds by Electronic Funds Transfer page appears.

Note: A form may appear to link your account to PayPal. Fill in the form and click the Add Bank Account link.

④ Click here and select your bank account.

⑤ Type the amount that you want to transfer.

⑥ Click Continue.

The Add Funds Confirmation page appears.

Verify that the information is correct.

⑦ Click Submit.

PayPal adds the funds to your account.

Did You Know?

After you sign up for PayPal, you need to add and then confirm your bank account. You also need to confirm your e-mail address. To add your bank account, click the My Account tab and then click the Add Checking Account link. Fill out the Add Bank Account form and click Add Bank Account. PayPal e-mails you instructions on how to confirm your e-mail address and bank account. To confirm your e-mail address, simply launch your e-mail application, open PayPal's e-mail, and click the link. Type your PayPal password. To confirm your bank account, PayPal makes two small deposits into it and then asks you to confirm them by checking your bank balance after two to three days.

WITHDRAW FUNDS
from PayPal

You can use your PayPal funds in many different ways. For example, you can transfer money that you make from selling items on eBay into your bank account. PayPal does not charge for these transfers. You can also leave the funds in your PayPal account and use them to buy items on eBay.

Be aware that transfers from PayPal to your account are not instantaneous and that you may have a delay between the time that you transfer funds and the time that they appear in your account. Although PayPal shows the transaction as complete, your bank

may not recognize the transfer, and so may not reflect the transfer. PayPal cannot verify when funds transfer to your bank account. If your transfer request has a problem, then your bank may take up to one week to notify PayPal. PayPal e-mails you if it learns of any problems.

Because you cannot cancel a withdrawal from your PayPal account, you must be sure that you want to withdraw the funds before doing so. For more information about PayPal, see Tasks #33 and #34.

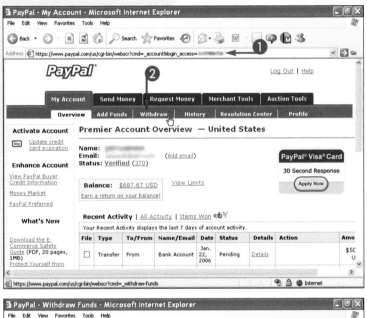

① Type **www.paypal.com** into your Web browser Address bar, and then press Enter.

   Note: You need to log in to the PayPal site, if you have not already done so.

② In the main PayPal page, click the Withdraw tab.

● PayPal displays your withdrawal options.

● The processing time and cost appear for each option.

③ Click the Transfer funds to your bank account link.

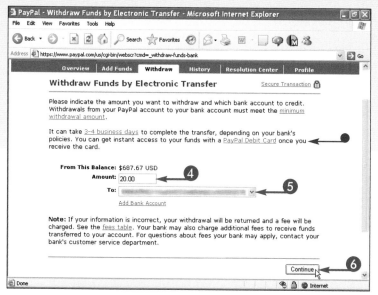

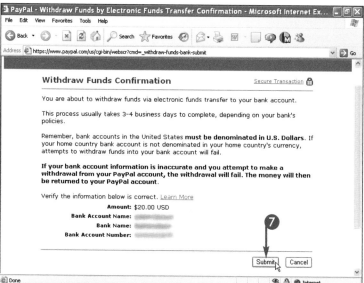

● The Withdraw Funds by Electronic Transfer page appears, and PayPal tells you that the transfer may take three to four business days.

④ Type the amount that you want to transfer.

⑤ Click here and select a bank account.

If you only have one bank account linked, then your account name and number appear in the To: field.

Note: *If you have not yet linked your bank account to PayPal, you need to do so.*

⑥ Click Continue.

The Withdraw Funds Confirmation page appears.

⑦ Click Submit.

PayPal processes your transfer.

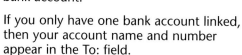

TIPS

More Options!

You can also request a check from PayPal, which takes one to two weeks and costs $1.50. Another option is to use a debit card, which allows you to receive 1 percent cash back on your purchases. To request a debit card, click the link at the bottom of any PayPal page.

Caution!

PayPal never asks you to send your password or financial information in an e-mail. You should only share this information when logged in to https://www.paypal.com.

eBay Savvy!

You can use your PayPal funds to purchase items from over 42,000 PayPal shops, through an online directory of businesses that accept PayPal. To access PayPal shops, click the Shops link at the bottom of any PayPal page.

USE ESCROW
to buy your item

You can protect yourself from fraud and ensure the quality of your purchase using an escrow service. An *escrow service* is a company that both buyer and seller trust to hold the buyer's payment until the buyer receives, inspects, and approves the item.

Both parties must agree to use escrow before the auction ends. You can check the seller's payment terms in the listing to see if they accept escrow. If you have any doubt, then you can use the Ask seller a question link to find out.

Although you can use escrow for any type of item, you generally use it for items worth $500 or more because of the level of risk involved and because the escrow service generally charges you for its use.

Because some fraudulent Web sites mimic actual escrow services, you should research the escrow company that you use. eBay recommends that U.S. and Canadian customers use escrow.com, and other escrow sites for users in other countries.

You must first register for an account with escrow.com to complete this task.

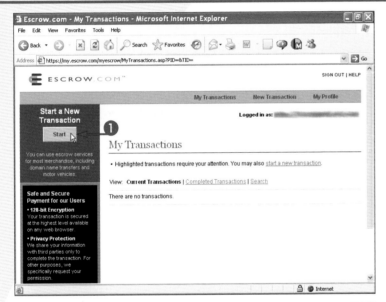

Log in to escrow.com.

The My Transactions page appears.

① Click Start.

The Select the Type of Transaction page appears.

② Click the icon for the transaction type that you want.

This example uses General Merchandise.

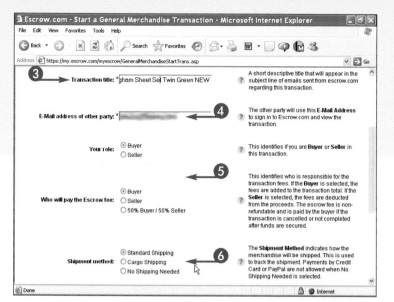

③ Type a transaction title.

④ Type the e-mail address of the seller.

⑤ Click to select a buyer or seller, as well as who will pay the escrow fee.

⑥ Click to select a shipment method, who will pay for the shipping, and the length of the inspection period.

⑦ Click Continue.

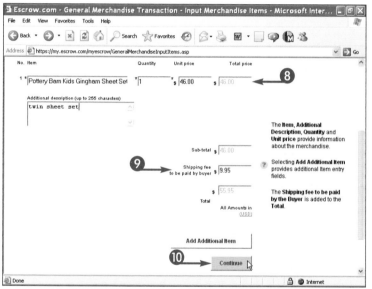

⑧ Type the item name, quantity, and price.

⑨ Type the shipping fee.

⑩ Click Continue.

Escrow.com prompts you to review the information and terms of the transaction.

⑪ Click I Agree.

Escrow.com initiates the escrow process.

Apply It!

To calculate your escrow fee, go to www.escrow.com/support/calculator.asp. In the Escrow Fees and Calculator page that appears, type the transaction value, and then click Calculate Your Fee. Your escrow fee appears for this transaction. Fees for escrow vary, depending on the price of the item. For example, the escrow fee for a $100 item is $25.00.

Did You Know?

Both seller and buyer must agree to the inspection period and the length of time that the buyer has to examine the item, which can be from 1 to 30 days. If the buyer rejects the item, then the seller has five days to examine the merchandise after the buyer returns it.

Troubleshoot
AFTER-SALE PROBLEMS

Although most transactions on eBay go smoothly, some unfortunately have problems. To protect your feedback rating, you need to handle problems carefully by following eBay's procedures.

Many sellers send a confirmation e-mail right away, including shipping fees, if necessary. If they do not, then you can request the total amount using the Ask seller a question link in the item's listing page.

If the seller does not contact you within three days, as stipulated in eBay's Item Won e-mail, then you can use eBay's Request a member's contact info form

to get the seller's phone number. For information about how to contact a seller, see Task #13.

If you get into a disagreement, then you can try to resolve the problem with the SquareTrade service. For more information about SquareTrade, see Task #38.

If your attempts to resolve a problem do not work, then you can file a fraud alert between 30 and 60 days after the auction ends. eBay sends you instructions as to how to file a protection claim, which you must file within 90 days after the auction ends.

① In the eBay home page, click the site map link at the top of the page.

The Site Map page appears.

● You can scroll to the Marketplace Safety section.

② Click the Security & Resolution Center link.

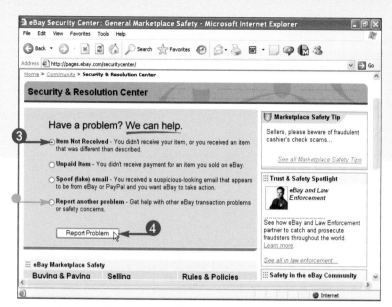

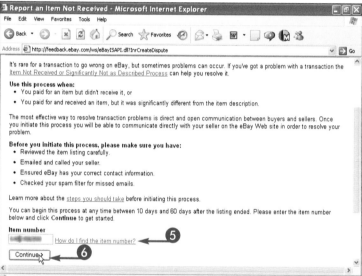

The Security & Resolution Center page appears.

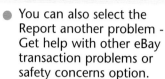

③ Click to select the Item Not Received - You didn't receive your item, or you received an item that was different than described option.

● You can also select the Report another problem - Get help with other eBay transaction problems or safety concerns option.

④ Click Report Problem.

The Report an Item Not Received page opens.

You may need to scroll down the page.

⑤ Type the item number.

⑥ Click Continue.

eBay guides you through the rest of the process for reporting the problem.

Did You Know?

Most credit card companies offer 100 percent consumer protection for online fraud or misrepresentation. eBay also offers buyer protection on items up to $200, minus a $25 processing fee. If you pay with PayPal, then you are eligible for up to $500 of coverage through PayPal's Buyer Protection program. To find out if you are covered, look for the PayPal Buyer Protection icon in the Seller Information box on an eBay View Item page. You must file a complaint within 45 days of the payment.

eBay Savvy!

Some eBay buyers complain that sellers give retaliatory negative feedback when they receive negative feedback. To protect your own feedback rating, leave negative or neutral feedback only as a last resort. For more information about the proper use of feedback, see Tasks #14 and #39.

Resolve payment disputes with
SQUARETRADE

You can use SquareTrade as a trusted third party to mediate a dispute between you and a seller or buyer.

SquareTrade is an eBay-recommended service that provides mediation for auction transaction disputes. It allows both seller and buyer to voluntarily work toward a positive solution in a safe, neutral setting.

To start the process, you can file a case through the SquareTrade site for eBay users. SquareTrade then contacts the other party in your dispute and instructs you both how to proceed. All information and communication related to the case appear on a password-protected Case Page.

The next step is for both parties to try to work out a resolution by communicating with each other through SquareTrade's Direct Negotiation, a free, completely automated Web-based tool.

If you and the other party cannot resolve the dispute using Direct Negotiation, then you can request a mediator's help. A *mediator* is a third party who helps both sides work through the issue and focus on a positive solution. If both sides agree, then the mediator recommends a solution, and you can resolve the dispute.

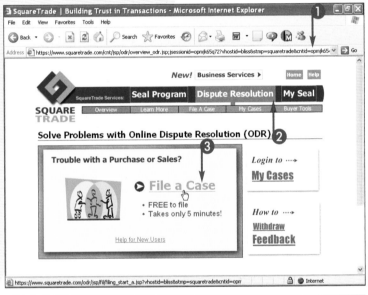

FILE A CASE

① Type **www.squaretrade.com** in the Address bar, and press Enter.

The SquareTrade home page appears.

② Click Dispute Login.

The Solve Problems with Online Dispute Resolution (ODR) page appears.

③ Click the File a Case link.

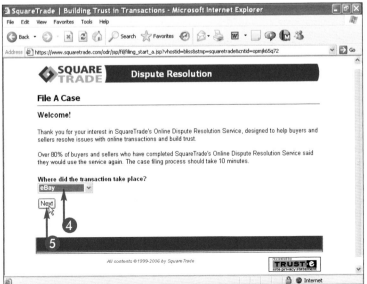

The File A Case page appears.

④ Click here and select eBay.

SquareTrade also offers options for eLance, Real Estate, Sony, econsumer.gov, VRBO, Cyberrentals, a1Vacations, Great Vacations, and Other.

⑤ Click Next.

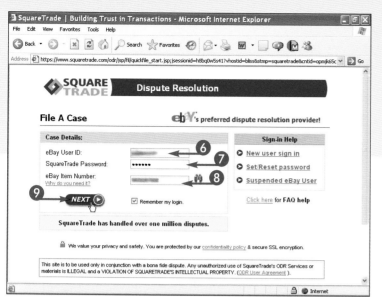

6 Type your eBay user ID.

7 Type your SquareTrade password.

8 Type the eBay item number in dispute.

9 Click Next.

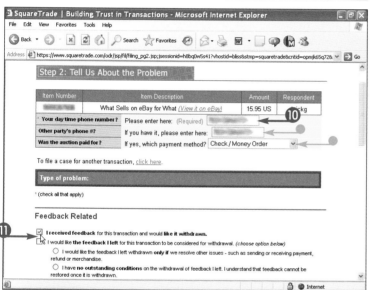

The Tell Us About the Problem page appears.

10 Type your phone number.

● You can type the other party's phone number and select a payment method option.

11 Click to select the types of problems that you are having.

12 Check to acknowledge that you read the SquareTrade ODR User Agreement.

13 Click Submit.

SquareTrade guides you through the mediation process.

TIPS

Did You Know?

SquareTrade allows you to suggest resolutions to your problem on its Step 3: Identify Potential Solutions page.

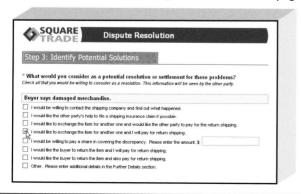

Did You Know?

You can have negative feedback removed or withdrawn. Select the option that you want feedback removed in the Type of problem section, and then explain the issues of your dispute in the Step 3: Identify Potential Solutions page. SquareTrade charges $20 for resolution services. For more information, click the SquareTrade Dispute Resolution link in the eBay site map, and then click How to Withdraw Feedback.

Use feedback to build
GOODWILL

Because buyers check feedback ratings before purchasing items, you can increase your desirability as a seller to eBay bidders by building a good feedback rating. You do this by giving positive feedback as often as possible to both your buyers and the sellers from whom you buy.

As a seller, the more positive feedback that you give to buyers, the more likely they are to return the favor. You can also request that your buyers leave feedback if they have not done so soon after purchasing an item.

In eBay's feedback forum, you can leave feedback concerning any transactions within the last 90 days. You can also review and respond to feedback that is left about you. This allows you to explain extenuating circumstances that may have led to a user leaving you negative feedback. You can also explain what you did to compensate them, if applicable.

If you are new to eBay, then one way to build your feedback quickly is to purchase many inexpensive items and to leave positive feedback promptly.

For more information about feedback, see Task #14.

① In the My eBay home page, click the Feedback link under the My Account heading.

You may need to scroll down the page.

eBay displays both your recent feedback and items awaiting feedback.

② Click Leave Feedback.

● You can also click the Go to Feedback Forum link in order to reply to or follow up on feedback.

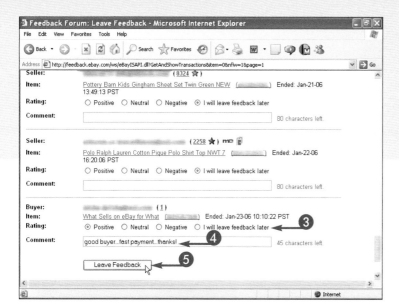

The Feedback Forum: Leave Feedback page appears.

③ Select an option for the feedback rating.

④ Type your feedback comments.

⑤ Click Leave Feedback.

DIFFICULTY LEVEL

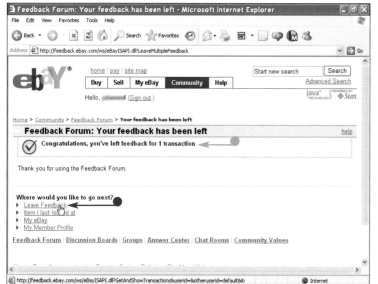

A new page appears, informing you that your feedback has been left.

● The number of times that you have left feedback appears here.

● If you want to leave additional feedback, then you can click the Leave Feedback link.

Did You Know?

You can discuss and get advice about feedback in eBay's Feedback discussion board, located in the Community area under the Discussion Boards link.

Did You Know?

In the Feedback Forum, eBay tells you that once you leave it, you cannot edit or retract feedback. However, in some cases, you can have a piece of negative feedback removed with SquareTrade, as explained in Task #38, or eBay's mutual feedback withdrawal, which you can read about at http://pages.ebay.com/help/feedback/questions/mutual-withdrawal.html. Unless you remove feedback via one of those methods, feedback stays on your record indefinitely. Some long-time eBayers have feedback that dates back to 1998, when eBay implemented its feedback policy.

Smart Selling on eBay

Selling items on eBay can be just as exciting as bidding on them because it brings a great deal of satisfaction — as well as extra cash. You can become a savvy seller by knowing what length to make your auction, the various listing options, and what to do when your highest bidder falls through. Adding pizzazz to your listing with a different design or color gives you an edge over the competition. Understanding listing fees and the pre-filled information feature saves you time and money.

Knowing how to list an item to match your situation is extremely important because listing formats determine how you conduct an auction. Regular auctions let buyers bid on an item until time runs out and the best bid wins.

However, if you want to set the prices of your item, then you can use a Fixed-Price auction. To allow both bidding and the option of a set price, you can add a Buy It Now feature. If you have multiple identical items to sell, then you can offer them in a single listing using a Dutch Auction.

To begin as a smart seller, you can register on your My eBay page and become familiar with the eBay policies page, which lists legal standards that you must follow. You can also ensure that eBay allows your item by checking the Prohibited and Restricted Items list. To avoid legal problems, you must follow the law, as well as eBay rules and guidelines.

Top 100

TRADEMARK PROTECTION

When you sell items on eBay, you must consider trademark and copyright protection. eBay prohibits infringing materials, which can include copyrighted items such as written works, music, movies, television shows, software, games, and artwork.

Intellectual property rights generally belong to the creator of the material. If you hold a copyright to materials that are being sold illegally on eBay, then you can join the Verified Rights Owner, or VeRO, Program to help keep illegal copies of your work from circulating. Because eBay cannot verify if an item is auctioned illegally, the owners of these properties must be vigilant.

In 1997, eBay created the VeRO Program to enlist owners of intellectual property rights to help keep eBay safe from trademark and copyright violations. As a member of VeRO, you can report and request the removal of listings that infringe on your ownership rights.

As a seller, it is your responsibility to make sure that the item you auction does not infringe upon the rights of the owners. If you are unsure, then you can check the VeRO Program participant's About Me pages.

① Type **pages.ebay.com/ help/policies/questions/ vero-ended-item.html** into your browser's Address bar, and press Enter.

The What is VeRO and why was my listing removed because of it? Help page appears.

You can read about why listings are removed due to VeRO.

② Scroll to the bottom of the page and click the eBay's Verified Rights Owner (VeRO) program link.

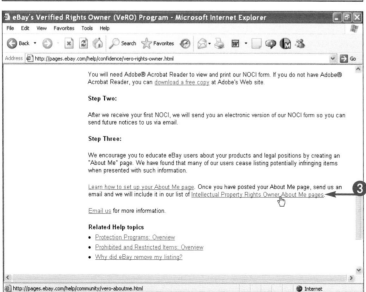

The eBay's Verified Rights Owner (VeRO) Program page appears.

You can read more about the program.

③ Scroll down the page and click the Intellectual Property Rights Owner About Me pages link.

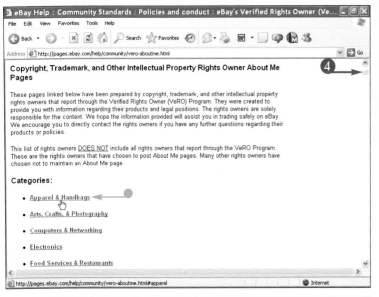

The Copyright, Trademark, and Other Intellectual Property Rights Owner About Me Pages page appears.

④ Scroll down until a list of categories appears.

● You can click a category to view a list of companies in that category which are members of VeRO.

⑤ Scroll down the page until you see the alphabetical listing of companies under a category title.

● You can click a link to view individual policies regarding copyrights and trademarks.

TIPS

eBay Savvy!

When you are unsure of what constitutes illegal use, let common sense guide you. For example, if an eBay auction offers a DVD, and that movie is still in theaters, then the DVD is clearly an illegal copy. Another example is a copyrighted photograph from a catalog being used to describe an item in a listing.

Caution!

If eBay removes your listing through VeRO, then you receive an e-mail explaining why. To find out what you did wrong, consult the VeRO About Me pages. If you believe the rights owner is in error and the item was legal for trade, then you can contact the owner directly and ask about the problem. The notification e-mail includes the rights owner's e-mail address.

ALLOWS YOUR ITEM

Before you start selling any items on eBay, you can check the policies list to make sure that eBay allows your items for auction. Some items, such as firearms, are absolutely prohibited. Other items may require some clarification before listing them on an auction. The eBay Web site features a variety of guidelines that you can consult regarding items that you plan to sell.

Some of the eBay item restrictions are fairly obvious. For example, you cannot sell hazardous materials, fireworks, or weapons and knives. Items such as autographed memorabilia require certificates of

authenticity. Because these items are easily forged, offering your buyers a certificate of authenticity can help reassure them that the item is legitimate.

If you end up selling an item that eBay does not allow, then eBay or a user can report you for a listing violation. If you accumulate several violations, then eBay can revoke your selling status.

If you have any doubts about whether or not the item that you want to sell is acceptable, then you should consult the Prohibited and Restricted Items list.

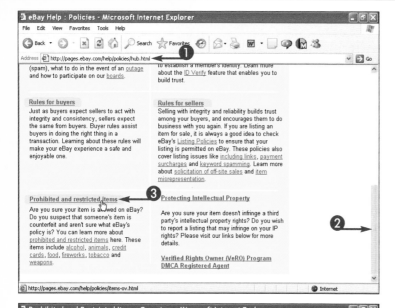

① Type **pages.ebay.com/help/policies/hub.html** into your browser's Address bar, and press Enter.

The eBay Policies page appears.

② Scroll to the bottom of the page.

③ Click the Prohibited and restricted items link.

The Prohibited and Restricted Items list appears.

● You can click a link to learn more about eBay's policies regarding an item category.

Set an
AUCTION LENGTH

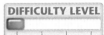
DIFFICULTY LEVEL

It takes practice and luck to determine proper auction length and timing. Depending on which length you choose — one, three, five, seven, or ten days — the auction ends at the exact time of the day on which it started.

For best results, you should enter an auction when the most potential bidders are online. Many experienced eBay users say that evenings and weekends are the best times to end an auction. If you plan to sell your items to eBay users overseas, then you must compensate for the time-zone changes when determining the auction start and end times.

You may also want to evaluate your own circumstances. For example, do you need to sell the item right away, or do you prefer a more leisurely pace? Some sellers believe that a ten-day auction attracts more potential buyers. Others say that a shorter auction appeals to impatient buyers who are unwilling to wait ten days to buy an item. Many buyers also look for shorter auctions around major gift-buying holidays. In general, the more popular an item is, the shorter the auction.

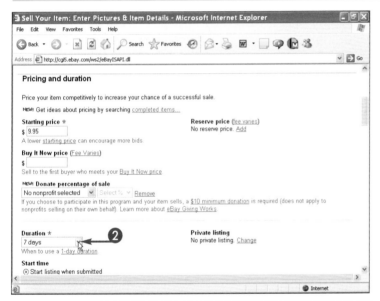

1 Begin filling out the eBay seller's form to create an auction listing.

Note: If you are new to selling, then go to the eBay help pages to learn how to become a registered seller and to set up an auction.

2 In the Sell Your Item: Enter Pictures & Item Details page, click here.

By default, eBay assigns a seven-day auction unless you specify otherwise.

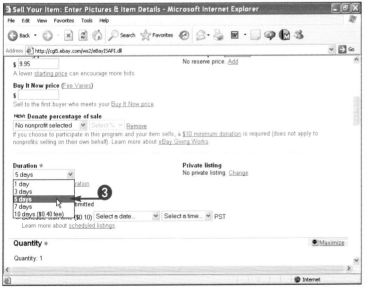

3 Click an auction length.

Note: A ten-day auction incurs an additional fee.

eBay assigns the length to your auction.

4 Finish filling out the seller form and list your item.

Note: For more information about listing items, see Tasks #64, #72, and #73.

The Buy It Now option allows buyers to purchase an item without going through the actual bidding process. This enables your bidder to end an auction early by paying the listed price. Essentially, your item becomes a real time-saver for impatient buyers, but still displays as a regular auction item.

When you add the Buy It Now option, a special button appears on the auction page. The option is only available until someone makes a bid on the item, at which time the button disappears.

When determining a reasonable price for your Buy It Now auction, you need to do some research. Setting the price too high drives off potential bidders who find that the price exceeds what they want to bid. If you set the price too low, then you risk selling the item for less than it is worth. For more information about researching prices for your items, see Task #3.

eBay's insertion fee for Buy It Now items varies, from $0.05 for items with a price from $0.01 to $9.99 to $0.25 for items priced $50 or more.

1 Fill out the eBay sellers form to create an auction listing.

2 In the Sell Your Item: Enter Pictures & Item Details page, scroll down to the Buy It Now price field.

3 Type the amount for which you are willing to sell the item.

   Note: You cannot use this option if the quantity of the item that you are selling is more than one.

4 Finish filling out the seller form and post your item.

● When you post your auction, the Buy It Now button appears along with the Buy It Now price.

   Note: The Buy It Now button disappears if someone places a bid on the item.

Create a
FIXED-PRICE LISTING

You can use the eBay Fixed-Price listing option to bypass bidding and offer a set price to anyone who looks at the item listing. Fixed-Price listings allow for an immediate transaction, without waiting for an auction to end. You use this listing to ensure that your item does not sell for less than its value, or to sell multiple items at the same price.

When you use the Fixed-Price listing, eBay lists the item with the Buy It Now feature, a button that appears on the item description page that allows buyers to purchase the item with a single click.

To use the new Fixed-Price listing option, you must be an established eBay seller, with a feedback rating of 30 or more.

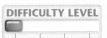

Although both Fixed-Price listings and Buy It Now auctions show the Buy It Now button, a Fixed-Price listing shows only the Buy It Now button, whereas a Buy It Now listing offers both a Place Bid and a Buy It Now option. For more information about the Buy It Now feature, see Tasks #19 and #43.

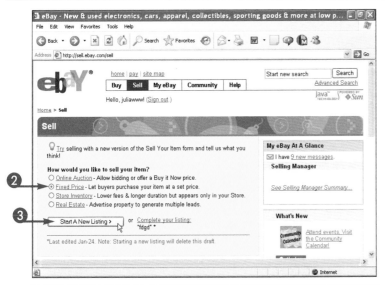

① Fill out the eBay Sell Your Item form to create an auction listing.

② In the Sell page under the How would you like to sell your item? heading, click the Fixed Price option.

③ Click Start a New Listing, and resume setting up your item listing.

④ In the Sell Your Item: Enter Pictures & Item Details page, scroll down to the Buy It Now price field.

⑤ Type the amount for which you are willing to sell the item.

eBay assigns the fixed price to your auction.

⑥ Finish filling out the seller form, and list your item.

SELL IN BULK
with Dutch Auctions

To sell a quantity of the same item quickly, you should consider offering a Dutch Auction — also called a *multiple item auction.* This is a format that allows multiple bidders to bid on a set quantity of identical items. For example, to sell ten tape measures without the Dutch Auction feature, you must sell them as a lot using a regular auction and hope for a good price, or set up ten different auctions for each item. However, if you offer the ten tape measures in a Dutch Auction with a minimum price, then you leverage your selling potential and only have to set up one auction listing.

What makes Dutch Auctions unique is the winning bid price — all winning bidders pay the lowest successful bid. If you have more buyers than goods, then the earliest successful bidders win the auction.

DIFFICULTY LEVEL

eBay does not allow a seller to list more than ten identical items as regular auctions. You can also use a Fixed-Price format or sell through your eBay Store, if you have one.

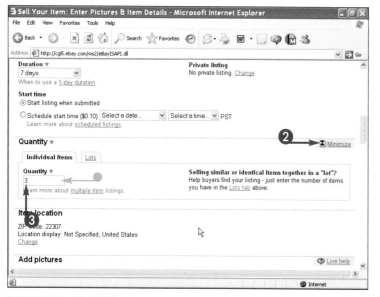

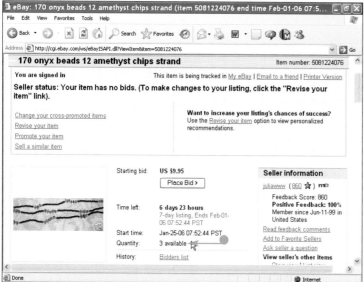

① Fill out the eBay Sell Your Item form to create an auction listing.

② When you scroll down to the Quantity section in the Sell Your Item: Enter Pictures & Item Details page, click here.

● The link changes from Maximize to Minimize, and the Quantity field appears.

③ Type an amount.

  eBay assigns Dutch Auction status.

④ Finish filling out the seller form, and post your Dutch Auction.

● The auction listing displays the quantity of items available.

  If the quantity is more than one item, then it is listed as a Dutch Auction.

PROTECT YOUR ITEM
with a Reserve

DIFFICULTY LEVEL

If you do not want to sell your auction item below a particular price, then you can assign a reserve price to the item. Hidden from the bidder in the auction listing, a *reserve price* is the lowest price for which you are willing to sell the item. You must make this price higher than the minimum bid price. Keep in mind that setting the reserve price too high may discourage buyers from continuing to bid for the item.

When you assign a reserve, eBay displays the phrase "Reserve not met" on the auction page. When the

bidding reaches the reserve price, the phrase disappears. If none of the bidders meet the reserve price by the end of the auction, then you reserve the right not to sell the item below the reserve price.

However, keep in mind that adding a reserve price to an auction incurs an additional listing fee. If your item sells above the reserve price, then eBay refunds the fee. If the item fails to sell, then eBay does not refund the fee.

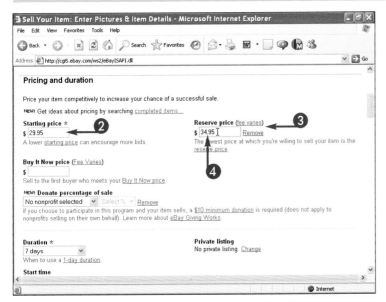

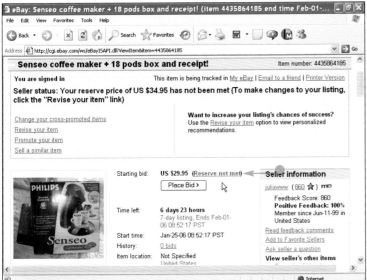

① Begin filling out the eBay Sell Your Item form to create an auction listing.

② When you scroll down to the Starting price field, type a minimum price.

③ Click the Add link under Reserve price to display the Reserve price field.

④ Type the minimum amount that you will accept as a final sale price.

eBay assigns the reserve status to your listing.

⑤ Finish filling out the seller form, and post your reserve price auction.

● The phrase "Reserve not met" displays in your auction listing until a bidder meets the reserve price.

LISTING FEES

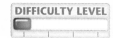

If you incur extra fees by adding too many extra features to your auctions, then you may reduce your profits by spending more than you intended. To help you limit your costs, you should evaluate the effectiveness of a feature before adding it to your listing.

You can save some money on your eBay listing fees by thinking creatively. For example, if you decide that you really must add a starting price or reserve price to an item, then first check out the insertion fees chart on eBay to see a breakdown of fee prices.

DIFFICULTY LEVEL

If you planned to sell the item in the $10 price range, then you may save money if you pay attention to how eBay defines its insertion fee brackets. Items priced from $1 to $9.99 cost $0.35 to list. Items priced from $10 to $24.99 cost $0.60 to list. As a result, by listing your item at $9.99 instead of $10, you save $0.25.

It is a good idea to regularly check the Fees Overview page on eBay to keep up with any fee changes.

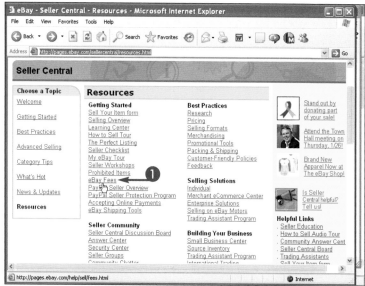

① From the eBay Seller Central Resources page at http://pages. ebay.com/sellercentral/resources. html, click the eBay Fees link.

*Note: You can also access the page by typing **selling fees** in the Help pages search field.*

The eBay.com Fees page appears.

● You can scroll through the page to view current fee tables, such as the Insertion Fees and Final Value Fees tables.

● You can click a link at the top of the page to view fees for eBay Specialty Sites such as eBay Motors.

BACKGROUND COLOR

DIFFICULTY LEVEL

By default, eBay auction pages use a white background. With some HTML coding for a table, you can add extra interest to your auction by assigning a unique background color to your page. Anything that you can do to make your auction seem more distinct can draw a buyer's attention. Color backgrounds can also display your personal style.

To designate a background color, you can enter HTML coding into the auction description text box when you fill out the seller's form. Valid HTML colors include teal, blue, aqua, fuchsia, green, lime, maroon, red, purple, yellow, olive, and silver. This example uses hot pink. You can type any of these color names in your HTML code to specify the corresponding background color. If you are familiar with hexadecimal numbers, then you can also use six-digit color codes that mix varying amounts of red, green, and blue.

When adding a background color, you should ensure that the color does not interfere with the buyer's ability to read your item description and instructions.

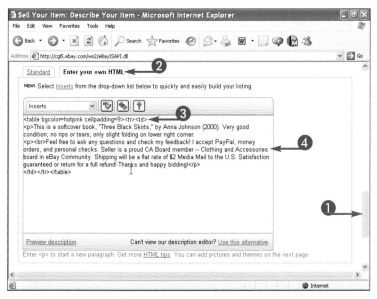

① In the eBay Sell Your Item: Describe Your Item page, scroll down to the item description text box.

② Click the Enter your own HTML tab.

③ Type **<table bgcolor=X cellpadding=9><tr><td>**, where **X** is the color that you want to use.

④ Type your description, and then type **</td></tr></table>**.

⑤ Click Preview description.

● A separate browser window appears, displaying your description with the background color.

⑥ Click Close Window.

The browser window disappears.

⑦ Continue filling out the information for your auction.

LISTING DESIGNER GRAPHICS

You can add interest to your auction listing by using graphics with the eBay Listing Designer feature. For an extra fee, you can add a graphical theme to make your listing more attractive to potential buyers. A Listing Designer theme sets a default font and background color for your listing that controls the appearance of the description area.

eBay's Listing Designer themes include holiday themes, themes related to collectible items — such as clothing — and generic graphical themes that add

color and liveliness to your description area. The Listing Designer also allows you to choose from a variety of layouts to customize the appearance of any photos that you display in the auction. For example, you can select a layout that displays your item photo prominently in the description area.

As with all features that enhance your listing, you should consider whether the price of your item justifies the extra design fee.

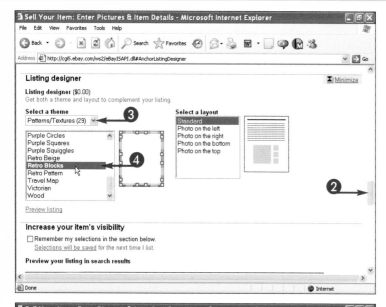

① Begin filling out the eBay seller's form to create an auction listing.

② In the Sell Your Item: Enter Pictures & Item Details page, scroll down the page to view the Listing designer section.

③ Click here and select the theme that you want to apply.

④ Select a design.

● A preview appears for the theme design.

⑤ Click a layout.

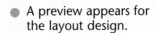
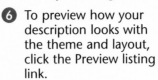

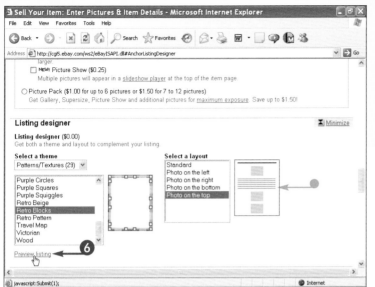

● A preview appears for the layout design.

⑥ To preview how your description looks with the theme and layout, click the Preview listing link.

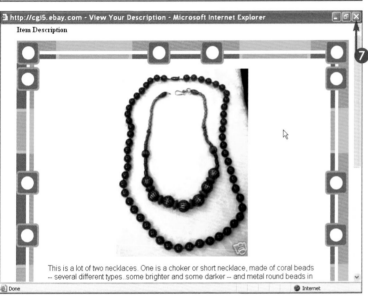

A preview window appears and displays your listing text and photos.

⑦ Click the Close button.

The preview window closes.

⑧ Continue filling out the information for your auction.

TIPS

Did You Know?

If you include HTML tags and JavaScript in your auction listing description, then you can still use the Listing Designer themes and layouts. However, keep in mind that if you set font color tags, then you should ensure that the colors do not conflict with the theme colors. For more on using HTML tags with your listing, see Task #64.

Did You Know?

You can also add your own graphics to an auction description. Graphic elements should never replace a photo of an item, but if you do not mind paying the extra fees to list them, then you can add graphic files just as you can add photo files.

Save time with
PRE-FILLED INFORMATION

You can make the process of listing your item much shorter by using eBay's Pre-filled Item Information feature. The feature is free, and it allows you to quickly and automatically place specific information in your auction's listing. This feature sometimes even provides a photograph for use in your listing, such as a book cover, which can save you from the time-consuming task of creating and editing your own picture.

The Pre-filled Item Information screen appears in the listing process after you select a category and subcategory for your item. This feature is only

available for certain types of items, such as books or movies.

The Pre-filled Item Information feature can include details such as a book's cover photograph, author, ISBN, and publisher. A third party provides the pre-filled information to eBay, and so eBay recommends that you confirm the accuracy of the information before including it in your listing.

Keep in mind that you still need to add your own personal description to your auction listing to elaborate on your own item's specific features or flaws.

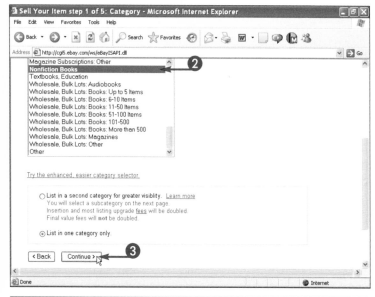

① Begin filling out the eBay seller's form to create an auction listing.

② At the Sell Your Item: Select Category screen, click here to select a subcategory for your item.

③ At the bottom of the page, click Continue.

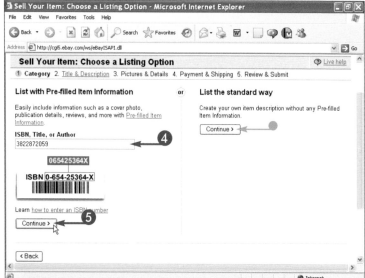

The Sell Your Item: Choose a Listing Option page appears.

You can scroll down the page to the List with Pre-filled Item Information section.

④ Click here and type an ISBN, title, or author.

⑤ Click Continue.

● You can also choose to list the standard way by clicking this Continue button.

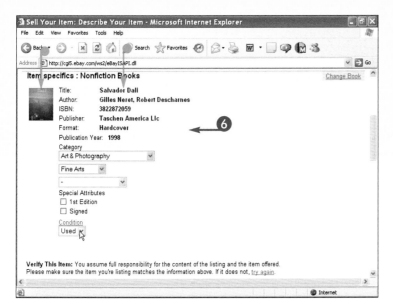

The Sell Your Item:
Describe Your Item
page appears.

● Prefilled item
information appears
about the book, as well
as a stock photo, if
available.

*Note: Although this
example uses a book,
you can use this feature
for DVDs and CDs,
although the options
may list differently.*

6 Check that the listed
information matches
your item.

You may need to scroll down the page.

● You can select the Include stock photo in
this listing option.

● You can select the Include additional
information option.

7 Continue filling out the information for
your auction.

TIPS

Did You Know?

In some categories, eBay offers another
time-saving listing feature called Item Specifics,
which are available as options for your selection
in the Sell Your Item: Describe Your Item form.
For example, in the Women's Pants subcategory,
eBay provides options for style, such as khakis.

Did You Know?

Some eBay sellers list items such as books and
CDs on amazon.com as well, which also allows
you to use pre-filled information. First, create a
seller account. In an amazon.com item page,
click Sell yours here. Select a condition, such as
Used: Acceptable. Type a description in the
comments field, and click Continue. In the Enter
the price for your item page, type a price, and
your ZIP code, then select a shipping method.
Confirm the details and click List item for sale.

Make a
SECOND-CHANCE OFFER

If your winning bidder fails to complete a sale, then you can make a second-chance offer to the next-highest bidder, if you have one. You can also offer the item to any underbidder if you have duplicate items available. This allows you to sell multiple items for one listing fee. A second-chance offer allows you to leverage the bidders in an auction and sell an item without having to relist the item, or pay additional listing fees. You pay only a Final Value Fee if the bidder accepts the offer.

You can create a second-chance offer immediately after a listing ends, and for up to 60 days afterward.

However, bidders can opt not to receive the offer. For this reason, you should first attempt to complete the sale with the original winning bidder before making a second-chance offer.

You can create a Second-Chance offer from your closed listing's page. A "second chance offer" link is only available for closed items with at least one underbidder.

Second-Chance offers are not available for multiple-item auctions, also known as Dutch Auctions. For more information about Dutch Auctions, see Task #45.

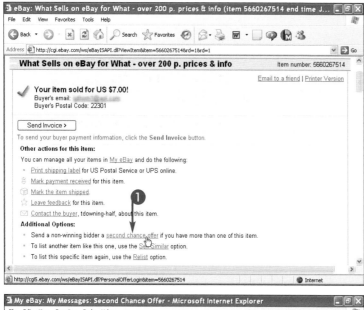

① From your item's closed listing page, click the "second chance offer" link.

This link only appears for closed listings that have at least one underbidder.

The Second Chance Offer page appears.

● You can read the rules for using a Second Chance Offer.

② Type the item number.

③ Click Continue.

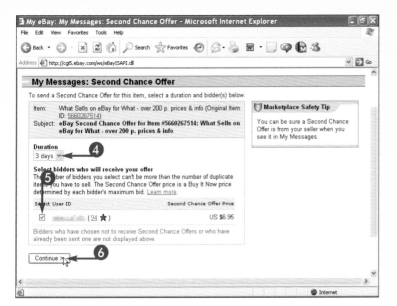

The Second Chance Offer setup page appears.

④ Click here and select how long you want the offer to last.

⑤ Click to select the bidder to whom you want to make the offer.

Note: You can select as many bidders as you have items to sell.

⑥ Click Continue.

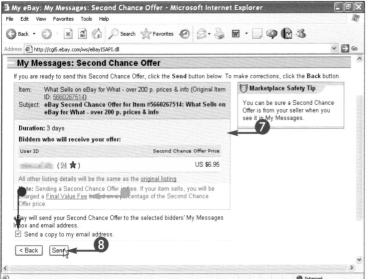

The Second Chance Offer review screen appears.

⑦ Review your offer details for accuracy.

● eBay charges a final value fee if your item sells.

● You can select the Send a copy to my email address option.

⑧ Click Send.

eBay sends a Second Chance Offer to the designated underbidder.

Did You Know?

You can make a Second Chance Offer to underbidders in a reserve-price auction that ends without the reserve price being met. In addition, eBay refunds the reserve fee to you if the bidder accepts your Second Chance Offer. For more information about eBay's Second Chance Offer, go to http://pages.ebay.com/help/sell/second_chance_offer.html.

Did You Know?

You can leave feedback for your original winning bidder as well as for the buyer or buyers in your Second Chance Offer sale. Your buyers can also leave feedback for you. eBay protection services cover Second Chance Offer sales. For more on eBay's fraud protection and related programs, see Task #37. For more on giving and receiving feedback, see Tasks #14 and #39.

Maximizing Your Efficiency with Seller Tools

When you use the eBay marketplace as a seller, you gain access to a whole new world of eBay features and expertise. To help you gain more experience, this chapter shows you some practical ways to sell more efficiently online.

Savvy eBay sellers know that it pays to invest in a quality image-editing program. Whether you take a snapshot of your item with a digital camera and download it to your computer, or scan a picture, you should edit the picture in an image-editing program to make your item look its best. Most image-editing programs offer features to cover up imperfections in a photo's quality, to improve tone and contrast, and to crop out parts of the picture that detract from the subject.

Another way to optimize your selling potential is to take advantage of eBay's tools, such as the auction scheduler, and the free counters that track how many people visit your listing page. These tools are available on the seller's form when you create a new auction listing.

eBay also offers several additional tools that you can download, such as the popular Turbo Lister, which enables you to prepare listings offline.

Another way to sell more efficiently is to take advantage of the many third-party auction tools that are available on the Web, such as DeepAnalysis and Andale. These tools help you to examine eBay data, such as which items are hot sellers, and the marketing values for various items.

Top 100

Use Photoshop Elements to
EDIT A PICTURE

Because photos show the buyer exactly what they are bidding on, it is extremely important to show an accurate representation of your item. To do this, you should take clear and well-lit color photographs. You can then use a photo-editing program to improve your photo's quality before posting it in your auction listing. To avoid after-sale problems, the photo should clearly show any flaws in the item.

Photoshop Elements is one of the best photo-editing programs on the market today, and retails for less than $90. Adobe also offers a free trial of Elements at http://adobe.com/products/tryadobe/main.jsp. The

program can handle all of your photo-editing needs for eBay auctions. For example, you can use Photoshop Elements to edit picture size, and improve focus, brightness, and contrast. You can also use the Auto Levels feature to quickly adjust tone and contrast. Finally, you can crop your image to eliminate extra background, and to minimize the file size, thus making the photo faster to load in your auction.

When you finish editing the picture, you can then save it as a GIF, JPEG, or PNG file to upload to the eBay Web site.

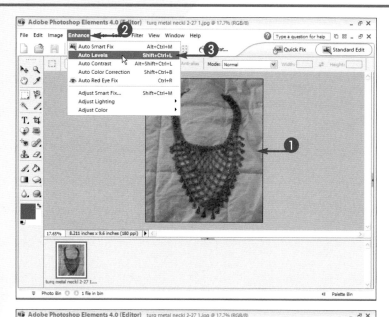

ADJUST TONE AND CONTRAST

1 Launch Photoshop Elements, and open the image file that you want to edit.

2 Click Enhance.

3 Click Auto Levels.

Note: You can use similar commands in other image-editing programs.

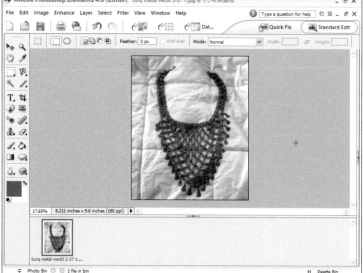

Photoshop Elements corrects the shadows, midtones, and highlights of the image.

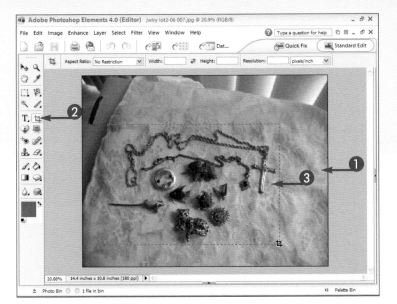

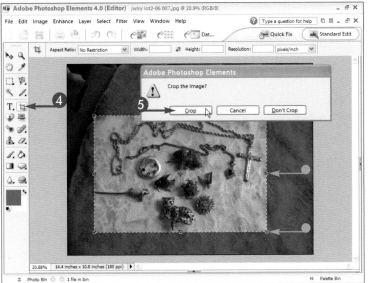

CROP A PHOTO

1 Open the image file that you want to edit in Photoshop Elements.

2 Click the Crop tool.

3 Click and drag a cropping boundary around the area that you want to crop.

 # 52

DIFFICULTY LEVEL

● You can drag the side and corner handles to move the cropping boundary.

4 Click the Crop tool.

5 Click Crop on the form that appears.

Photoshop Elements crops the image, deleting the pixels outside of the cropping boundary.

---

eBay Savvy!

You should use a neutral background when taking a picture of an eBay auction item because a busy background, such as a pattern, distracts the viewer from the item. You should also shoot an item from a flattering angle instead of straight on, so that the viewer can see more than one side of it. If you are selling a collection of items, then include at least one group photo. Be sure to take several snapshots so that you can choose from among the best ones for posting in your auction listing.

More Options!

Some other popular image-editing programs include IrfanView, which is free at www.irfanview.com; Corel Paint Shop Pro X, which is $99.00 at www.corel.com; and Ulead PhotoImpact 11, which is $89.99 at www.ulead.com/pi.

COPYRIGHT
your auction photographs

If you take a good photograph of your auction item, then other eBay users may use it in their own auctions. Although eBay disapproves of this behavior, which infringes on copyright laws, it is not an uncommon practice. To prevent this, you can place a text line discreetly in the image.

Most photo-editing programs, including Photoshop Elements, offer a text-editing feature that you can use to add your user ID number and a superimposed copyright symbol to the photo. If someone co-opts your image for use on their site, then bidders can

clearly see that the image does not belong to the seller.

If someone does use your image without your permission, then you can contact eBay and report the infringement, including the auction item number as well as your original auction item number. However, you must enroll in eBay's VeRO program for eBay to take action on your behalf. For more information about VeRO, see Task #40. eBay may take a few days to investigate, at which point they may remove the auction and notify the seller of the offense.

1 In Photoshop Elements, open the image file to which you want to add a copyright symbol.

2 Click the Type tool.

3 Click where you want the line of text to appear.

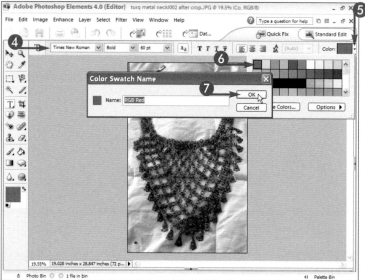

4 Click here to select a font, style, and size for your text.

5 Click the drop-down arrow next to the Color box.

6 Click a color.

A Color Swatch name confirmation box opens.

7 Click OK.

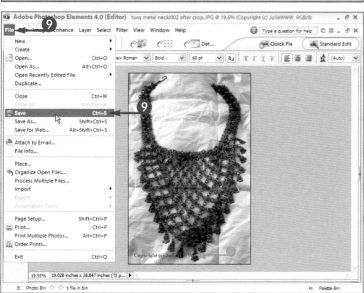

8 Click where you want your text to appear and type your copyright text.

To create a copyright symbol, you can type **(c)**.

● The image displays the text that you typed.

9 Click the File menu and select Save.

You can also type Ctrl+S.

Choose an Image and Layer compression and other options, and click OK.

Your photo is now copyrighted.

TIPS

More Options!

You can choose from a large variety of colors for the text in your copyright notice. Before you click the Type tool, click the top square of the color picker, located near the bottom of the Photoshop Elements toolbar. Click within the square to select a color. Click OK. Click the type tool and click the image where you want to place your text. The text appears as the color that you specify.

Caution!

When selecting a color for text, ensure that it does not conflict with the image or distract the buyer from viewing the item.

Track listing visits with a
FREE COUNTER

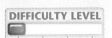

You can use a counter on your auction listing page to keep track of how many people view your listing. Counting the number of visits can help you to determine the marketability of your item, as well as how popular or unpopular your item is with other eBay bidders. You can use counters from third-party sources, or you can use a free counter from Andale.

Andale counters count every visit to your item listing, even if a person looks at your item more than once. The Andale counter has two different designs from

which you can choose. You can also keep the counter hidden from the bidders' view. Counters appear as graphics at the bottom of your auction listing page.

DIFFICULTY LEVEL

If you want to hide your counter, then visitors see only a "Thanks for looking" graphic instead of the usual counter graphic. With a hidden counter, only you, the seller, can see how many people visit your listing.

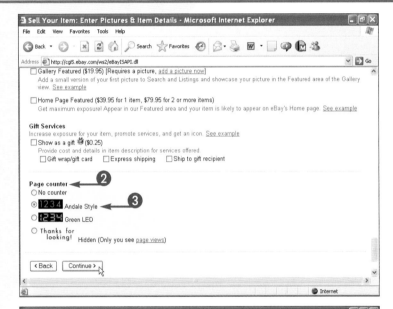

① Begin filling out the eBay seller's form to create an auction listing.

② In the Sell Your Item: Enter Pictures & Item Details page, scroll down the page to locate the Page counter section.

Note: if no counter styles display, then click the Change link.

③ Click to select a counter style.

④ Finish filling out the seller form, and post your item.

⑤ View your finished listing page in a Web browser.

● The auction listing displays the counter.

Start an auction with the
SCHEDULER

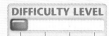

DIFFICULTY LEVEL

You can use eBay's built-in scheduling feature to help you schedule auctions for the best times, even when you are not present to post your listings. For a small fee, the eBay scheduler allows you to pick a day and time to start the auction.

You can use the scheduler to schedule up to 3,000 auction listings, up to three weeks in advance. For example, if you know you are going to be out of town when you want to begin a seven-day auction, then you can use the scheduler to designate the date

and time for you. You may find that your item sells best when you start an auction on a particular day of the week, or that your item gets more bids when an auction closes at the end of the day rather than earlier. The scheduler allows you to select the date and time that works best for your particular item.

In addition to the eBay scheduler, you can also find third-party schedulers that you can use to list your items.

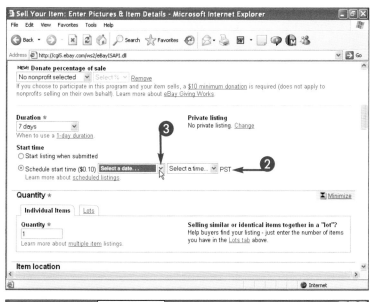

① Begin typing information in the eBay seller's form to create an auction listing.

② In the Sell Your Item: Enter Pictures & Item Details page, click to select the Schedule start time option.

③ Click here.

④ Click a start date.

   You can schedule up to three weeks in advance.

⑤ Click here and select a start time.

   Finish typing your information into the seller's form, and post your item.

   eBay posts your auction at the date and time that you specified.

Determine the
BEST AUCTION DAYS

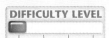

DIFFICULTY LEVEL

Although there is no magic formula for determining what times and days are the best for online auctions, some users argue that certain days are better than others. For example, the AuctionBytes Web site offers a useful calendar that you can reference when determining which days are best to start your auctions, with weather-related icons that identify good days and bad days.

The AuctionBytes calendar lists optimum days to end auctions, based on the number of days that you set for your auction listing. For example, starting a

three-day auction on a Monday is good because Thursday is considered a good day to end your auction.

However, keep in mind that anomalies exist with any eBay formula; no one can predict with any certainty when a bidder may bid on an item. Trial and error and your own experiences are the best way to gauge how to sell items online. In fact, you may find that the market for your item contradicts popular eBay listing theories completely.

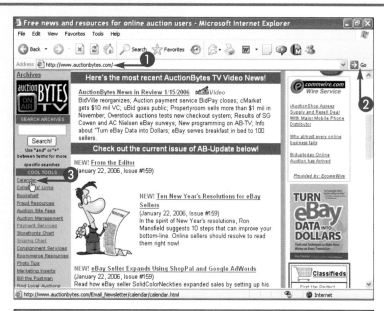

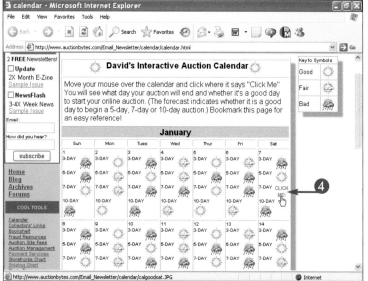

① In the Address bar of your Web browser, type **www.auctionbytes.com**.

② Click Go or press Enter.

The AuctionBytes Web page appears.

③ Click the Calendar link.

The Auction Calendar page appears.

④ Move the mouse pointer over an auction-listing icon, and click when the icon changes to a CLICK ME icon.

A Web page displays information about that particular type of listing and auction length.

View eBay
SELLER TIPS

#57

DIFFICULTY LEVEL

A great way to stay current with the latest news about any particular eBay auction category is to view the Category Tips section, located in the eBay Seller Central page.

For each category, you can view a regularly updated article called Seller's Edge, which is published monthly and features insider strategies, features, and insights. For example, the Antiques Seller's Edge article is specific to online antique sellers, while the Entertainment Seller's Edge article is specific to entertainment products.

eBay also features a different seller each month in its Seller Profiles section.

You can also view a list of the hottest-selling items for a particular category, called In Demand, as well as links to useful eBay tools and information. Be sure to look at the Category Tips section each month to find out the latest news about your category of interest.

If you are new to selling items on eBay, then start by reading tips for just one or two categories until you are ready to explore others. For information on various industry newsletters, see Task #95.

① In the Address bar of your Web browser, type **http://pages. ebay.com/sellercentral/ sellbycategory.html**.

② Click Go or press Enter.

The Seller Central page appears, displaying the Category Tips section.

③ Click the Seller's Edge link below a category that interests you.

● You can also click the Seller Profiles or In Demand links.

eBay displays the Seller's Edge page for that category.

You can read this section to learn valuable information about your category of interest.

Create auction listings with
TURBO LISTER

You can use the eBay Turbo Lister program to give your eBay auction listings a more uniform and professional appearance. After you download Turbo Lister for free from eBay, you can use it to build your auction listings offline. When you are ready to post the auctions on eBay, Turbo Lister posts the listings for you.

Turbo Lister, available at http://pages.ebay.com/turbolister/download.html, offers you a choice of several themes for your listing, and you can also select from several layouts for photo placement.

You can add your description text and format it just as you would with a word-processing program. You can also view your listing in HTML format and add HTML tags to your text.

One of the most attractive features in Turbo Lister is the ability to duplicate listings for similar items without having to retype your information. For example, after you design and type a listing for a collectible item, you can duplicate that same listing for a second, similar item and then make small changes to describe the second item.

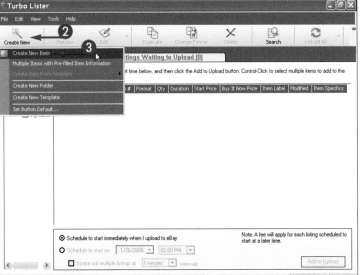

① Double-click the eBay Turbo Lister shortcut icon.

Note: This shortcut icon appears on the Windows XP desktop after you download and install the free Turbo Lister program from eBay.

The Turbo Lister program window opens.

Note: The first time you open Turbo Lister, you must set up your eBay account to work with it by following the onscreen prompts.

② Click Create New.

③ Click Create New Item.

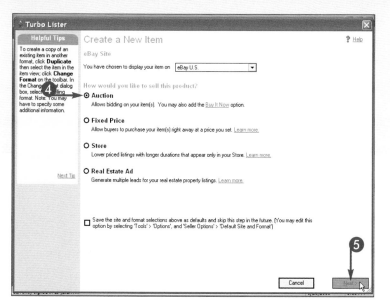

The Create a New Item page appears.

④ Click to select the type of listing that you want to create.

Note: The Store option only shows if you have an eBay Store.

⑤ Click Next.

 # 58

DIFFICULTY LEVEL

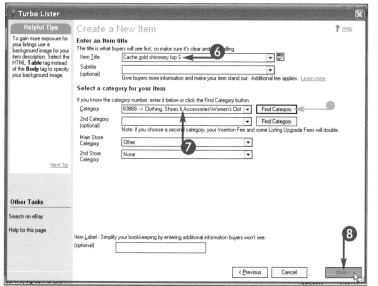

The next Create a New Item page appears.

⑥ Type a title that describes your item.

⑦ Type a category number.

● You can also click Find Category and select your category.

⑧ Click Next.

Note: You may be prompted to type item specifics, depending on the eBay category that you choose.

Did You Know?

You can download a copy of Turbo Lister for free from eBay at http://pages.ebay.com/turbolister/download.html. TurboLister offers both a Web Setup, which checks your computer for previously installed components and downloads only those that are needed, and a Full Setup. After installing the software, a shortcut icon for Turbo Lister appears on the Windows desktop. You can double-click the icon to open the program. Turbo Lister does not currently support the Macintosh platform.

eBay Savvy!

Turbo Lister can also import delimited data files. This means that you can use database core programs, such as inventory-management programs or order-accounting programs, with Turbo Lister.

Create auction listings with
TURBO LISTER

If you plan to sell items frequently on eBay, then you can definitely benefit from downloading Turbo Lister. Turbo Lister helps you to sell your items more efficiently, and you always have a list of your auctions ready to view or edit.

Turbo Lister presents a seller's form similar to the one on the eBay site; however, creating your listing with Turbo Lister is much faster than creating an online eBay listing. You can check your work for errors without the pressure to complete your listing

online. You can also save your work and edit it later before posting the auction on eBay.

Turbo Lister's themes and photo layouts are the same as those that are available with the Listing Designer feature on eBay's online seller's form. You are charged a small fee for each auction for using Listing Designer with Turbo Lister. Other items that you apply in Turbo Lister still incur a fee on eBay, such as adding a second category, adding a Bid Now option, or including more than one photo with the listing.

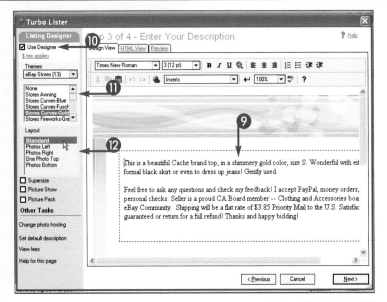

⑨ Type your auction listing text.

⑩ Click to select the Use Designer option.

⑪ Click a theme type and theme.

⑫ Click a photo layout.

⑬ Click anywhere beneath the text box to insert a picture.

The Insert Picture dialog box appears.

⑭ Click the picture that you want to add to your auction listing.

● You can click here to resize the picture.

⑮ Click Insert.

The Insert Picture dialog box closes.

⑯ Click Next.

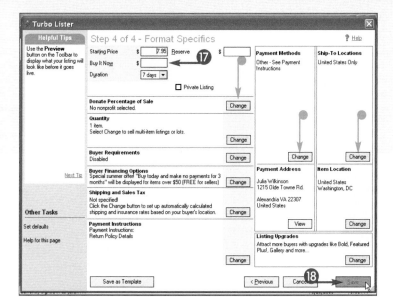

The Format Specifics page appears.

⑰ Type information in the form just as you would the eBay seller's form, specifying auction duration and price.

● You can click Change to edit information.

⑱ Click Save.

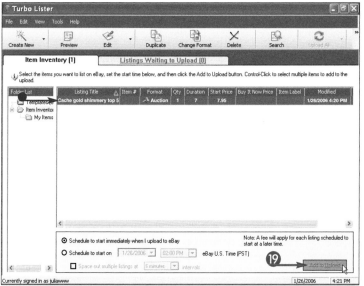

● Turbo Lister saves the listing to your Item Inventory list.

You can continue adding more auction listings to your inventory.

⑲ When you are ready to post the listings, select the listings and click Add to Upload, log on to the Internet, and upload your auction to eBay.

eBay Savvy!

When you upload your auction listings from Turbo Lister to eBay, eBay schedules the auction to start at the time that you upload. If you prefer to start an auction at a later time, then you must use the scheduler, which incurs a listing fee. For that reason, you may prefer to log in to your Internet connection and upload the listings at the most convenient time for your auctions. Remember that the start time on eBay's listing form is in Pacific Standard Time, or PST.

Did You Know?

Every time you upload listings to eBay from Turbo Lister, the program also checks for system updates. Any updates display in an Update Status message.

Research auctions with
DEEPANALYSIS

You can use a variety of third-party auction tools to research the eBay marketplace. For example, a search for the keywords *auction tools* using a Web search engine such as google.com displays a variety of shareware and freeware tools that you can download and use, including the popular DeepAnalysis program from HammerTap.

DeepAnalysis is an eBay market research program that you can use to analyze and extract auction sales information and eBay statistics. You can download a trial version of the program for $1 from the HammerTap Web site at www.hammertap.com. Once you install the program, you can specify

what sort of auction data you want to research. DeepAnalysis helps you to log in to eBay and extract the data. DeepAnalysis then displays the data by seller and item.

You can use the full version of DeepAnalysis to view sell-through rates, see the average sale price for each item, view average bids for each item, discover the highest-priced items, and create reports about the data that you analyze.

The program also features a Statistics tab for viewing eBay statistics about the item that you are researching.

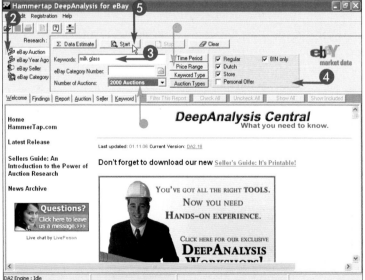

① Double-click the DeepAnalysis shortcut icon.

Note: This shortcut icon appears on your desktop after you download and install the trial version of the program from www.hammertap.com.

The DeepAnalysis program window appears.

② Click the type of analysis that you want to perform.

③ Type the keywords here.

Note: Not all analyses require keywords.

④ Click here and select Auction Types.

● You can also select a price range.

● You can select the number of auctions to analyze.

⑤ Click Start.

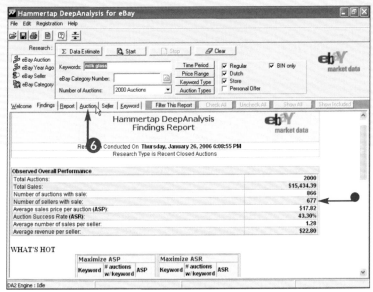

DeepAnalysis analyzes the site.

This process may take a few minutes.

The DeepAnalysis Findings Report appears.

- You can view the total sales and other data.

⑥ Click the Auction tab.

59

DIFFICULTY LEVEL

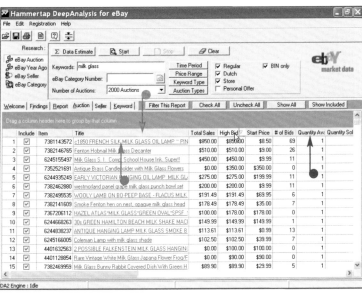

The Auction page appears.

- You can view data for the individual auctions, including title, total sales, and high bid.

- You can click a title to view the auction page.

- You can click a column heading to sort the results by that option.

TIPS

More Options!

The latest version of DeepAnalysis has an "eBay Year Ago" feature that you can use to find long-term results and trends. In the DeepAnalysis main screen, click eBay Year Ago, type the keywords or eBay category number of your choice, and then click Start. The results appear for the selected time period a year ago. You can select up to 30 days of data in a time period.

eBay Savvy!

DeepAnalysis enables you to quickly see which eBay sellers are doing well in the marketplace and examine their techniques and product lines. You can also use the data that you research to find out which categories work best for your own items, as well as which items receive the most bids.

Boosting Your Sales with Advanced Selling Techniques

Once you master the basics of selling on eBay, you can learn new skills to manage and increase your sales.

If you consistently sell enough items on eBay, then you can earn the prestigious title of PowerSeller, which brings many benefits, such as icons that you can use in your auctions, a dedicated message board, and a health care program.

As you sell more items, your image fees may add up, especially if you list multiple images of each item. You can save money by using third-party image-hosting companies, such as inkFrog.com. To give your bidders a more complete view of your products, you may also want to display multiple images of your items in a slideshow format.

eBay's tools, such as Selling Manager Pro, can help you to keep track of sales, shipping, and payments. They also enable you to archive sales records, and download statistics into a format that

you can read with accounting applications, such as Microsoft Excel. Selling Manager Pro also enables you to expedite the many chores associated with eBay sales, such as contacting buyers, managing payments, and tracking shipments.

You can improve the appearance of your auctions by using eBay's built-in text editor, which enables you to make your auction look much more professional without knowing HTML. You can add many text attributes, such as bold and color, and select different fonts, to make parts of your item description stand out.

You can create an even more professional image by opening your own eBay Store, which enables you to use listing management tools and many cross-promotion features. If you sell items that complement each other, such as men's neckties and shirts, then you can use these options to show more of your related items to your customers.

Top 100

Save money with
IMAGE HOSTING

Because eBay charges for each picture that you upload to host auction images, you can save money by using a third-party image-hosting service. The first image on eBay's image-hosting service is free, but each subsequent image costs $0.15. As a result, your picture fees can add up to a significant amount of money. For example, if you upload four images for each auction, and you list ten auctions each week, then your image-hosting fees on eBay are $4.50 each week, or about $18 every month.

With the same number of images, you can have a service, such as inkFrog.com, host your images for

one flat rate of $4.95 each month, a savings of $13.05 or more each month, depending on how many auctions you list. inkFrog also offers other pricing plans.

You should not make your photo files larger than 50KB, or they will load slowly on eBay. See Task #52 for information on cropping your image.

Before you can perform the steps in this task, you must first register at inkFrog.com. For information on adding multiple images in a slideshow format, see Task #61.

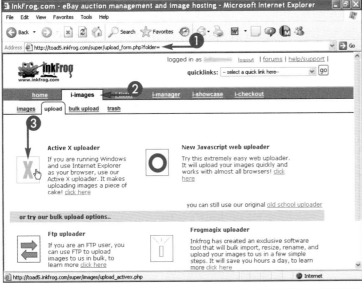

① Log in to the inkFrog.com Web site.

The inkFrog picture & auction management page opens.

② Click the i-images tab.

③ Click to select an uploader option.

If you are using Internet Explorer, then inkFrog suggests that you use ActiveX.

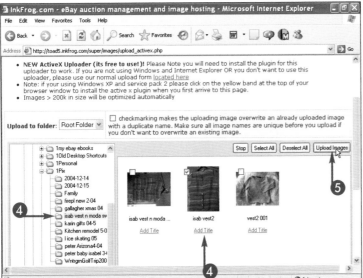

inkFrog prompts you to download the software if you have not done so.

The Images Section appears.

④ Navigate to the image that you want to upload and select it.

Note: To make your image eBay-ready, see Task #52.

⑤ Click Upload Images.

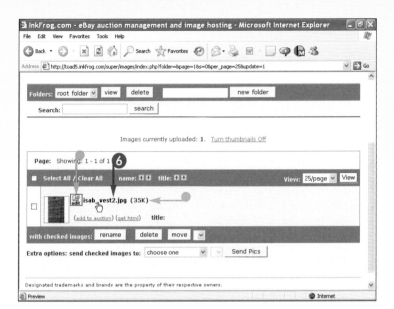

 # 60

DIFFICULTY LEVEL

inkFrog tells you that your image is uploaded.

● The file size appears here.

If your file size is larger than 50KB, then the image loads slowly on eBay.

● You can click here to edit the image.

6 Click the filename link.

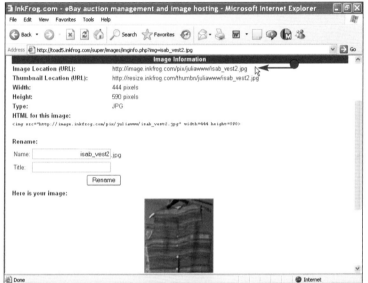

● inkFrog displays the image location, or URL.

inkFrog hosts your picture.

You can type the URL into the Picture URL box on eBay's listing page to add the picture to your eBay auction.

More Options!

You can use other third-party image-hosting services, such as SpareDollar, Andale, or Vendio. SpareDollar offers 50MB of image storage space that holds approximately 1,000 images, for $8.95 each month. Andale offers a $3 monthly plan for up to 50 images. You can read about their pricing plans at www.sparedollar.com/corp/pricing.asp, www.andale.com/corp/pricing_corp.jsp, and www.vendio.com/pricing.html. Shop around and decide which is best for you. Consider the volume and size of images that you host each week or month.

More Options!

inkFrog offers a premium plan at $7.95 each month, which includes 400 images and auction-listing tools, such as professional-looking templates. It also offers a pro plan at $12.95 each month, which includes 1,000 images, thumbnails, cropping, and bulk-listing tools.

Add multiple images in
SLIDESHOW FORMAT

Using eBay's image-listing options, you can increase your sales by showing your prospective buyers different angles of an item using multiple images in a slideshow format. eBay buyers are savvy, and they like to know exactly what they are getting. For example, they bid more confidently if they can view both sides of a garment instead of only the front view.

You can upload up to a total of six images with eBay's image-hosting service. The first image for an auction is free, and each additional image is $0.15.

eBay does not charge an additional fee for rotating the images in slideshow format.

Because costs for images and a slideshow add up, you should make sure that the estimated final price of the auction item justifies adding them. For example, you may decide that it makes sense to post multiple images and a slideshow for an item worth $50, but not for an item worth only $10.

For more information about image hosting, see Task #60.

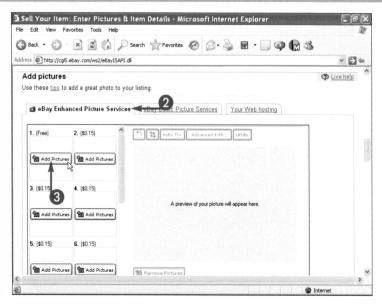

1 In the eBay home page, click the Sell tab.

eBay guides you through the process of selling your item.

2 In the Sell Your Item: Enter Pictures & Item Details page, scroll to the eBay Enhanced Picture Services tab.

Note: If this is the first time that you use eBay Enhanced Picture Services, then you must click the Set up Picture Services button and install it.

3 Click Add Pictures.

The Open dialog box appears.

4 Double-click the folder that contains your photo file.

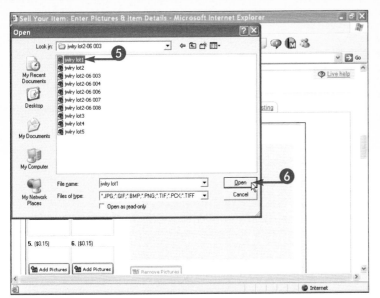

The folder displays the files.

⑤ Click the file that you want to upload.

⑥ Click Open.

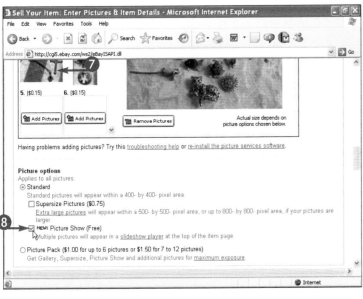

The photo appears in the Picture 1 box.

⑦ Repeat steps **4** to **6** for each additional photo that you want to add.

⑧ Scroll down the page, and click to select the Picture Show option.

⑨ Continue the listing process by completing the Sell Your Item form.

eBay adds a slideshow of the selected images to your listing.

Did You Know?

You can use between two and six images to create an animated effect with a slideshow. Keep in mind that you cannot have still pictures and a slideshow in the same listing with eBay's picture services. You can also increase the size of your pictures, or super size them, up to 800 pixels wide by 800 pixels high, for $0.75. Images must be at least 440 pixels on their longest side to qualify for the Supersize Picture option.

More Options!

You can create slideshows with some third-party image-hosting companies, such as Andale at www.andale.com. You can also find some companies that provide free image hosting, such as www.mpire.com. For more information about third-party image hosting, see Task #60.

Use statistics to MEASURE SALES

If you sell items regularly on eBay, then you may find it time-consuming and difficult to keep track of all of your sales records for business and tax purposes. The Selling Manager Pro tool makes this tedious chore a lot easier.

You can download your sales records with eBay's Selling Manager Pro tool in a comma-delimited file format, so that you can read them in a software application such as Microsoft Excel. You can also retrieve an estimate of your total active and past sales with Selling Manager Pro's Quick Stats, which measures weekly or monthly profits, as well as tax records.

You can download sales records for periods ranging from yesterday to the last 90 days, or select a specific date. Because eBay only retains sales records for four months, you should download them regularly to ensure that you have all of the information that you need for the entire tax year.

Selling Manager Pro costs $15.99 each month, and eBay offers a free 30-day trial. For a tour of Selling Manager, go to http://pages.ebay.com/selling_manager/tour.html.

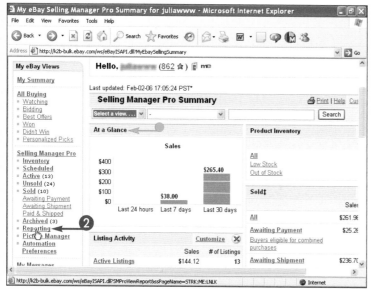

① In any eBay page, click My eBay.

Note: You must first subscribe to Selling Manager Pro.

The My eBay Selling Manager Pro Summary page opens.

● You can view your sales at a glance.

② Click the Reporting link.

eBay tells you that it may take up to 60 minutes to generate your report.

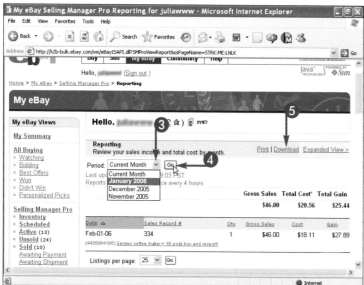

The My eBay Reporting page opens.

③ Click here and select the month for which you want to download data.

④ Click Go.

The data appears for the month that you selected.

⑤ Click Download.

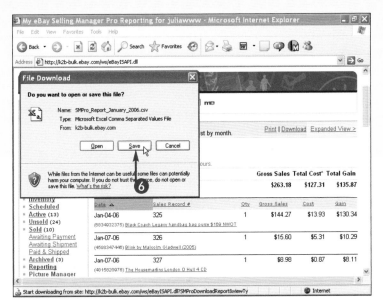

The File Download dialog box appears.

6 Click Save.

eBay guides you through the process of saving your data.

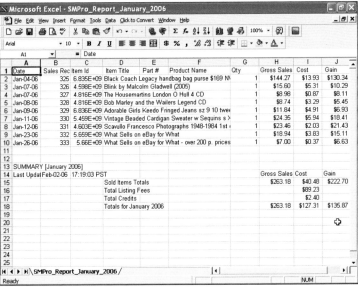

7 Launch your spreadsheet application and open the file that contains your data.

You can view your sales statistics.

TIPS

More Options!

Selling Manager and Selling Manager Pro can help you keep track of when you ship items and when buyers pay for them. You can mark sold items as awaiting payment, awaiting shipment, and paid and shipped. From the main Selling Manager or Selling Manager Pro screen in My eBay, click a link under Sold, such as Awaiting Shipment. Select the box next to the items. Click the Change Status menu and select an option, such as Shipped, then click Select, and then click Confirm Status. Sales Manager tells you that your Sales records status updated successfully.

Did You Know?

Some third-party tools, such as Andale, at www.andale.com, also allow you to organize statistics. Andale's Sales Analyzer tool displays what percentage of your sales are successful.

Get organized with
SELLING MANAGER

You can save time on many administrative tasks and be more efficient and organized with eBay's Selling Manager or Selling Manager Pro. These are online tools that enable you to track and manage your sales. With Selling Manager, you can easily do all of the following: keep track of items that have sold, been paid for, and shipped; relist items in bulk; archive auction records; and print invoices and shipping labels directly from your sales records.

Selling Manager is most useful for sellers with medium- to high-volume sales. If you have low-volume sales, then you may not need Selling

Manager. You get the most out of Selling Manager if you use it in tandem with eBay's free Turbo Lister tool.

Although the examples in this task use Selling Manager Pro, the same features are available with Selling Manager.

You can try Selling Manager for free for 30 days. After the free trial, Selling Manager costs $4.99 each month. For information about Selling Manager Pro, see Task #62. To sign up for Selling Manager, you can go to http://pages.ebay.com/selling_manager/products.html.

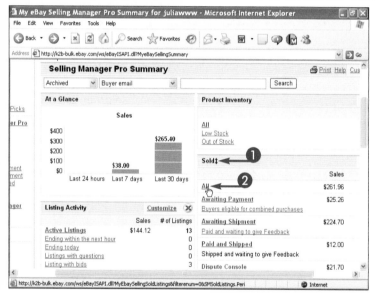

① From the My eBay page, scroll to the Sold heading in the Selling Manager Pro Summary tab.

Note: This summary appears only after you subscribe to Selling Manager or Manager Pro.

② Click the All link.

A list of your sold items appears.

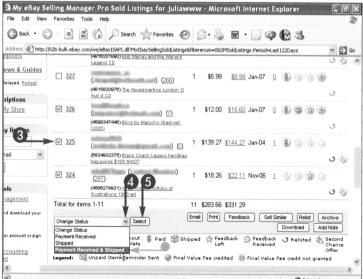

③ Click to select an item or items.

④ Click the Change Status drop-down menu and select the Payment Received & Shipped option.

● You can also click either Payment Received or Shipped.

⑤ Click Select.

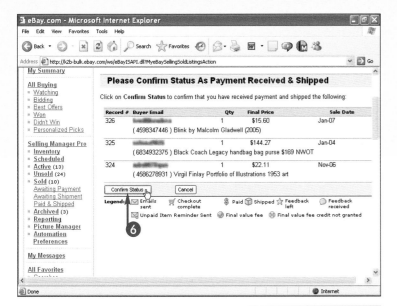

The Please Confirm Status as Payment Received & Shipped screen appears.

6 Click Confirm Status.

63

DIFFICULTY LEVEL

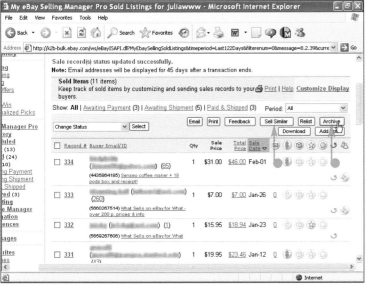

Sales Manager tells you that your sale records status has updated successfully.

Sales Manager updates the numbers on the Summary page, next to Paid and shipped.

● You can click either Sell Similar or Archive.

Sales Manager helps you to keep track of your payments and shipments.

More Options!

If you are a high-volume eBay seller and list hundreds of items each month, then you can use eBay's Selling Manager Pro, which offers all of the features of Selling Manager, as well as inventory management. These tools can help you to do the following: determine your products' success ratio and average selling price; send and track feedback and invoices; use customizable seller e-mail templates; and bulk e-mail to buyers. For a complete list of features, go to http://pages.ebay.com/selling_manager_pro/faq.html. Selling Manager Pro is free for 30 days and then costs $15.99 monthly.

Did You Know?

You may want to use eBay's Turbo Lister tool if you sell in volume. For more about Turbo Lister, see Task #57.

Improve your listings with eBay's
EDITOR

You can use basic HTML attributes to format your listings so that they are clear, well organized, and have a nice appearance. Your prospective bidders take you more seriously when your listings look professional, and this can lead to more sales.

eBay makes it very easy to use HTML, because it provides an editing toolbar that allows you to apply HTML text attributes within the auction-listing page. You simply select from a menu of buttons that represent different HTML attributes, and highlight the text to which you want to apply those attributes.

The HTML editor allows you to place your text in bold and italics, and select a font, size, and color for your text. You can also center, right- or left-justify it, or create bulleted or numbered lists.

If you prefer, you can use the Enter your own HTML tab. By adding a few HTML attributes to your listings, you can even transform a long, monotonous piece of text into a series of neatly separated and defined paragraphs.

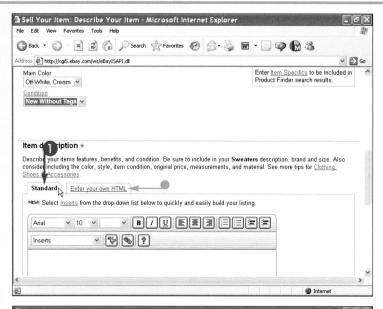

① In the Sell Your Item: Describe Your Item page, in the Item description section, click the Standard tab if it is not already selected.

● You can click here to enter your own HTML formatting.

② Type your text into the text box, and select the text that you want to change.

③ Click a formatting option.

● You can click here and select a font size.

● You can click here and select a font.

● You can also click here to change the text color.

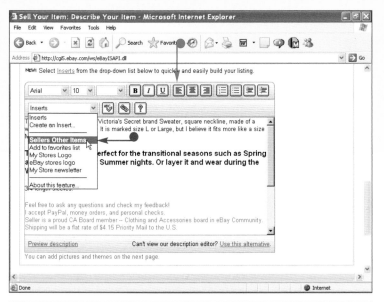

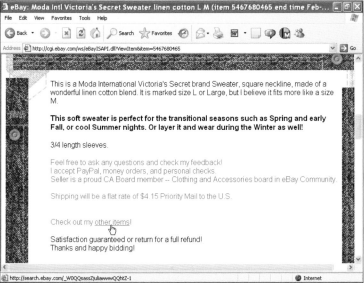

● You can click these options to change the format of your text.

bold

italic

underline

left-justify

center

right-justify

numbered list

bulleted list

● You can click here and select an Insert option, such as Sellers Other Items.

④ Scroll down and Click Continue.

Your item description appears with your HTML attributes when eBay users view it.

This example shows text that has been changed to bold, with a font size of 12, and red text to emphasize different parts of the listing.

TIPS

More Options!

If you choose the Enter your own HTML tab in the Sell Your Item: Describe Your Item page, then you can use basic HTML such as a <p> tag to separate your paragraphs, a <br> tag to start a new line without skipping a space, and the <hr> tag to add a horizontal rule with your text above and below it. You can also create different-sized headings with the <h1></h1> through <h6></h6> tags.

Did You Know?

The Web offers a number of free HTML tutorials, such as www.pagetutor.com, www.htmlgoodies.com, or Dave's HTML guide at www.davesite.com/webstation/html. You can also do a search for HTML tutorials using your favorite search engine.

Market your goods with an
EBAY STORE

You can open an eBay Store to create a unique presence and to instill confidence in your customers that you are a reputable seller. An eBay Store is an area within eBay that you can customize with graphics and your own categories. You can also use the eBay Store listing-management tools to receive monthly sales reports.

eBay Stores offer the following advantages: your own directory page and search engine; a chance to feature the store on the main Stores page; promotion on all of your item listings and on the related Stores area within eBay's search results pages; and a general eBay Stores link in the eBay home page.

eBay offers a free 30-day trial for stores, after which pricing starts at $15.95 each month for a Basic eBay Store.

To qualify for an eBay Store, you must have a PayPal account or be ID-verified

Even if you have an eBay Store, you should also list items within the non-store part of eBay. Although Store items now appear after matching Online Auction and Fixed Price listings in eBay search and browse results, depending on how many of those results appear, the Store listings may not be easy for eBayers to find.

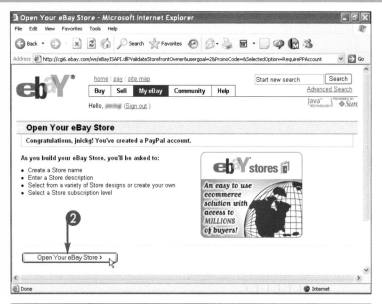

① In the eBay home page, click the eBay Stores link, or go to http://stores.ebay.com and then click Open a Store.

eBay guides you to the Open Your eBay Store page.

You may be asked to create a PayPal account or become ID verified.

② Click Open Your eBay Store.

The Select Theme page opens.

③ Click to select a theme.

④ Scroll down the page, and click Continue.

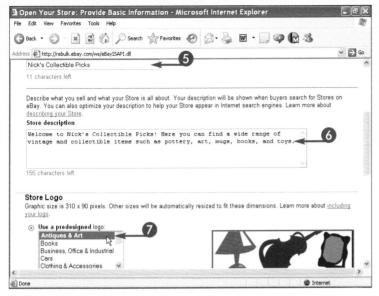

5 Type a Store name.

6 Type a Store description.

7 Choose a Store logo.

You can choose a predesigned logo, upload your own logo, or choose not to use a logo.

eBay guides you through the rest of the Store-building process.

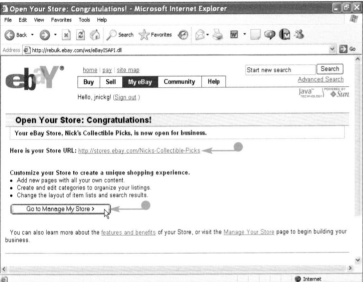

● eBay tells you that your store is open and displays your Store URL.

● You can click Go to Manage My Store.

More Options!

In addition to the Basic Store, eBay offers Featured Stores for $49.95 each month, and Anchor Stores for $499.95 each month. Both Featured and Anchor Stores get priority placement in eBay's onsite promotions, such as rotation in the eBay Stores homepage. eBay also gives Featured Stores $30 worth of prepaid eBay Keywords promotions each month, and Anchor Stores $100 worth of eBay Keywords promotions each month.

Did You Know?

You can make changes to your Store after you create it by using the Store Builder tool. To make changes, go to your Store's home page, click the Seller, manage store link, and then select one of the Store Design or Store Marketing links.

Cross-promote your
EBAY STORE ITEMS

A great feature of an eBay Store is that shoppers can see thumbnail images of items that you designate at the bottom of a Store listing. They can then go directly to an item that interests them and bid on it, which can lead to more sales for you. You can designate what types of items you cross-promote through the Manage My Store page.

You have several options for cross-promoting. For example, you can cross-promote items by Selling format, such as only Buy It Now items or only Store inventory items. You can either show items with

Gallery images first, or only show items with Gallery images. You can also select items by when they end, such as those ending soonest or last. If you prefer, you can have eBay show your highest-priced items first.

For information on cross-promoting by Store category, see Task #67. For more on eBay Stores, see Task #65. You can also attract eBay buyers to your auctions using eBay Keywords and your About Me page, as illustrated in Tasks #68 and #69.

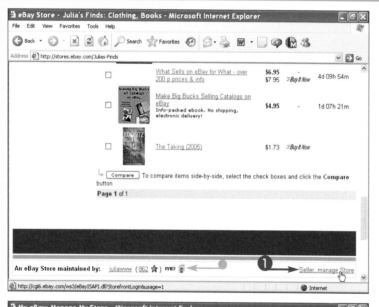

1 From your eBay Store main page, click the Seller, manage Store link.

● You can click the Stores icon near the top of the My eBay page to go to your Store, or just click the Stores icon from any of your eBay listings.

The Manage My Store page opens.

2 Click the Default Cross Promotions link.

● You can click here to manage your Store Vacation Settings.

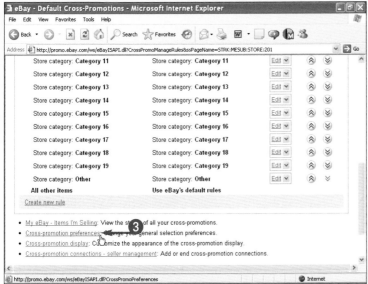

The Default Cross-Promotions page opens.

③ Scroll down and click the Cross-promotion preferences link.

DIFFICULTY LEVEL

The Manage Your Cross-Promotions page opens.

④ Click to select the Cross-promote my items option.

● You can also select Cross-promote in checkout and Cross-promote in all other available areas.

● You can also choose Do not cross-promote my items.

⑤ Select your cross-promotion display preferences for when someone views your items.

⑥ Click Save Settings at the bottom of the page.

eBay saves your settings.

More Options!

To quickly cross-promote your eBay Store, include item descriptions that encourage users to view your other Store items. Prospective bidders can click the eBay Stores icon to access your Store. To make this technique effective, you should list auctions as well as fixed-price Store listings; this is because fixed-price listings appear in eBay's regular search beneath regular auction format items, and are therefore sometimes not as visible.

More Options!

You can select options for when someone bids on or wins your items, as well as for when someone views your items. From the Participate in Cross-Promotions page, scroll down past the When someone views my items section. You can cross-promote your items by selling format, by Gallery images, or by ending times.

Manage
CROSS-PROMOTED ITEMS

Using eBay's Store Merchandising Manager, you can boost your Store sales by designating which types of items your eBay Store cross-promotes to eBay users.

eBay shoppers can see thumbnail images at the bottom of a Store listing of items in the same category, or of items in the category that you designate. eBay automatically cross-promotes items that are in the same Store category, but Merchandising Manager allows you to specify which categories of items you want users to see when they view and bid on your items.

In most cases, you may want to promote items in the same category. For example, from a listing in a Books category, you may want to promote other items in the Books category. However, in some cases you may want to promote an item that complements a particular item, but is in a different category. For example, you may want to promote a book light in a book listing.

For more information about cross-promoting your eBay Store items, see Task #66.

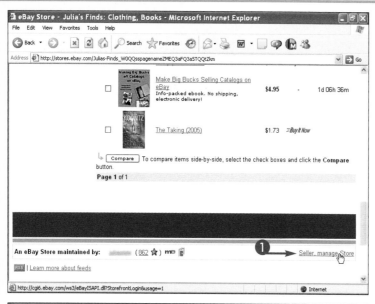

1 In your Store page, click the Seller, manage Store link.

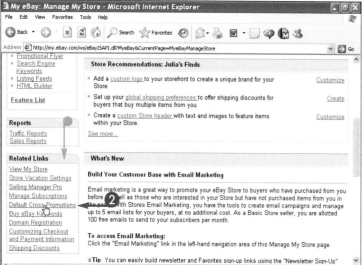

The Manage My Store page opens.

2 Click the Default Cross Promotions link.

● You can also click the Customizing Checkout and Payment Information link, as well as other Store management options.

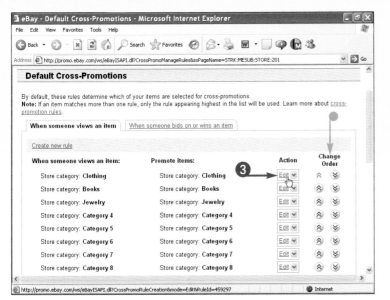

The Default Cross-Promotions page opens.

③ Click the Edit link under the category that you want.

● You can click here to change the order of your categories.

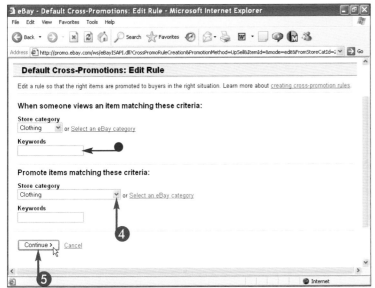

The Default Cross-Promotions: Edit Rule page opens.

● You can type keywords from your item titles here.

④ Click here and select a category that users see when they view an item.

⑤ Click Continue.

eBay prompts you to verify your changes and promotes items from the category that you designate for the items.

More Options!

You can see which of your Store items have manual and automatic cross-promotions, as well as which ended items have had their cross-promotions replaced. To do this, in the Default Cross Promotions page, click the My eBay - Items I'm Selling link to view the status of all of your cross-promotions.

Did You Know?

You can turn cross-promotion of your items on or off, and specify different cross-promotion display settings. From the Manage My Store page, click the Default Cross Promotions link. You can select various display options, such as Show only items with a Buy It Now price, or Show any item. You can also specify how to cross-promote Gallery items and how to sort cross-promoted items.

Chapter 8

Maximizing Your Items' Exposure

eBay and some third-party developers offer many ways to attract attention to your items to increase your sales. One way to promote both your auctions and your business is to set up an About Me page. The About Me page is the only place on eBay where you may post links to your Web site, or to other Web sites.

You can also use eBay's Gallery feature, which offers a good value at only $0.35. With Gallery, eBay users can preview a photo of your item when searching and browsing, and therefore are more likely to view the auction.

You can buy your way to a better placement within eBay's many pages by using a Featured Plus! listing for an extra $19.95. You can also time your auctions more strategically using the eBay Merchandising Calendar, and create your own ad using eBay Keywords.

While not as high in profile, other tactics can also be effective, such as using the bold or highlighting listing option, and mentioning your other auctions within your auction text.

Sophisticated techniques, such as Andale's Gallery tool, showcase thumbnails of your other auctions in your listings. You can also list a strategic item to attract attention to all of your auctions and gain buyers' confidence with a SquareTrade Seal of Approval.

Experiment to see which techniques work best for you, and watch your sales increase.

Top 100

USE EBAY KEYWORDS
to attract traffic

You can attract bidders who search for auctions using related words by running ads with eBay Keywords. eBay shoppers use the search field millions of times each day, and so an eBay Keywords ad can significantly boost your auctions' visibility.

Your banner or text ad runs on the search results page that eBay members see when they perform searches using the same keywords or phrases that you specify. You can link your ad to one or more auctions, or to your eBay store. The eBay Keywords site guides you through the creation of your ad, and also allows you to upload a graphic of your own.

You can designate your budget for the ad campaign, and your bid for the ad's cost-per-click. You only pay when someone clicks your ad. eBay automatically pauses your campaign when the auction to which the campaign is linked ends. You must be careful not to spend more than you can afford, especially with your first campaign.

To run an ad, you must first sign in to the service with your eBay Login at the eBay Keywords Web site at http://ebay.admarketplace.net.

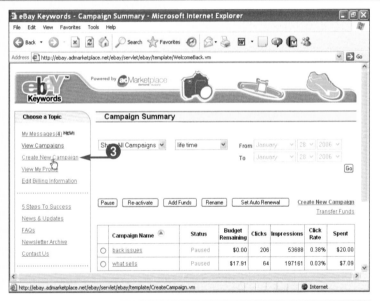

① Type **ebay.admarketplace.net** in the Address bar of your Web browser, and press Enter.

The eBay Keywords home page opens.

② Click Sign In to login to the site.

Your Campaign Summary page opens, with information about any current or previous campaigns.

Note: *If you have no campaigns running, the Campaign Creation page appears.*

③ Click the Create New Campaign link.

The Campaign Creation page opens.

④ Type a campaign name in the text box.

⑤ Type an amount for your campaign budget.

The minimum budget is $20.

⑥ Click Create Ad.

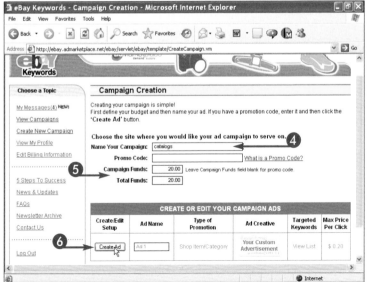

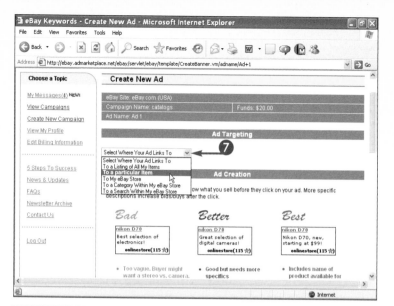

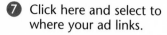

The Create New Ad page opens.

7 Click here and select to where your ad links.

8 Scroll down the page and type an ad title and description.

9 Click Proceed to Keyword Selection.

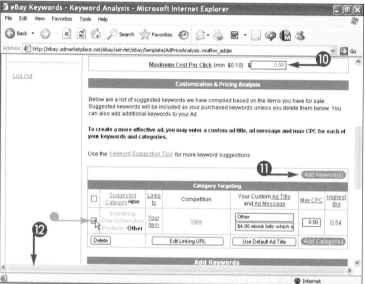

The Keyword Analysis page opens.

10 Type a maximum cost per click.

11 Click Add Keyword(s).

12 Scroll down the page and type your keywords in the text box.

● You can select a suggested category.

13 Click OK.

14 Click Proceed to Ad Review.

eBay guides you through the rest of the ad creation process.

---

eBay Savvy!

When you follow these steps, you produce an ad that eBay users see at the top of a search results list, as shown in this figure. You can also create your own graphic and upload it if you want to use a custom ad design.

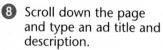

Sell catalogs Click Here

$4.95 ebook tells which sell for the most.

juliawww (860 ⭐)

Emphasize listings with your
ABOUT ME PAGE

You can attract viewers to your auctions and post links to resources outside of eBay by using your About Me page. Although eBay does not allow members to post links to their own Web sites in auction listings, it does allow the posting of these links on members' About Me pages.

eBay users can access your About Me page by clicking the blue-and-red me icon next to your eBay user ID. You can also place text in your auction listings that directs people to your About Me page.

Some eBay sellers use the About Me page to post helpful information and resources about their field of expertise. For example, several purse experts use the About Me pages to showcase information about how to tell authentic brand bags from fake bags. You can do the same thing with your About Me page, giving eBay buyers a reason to visit your page, and therefore getting more eBay buyers to follow links to your auctions.

This task assumes that you already have an About Me page. For more information, see http://pages.ebay.com/help/feedback/about_me.html.

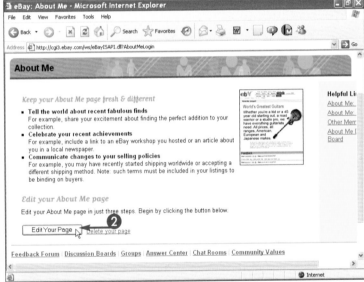

① From the eBay Community page, click the Create an About Me page link.

The About Me page opens.

② Click Edit Your Page.

If you do not already have an About Me page, then eBay guides you through the process of creating one.

The About Me: Choose Your Editing Option page opens.

③ Click to select an editing option.

● You can either select eBay's step-by-step process, or enter your own HTML code.

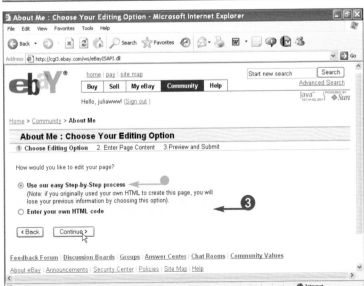

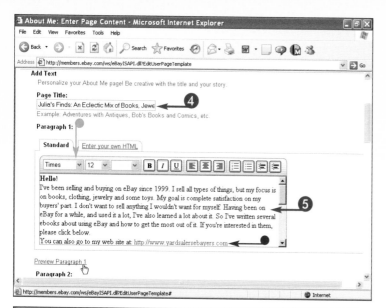

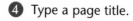

The About Me: Enter Page content page opens.

④ Type a page title.

⑤ Type information about yourself and your business.

● To format the text, you can select a font and other options.

● You can also include links to your Web site.

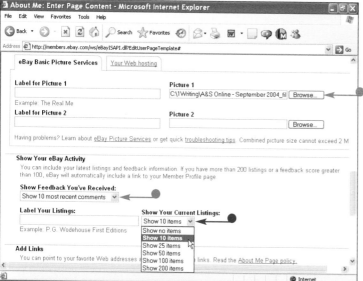

● You can click Browse to add a picture.

● You can click here and select a feedback option.

● You can click here and select a current listings option.

⑥ Click Continue.

eBay guides you through the rest of the process and saves your About Me page.

More Options!

You can choose one of three different layouts for your About Me page, with different arrangements of images and text. Once you select a layout, click Submit. eBay then tells you that your About Me page has been edited and displays a link to view the page. The link is http://members.ebay.com/ws/eBayISAPI.dll?ViewUserPage&userid=X, where X is your user ID.

Julia's Finds: An Eclectic Mix of Books, Jewelry & Clothing

Hello!

I've been selling and buying on eBay since 1999. I sell all types of things, but my focus is on books, clothing, jewelry and some toys. My goal is complete satisfaction on my buyers' part. I don't want to sell anything I wouldn't want for myself. Having been on eBay for a while, and used it a lot, I've also learned a lot about it. So I've written several ebooks about using eBay and how to get the most out of it. If you're interested in them, please click below.

You can also go to my web site at: http://www.yardsalersebayers.com

My books include: eBay Top 100 Simplified Tips & Tricks, Wiley, 2004 (http://www.amazon.com/gp/product/0764555952)

Give shoppers a preview with GALLERY

You can use the Gallery feature to show eBay shoppers a miniature image, or thumbnail, of your auction item when they browse or search in your lists of items. According to some reports, you can get from 25 percent to 200 percent more bids by using the Gallery feature. At a cost of only $0.35, the Gallery feature may be your best investment in your auction beyond the basic listing fees.

Because your items are competing against so many other items on eBay, anything that you do to help them stand out increases the chances that people will bid on them. Some shoppers browse through so many pages of listings so quickly that they may not even take the time to view your item if you do not use the Gallery feature.

You can choose the Gallery feature in the Sell Your Item: Enter Pictures & Item Details page during the eBay listing process. After you submit your listing, eBay may take a few minutes to recognize your item in its search engine.

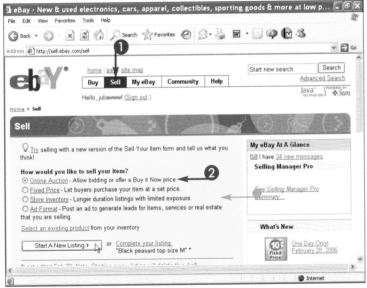

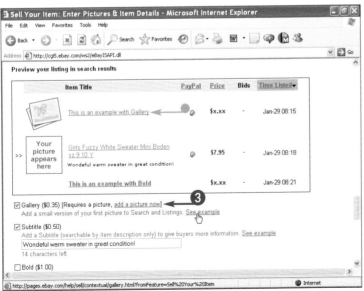

LIST YOUR AUCTION

1 In the eBay home page, click Sell.

The Sell page opens.

2 Click to select the Online Auction option.

● You can also select the Fixed Price, Store Inventory, or Real Estate options.

The Store Inventory option only shows if you have an eBay Store.

eBay guides you through the listing process.

3 In the Sell Your Item: Enter Pictures & Item Details page, click to select the Gallery option.

● You can click this link to see an example of a Gallery listing.

eBay continues to guide you through the listing process.

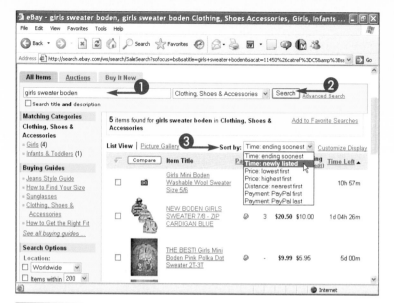

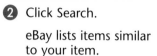

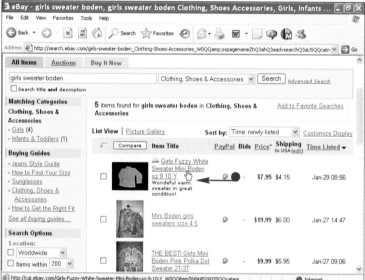

#70

DIFFICULTY LEVEL

1 In the eBay category where you list your item, or eBay's main Search page, type keywords from your item's title in the Search text box.

2 Click Search.

eBay lists items similar to your item.

3 Click here and select the Time: newly listed option.

The most recently listed auctions appear.

● You can view your item with a Gallery preview.

eBay shoppers see this photo preview when they browse or search.

TIPS

More Options!

When you shop on eBay, try browsing with the Picture Gallery view feature, instead of viewing the search results in the default view. To do this, click the Picture Gallery link on the left side of an eBay search or browse results page next to the List View heading. eBay displays auctions on the page in horizontal rows of gallery images, allowing you to view many photos of items on one page. For more information about the Picture Gallery feature, see Task #20.

eBay Savvy!

Although the Gallery feature is relatively inexpensive, if your profit margins are slim, then this feature may not be worthwhile for you.

Place your item on
EBAY'S HOME PAGE

Every day, eBay features specific categories and subcategories on its home page, the first page that people see when they navigate to www.ebay.com on the Web. You can take advantage of the top-level exposure that these categories receive, and therefore get more exposure for your own items, by using eBay's Merchandising Calendar.

The eBay Merchandising Calendar is a schedule of which categories eBay plans to feature on its home page in the upcoming weeks. You can plan to list

items that match those categories during that time. You can find this calendar in the What's Hot area, located in the Seller Central section of eBay, and accessible through the site map.

Because the schedule is subject to change without notice, you may want to check the calendar shortly before you plan to list the items for which you want front-page category exposure. eBay says that they make every effort to update the calendar as soon as any changes occur.

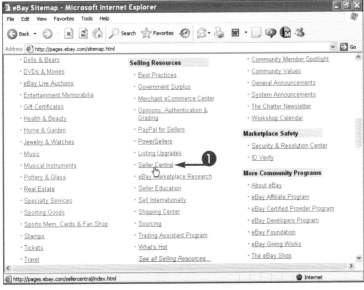

1 In the eBay site map, click the Seller Central link.

The Seller Central page opens.

● The Best Practices link appears, along with other resource links.

2 Click the What's Hot link.

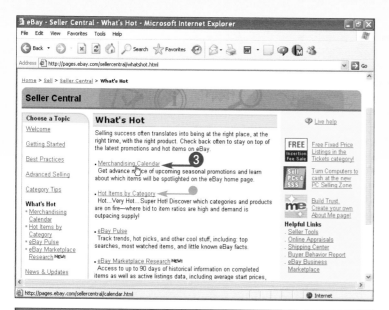

The What's Hot page opens.

● You can click the Hot Items by Category link to view popular categories and products.

③ Click the Merchandising Calendar link.

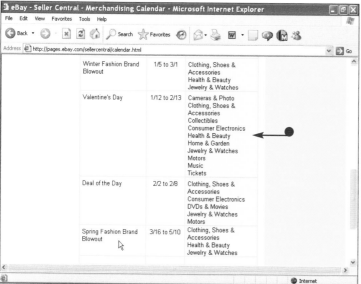

The Merchandising Calendar page opens.

● eBay lists the categories that it will feature in upcoming weeks.

By listing the types of items that are specified during the listed weeks, you ensure that your items' categories receive maximum exposure on the eBay home page.

Note: For more information about emphasizing a listing, see Tasks #69 and #72.

TIPS

eBay Savvy!

You can time your auctions to maximize their effectiveness by using David's Interactive Auction Calendar at www.auctionbytes.com/Email_Newsletter/calendar/calendar.html.

More Options!

For $39.95, you can receive a link to your item directly on the eBay home page with the Home Page Featured listing option. For more information about the Home Page Featured listing option, see Task #73.

eBay Savvy!

To immediately receive front-page exposure for auctions, make a note of which categories eBay promotes on a given day and list any of your inventory that fits into those categories. For example, if the home page promotes Fisher-Price toys, then you can quickly list one that you have to sell and benefit from eBay's top-level category exposure.

Use bold and highlighting to
EMPHASIZE AUCTIONS

You can make your item stand out in the sea of auction items on eBay by using the Bold or Highlight Listing upgrade. This feature is especially helpful when eBay has many items similar to yours, and you do not want your item to be lost in the competition. By some estimates, placing the title of your auction in bold text, or in highlighted format, increases your chances of receiving more bids by as much as 25 to 35 percent.

The bold listing option costs $1.00, which is a good deal when you sell an item that is of a high-enough estimated value to justify the cost of the feature. The highlight listing option is more expensive, at $5, which you can only justify for more-expensive items.

You may not want to use bold or highlighted text for every listing. For low-priced items or rare items that do not have much competition, the added fees for emphasized text may not be worth it. You can experiment with your auctions to see where these options are most effective.

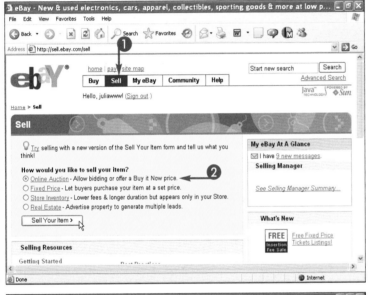

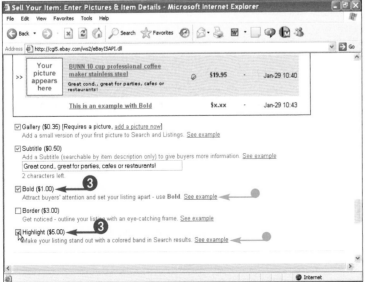

SELECT THE BOLD OR HIGHLIGHT OPTION

① In the eBay home page, click Sell.

The Sell page opens.

② Click to select the Online Auction option.

eBay guides you through the listing process.

③ In the Sell Your Item: Enter Pictures & Item Details page, click to select the Bold and/or the Highlight option.

● You can click these links to see an example of the emphasized listing.

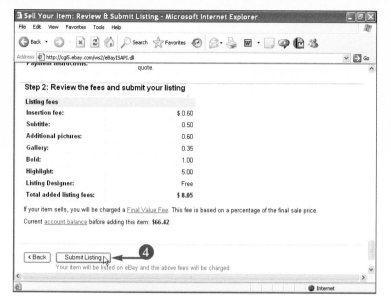

eBay continues to guide you through the listing process.

④ At the end of the listing pages, click Submit Listing.

eBay tells you that you have successfully listed your item.

DIFFICULTY LEVEL

VIEW FORMATTING

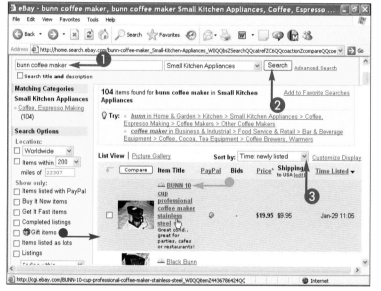

① In the eBay category where you listed your item, type search words that describe your item.

② Click Search.

③ Click here and select Time: newly listed.

● The search results appear with your item listing in bold, emphasized text.

● The highlight feature creates a shaded background.

Did You Know?

eBay sometimes changes fees for additional features, such as bold and featured listings. You should check the eBay Announcements section at www2.ebay.com/aw/marketing.shtml periodically, or pay close attention to the prices on the Sell Your Item form. eBay reduced the fee for bold listings in regular U.S. auctions from $2 to $1 in March 2003. eBay also reduced the fees for bold text in eBay Stores, depending on the duration of the eBay Store listing. For more information, see http://pages.ebay.com/community/news/changes.html.

More Options!

You can also use HTML to apply bold formatting to parts of your item description text to make it stand out. For more information about using HTML in auction listings, see Task #64.

Maximize visibility with
FEATURED AUCTIONS

You can use the Featured Auction listing option to increase the visibility of your auctions. When you apply the Featured Auction option to your listings, they appear above the other auctions in their category.

eBay currently offers two kinds of Featured listings. The first kind, Featured Plus!, costs $19.95. Featured Plus! auctions appear at the top of the listings page for that category. eBay also randomly selects Featured Plus! auctions for display in the Featured Items section of related category pages.

The other type of Featured listing is the Home Page Featured Auction listing, which costs $39.95, or $79.95 for multiple-quantity listings. When you select the option, your item appears at the top of eBay's all featured items page. Several lucky auctions randomly appear on the eBay home page in the Featured display section, and in the Featured Items section of related category home pages.

For other ways to emphasize your listings using formatting, see Tasks #64 and #72.

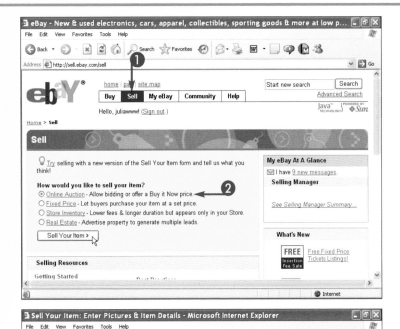

1 In the eBay home page, click Sell.

The Sell page opens.

2 Click to select the Online Auction option.

eBay guides you through the listing process.

3 In the Sell Your Item: Pictures & Details page, click to select the Featured Plus! option.

You must have a feedback rating of 10 or more to use this option.

● You can click this link to see an example of a Featured Plus! listing.

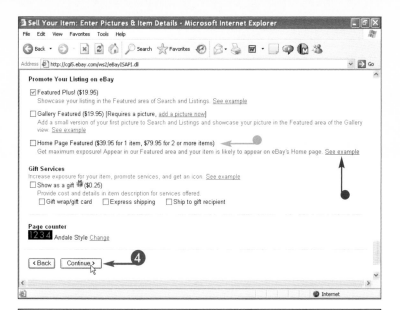

● You can also select the Home Page Featured option.

You must have a feedback rating of 10 or more to use this option.

● You can click here to see an example of a Home Page Featured listing.

④ Click Continue.

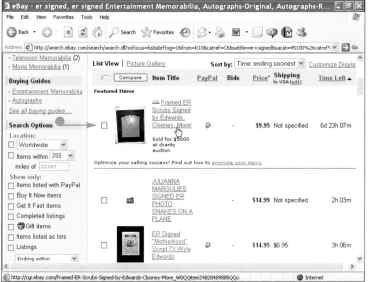

eBay guides you through the rest of the listing process.

To view your Featured listing, navigate to the category in which your item is listed.

● Your item appears in the Featured Items section above the non-featured items.

Did You Know?

You need to scroll to the bottom of the eBay home page to see the Home Page Featured Items. Conditions for using the Featured Items options include that the auction item cannot be of an adult nature or in poor taste. For a complete list of prohibited items, see http://pages.ebay.com/help/sell/hpf.html. For more on what items eBay allows, see Task #1.

Call attention to your
OTHER AUCTIONS

An easy way to notify eBay shoppers about all of your other auctions is to write a sentence or two in your auction descriptions that invite people to view your other auctions. Calling attention to other auctions is especially effective when you list a popular or otherwise attention-getting item, and when your other auctions are for related items.

You can use bold, italic, or other formatting to highlight the sentence that describes your other auctions. You can use eBay's built-in HTML editor or enter your own HTML. eBay shoppers can then go to

your other auctions using the View seller's other items link, located in the blue Seller information box. eBay buyers can also access your eBay Store, if you have one, through its link, which appears beneath the View seller's other items link. For more on using HTML tags, see Task #64.

To perform this task, you should know how to create a basic eBay listing. For more information about attracting eBay buyers to related auctions, see Task #75.

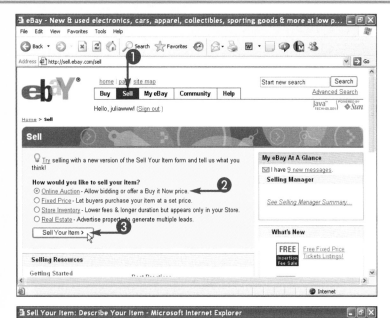

REFERENCE YOUR OTHER
AUCTIONS AS A SELLER

① In eBay's home page, click Sell.

② In the Sell page, click to select the Online Auction option.

③ Click Sell Your Item.

eBay prompts you to select a category and guides you through the auction listing process.

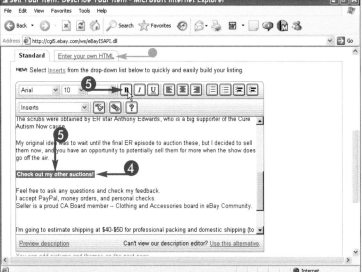

④ In the Item Description section, type text that invites buyers to your other auctions.

⑤ Select this text and click here to apply bold formatting to it.

● You can also click this tab and type HTML manually.

eBay guides you through the listing process.

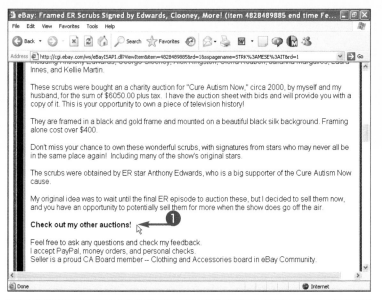

① In an item's listing page, look for text referring to the seller's other auctions.

② Scroll up the page to view the Seller Information section.

③ Click the View seller's other items link.

Because buyers can view the seller's other items, the seller may get more bids.

TIPS

eBay Savvy!

You can create a direct link to your other auctions in your item's listing page. Go to any of your auctions and click the View seller's other items link. Copy the URL that appears in your browser's Address bar and paste it into your new auction's description. Add the <a href= tag in front of the http tag, the > tag after the 50, and the </a> tag at the end. For example, where xxxx is your seller ID, type the following: **<a href=http://cgi6.ebay.com/ws/ eBayISAPI.dll?ViewSellersOtherItems&userid=xxxx&i nclude=0&since=-1&sort=3&rows=50>Click HERE to see my other auctions!</a>.**

More Options!

Although you cannot post links to your Web site in your auctions, you can post them in your About Me page, which is discussed in Task #69.

Showcase thumbnails of
RELATED AUCTION ITEMS

You can use Andale's Gallery tool to show eBay shoppers thumbnail images of your related auction items. This enables eBay users to view small images of your other auction items from your auction descriptions. When eBay shoppers can easily view and access your other auctions, it means increased sales for you.

Andale is a third-party auction management service with products that enable you to list and research your auctions, and analyze your sales. You can purchase Gallery as a separate service from Andale, or combine it with some of Andale's other tools.

Andale provides graphics templates so that you can customize the appearance of your Gallery. You can also select whether to have your thumbnail images available from a button in your listing, or directly embedded into your listing.

Andale Gallery plans start at $5.95 each month for up to 100 listings, and an extra $0.07 for each additional listing.

To perform this task, you must first sign up for the Andale Gallery service at www.andale.com, and log in to the Andale site.

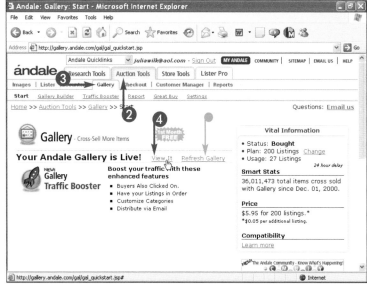

① Type **www.andale.com** into your Web browser Address bar, and press Enter.

② Click the Auction Tools tab.

③ Click Gallery.

Andale prompts you to buy the Gallery feature if you have not already.

● You can click here to reload your Gallery at any time.

④ Click View It.

Your Gallery Showcase appears.

● You can click a category option.

● You can click an eBay specialty site option.

⑤ Click an auction link to view one of your eBay auctions.

Your eBay auction opens in a new window.

6 Scroll down to the Description section.

7 Click Andale Gallery.

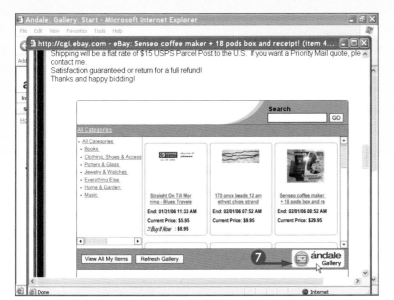

Andale displays thumbnail images of your other auction items.

● You can click a category or the View All My Items button.

● You can scroll through the images.

● Buyers can see your other auctions and click a link to bid on one.

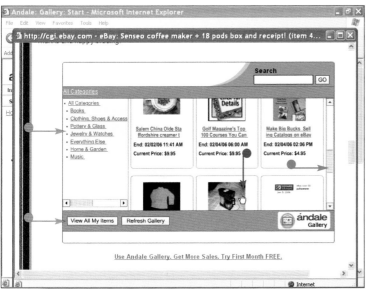

TIP

More Options!

You can customize your Gallery so that your thumbnail images appear directly beneath your item's photo in an auction page. From the Andale Gallery page, click Gallery Builder, and then select the Gallery in listing option, which displays up to 50 items in your listing. Click Continue. You can also select an option from a menu of design themes, color themes, and fonts. You can select an option to place the Gallery in the bottom or the top of the listing, and you can type a business name and promotion text. You can also create an About Me page. Click Done to save your settings.

Appeal to buyers with SquareTrade's
SEAL OF APPROVAL

You can attract more buyers to your auctions and inspire more confidence in your bidders with a SquareTrade Seal of Approval. SquareTrade Seal benefits include automatic insertion of the Seal into your eBay listings, notification when you receive negative feedback, and up to $750 in buyer protection. You also receive activity reports that show you when buyers view your auctions the most, as well as buyer alert e-mails that tell bidders that you are a SquareTrade Seal member who cares about giving them a positive buying experience.

To sign up for a SquareTrade Seal of Approval, you can go to the SquareTrade home page at www.squaretrade.com. The SquareTrade Seal costs $9.50 each month after your 30-day free trial. You can also prepay $85.50 for a year, saving 25 percent off the monthly fees, and get the premium features, which include sales reports, discounts off mediation services, and increased buyer protection.

For more information about using SquareTrade, including mediating a dispute, see Task #38.

① Type **www.squaretrade.com** in the Address bar of your Web browser, and press Enter.

● You can click here to read about the SquareTrade company.

● You can click here to read about SquareTrade's Buyer services.

② Click Seller Services.

The SquareTrade Seller Services Overview page opens.

● You can click here to read about the various SquareTrade seller services.

③ Click Go under Apply for Seal Membership.

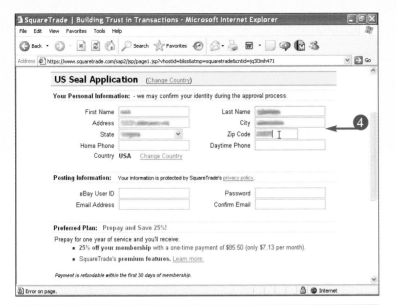

The SquareTrade Seal application page opens.

④ Type your profile information into the text boxes in the form.

SquareTrade guides you through the application process.

DIFFICULTY LEVEL

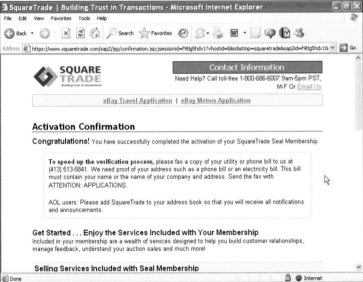

SquareTrade confirms that you have completed the activation of your membership.

SquareTrade may ask you to confirm your address.

When SquareTrade confirms your identity and activates your account, you receive the SquareTrade Seal of Approval, and eBay inserts the SquareTrade logo into your auction listings.

More Options!

You can get a customized SquareTrade Seal to use in your auctions. SquareTrade personalizes the Seal with your eBay user ID and that day's date on your eBay listings. This shows buyers that the Seal is really yours, and protects you from unauthorized use of your Seal. To customize your Seal, log in, click Seal/Policy Posting, and then click Customize your seal now!

More Options!

You can get SquareTrade Seal Activity and Sales Reports to help you analyze your sales. The reports feature information such as how often your Seal is viewed, how much you are earning, the average selling price of your successful auctions, a comparison of the average start price of your sold listings to your unsold listings, and more.

Boost all auctions with a
STRATEGIC ITEM

You can attract more bidders to all of your auctions by listing one special item that attracts a lot of attention. Even if your other items are not as unique or expensive as your strategic item, more bidders are likely to view these auctions. Many eBay sellers agree that this strategy works for getting bids for their other items.

If you have a limited inventory of big-ticket items, then you can spread out your strategic auctions over time. In this way, your other auctions benefit from being listed with the attention-drawing items for the longest period of time.

You can use various methods to attract bidders to your other auctions: bidders can simply click the View seller's other items link; you can reference the other auctions in your strategic auction description; or you can use the Andale Gallery tool to showcase thumbnail photos of your other items. For more on cross-promoting your auctions, see Tasks #66 and #67.

This task assumes that you know how to list an item. For more information, see Task #64 and Chapter 5.

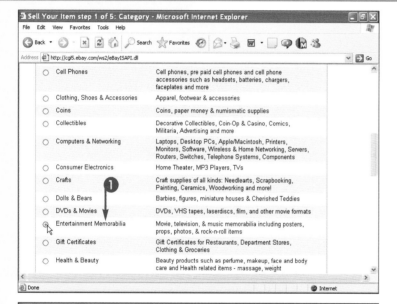

LIST A STRATEGIC ITEM AS A SELLER

① In the Sell Your Item: Select Category page, select the main category option for your strategic item.

You should choose a strategic item that is expensive or certain to attract attention, similar to a store window display item.

eBay guides you through selecting a subcategory.

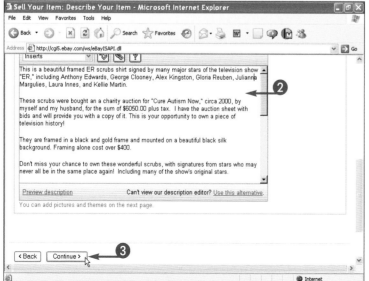

② In the Sell Your Item: Describe Your Item form, type a description of your strategic item.

You can mention any special details, including the item's retail value.

Note: *For more on attractive auction descriptions, see Task #64.*

③ Click Continue.

eBay guides you through the listing process and lists your item.

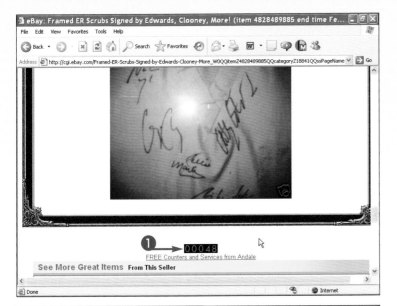

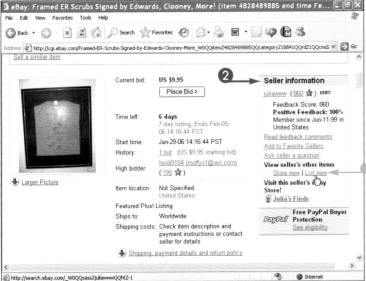

① In the item listing page for a strategic item, you can scroll down to the counter stats, which show the number of visits that your auction has received.

In this example, 48 people viewed this item in one day, which is a high number of people.

② Scroll up to the Seller Information section.

● Buyers can click the List View link under View seller's other items to check your other auctions.

Buyers who are attracted by your strategic item may bid on your other items.

eBay Savvy!

To learn the techniques of successful sellers, consider viewing their auctions for up to the past two weeks. You can do this by clicking the Advanced Search link, clicking the Items by Seller link, and then typing the seller's eBay user ID in the text box. Select the Include completed items option, and then click Search. You can also learn by participating in the eBay Community Forums. For more information about eBay's Discussion Boards, see Tasks #88 to #91.

eBay Savvy!

To improve the click-through rates in your auctions, you can add text to the title and description that reference an item's brand, age, or retail value. You can also use eBay abbreviations to conserve space in an auction title.

Chapter 9

Smart Shipping

Packaging and shipping items are among the least favorite tasks that eBay sellers must perform. However, with the tools described in this chapter, you can lighten your workload considerably in this area of your business. For example, you can easily look up shipping rates online, or use flat rates, thus eliminating the need to estimate shipping rates altogether.

You can empower your customers to find out their own shipping information by placing a shipping calculator in your auction listing. eBay customers also appreciate clearly written shipping and packaging terms.

You can keep your costs down by using services such as U-PIC's discount shipping insurance, ordering low-cost supplies, and even getting free packing supplies. You can pass these savings on to your customers and give yourself an edge over other sellers.

Shipping entails risk for both buyers and sellers. As a seller, you can protect yourself against loss by ordering delivery confirmation, insurance, or both.

Of all the shipping-related tasks, the least enjoyable for most eBay users is waiting in line at the post office. You can eliminate this task by buying and printing your own stamps and mailing labels. You can then either drop off your packages at given locations or have your mail carrier pick them up.

Special shippers, such as Craters and Freighters, can handle the shipping of large or awkward items. Once you are familiar with the various shipping services and methods that are available, you can decide what works best for you.

Top 100

Create good
TERMS OF SALE

You can attract more bidders to your auctions if you clearly state your packaging, shipping, and return policy in your auction listings. You can also save time answering e-mails from prospective bidders if you place as much detail as possible in your auctions regarding your terms of sale.

Although eBay prompts you for details about your terms of sale in the Sell Your Item pages, you should consider repeating them in the item description area. You should state what types of payment you accept, how you charge for shipping, and your return policy.

Many sellers charge separately for handling or packaging, and so you should be clear about these details. You risk getting negative feedback if you surprise buyers with added costs on top of what they pay for shipping. To determine shipping costs, see Task #79. To include a shipping calculator in your listing, see Task #80.

One successful eBay seller suggests phrasing your sale terms positively — I accept PayPal and money orders — rather than negatively — NO personal checks! — because negative wording may scare off bidders.

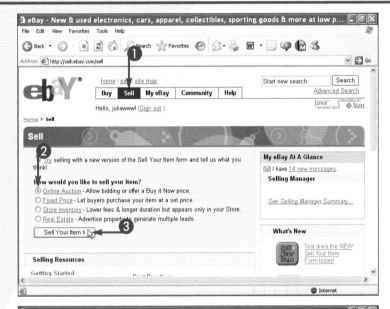

① In the eBay home page, click Sell.

The Sell page opens.

② Click to select the Online Auction option.

③ Click Sell your Item.

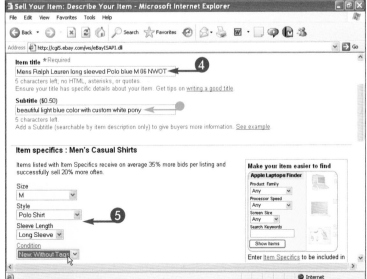

eBay prompts you to select a category.

The Sell Your Item: Describe Your Item page opens.

④ Type a title for your item.

● You can type an optional item subtitle.

⑤ Select the specific options that describe your item.

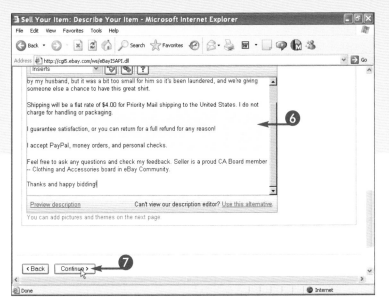

6 Type your shipping, return, and payment policy information in the item description text box.

7 Click Continue.

In the Enter Pictures & Item Details page, eBay guides you through specifying an auction duration, starting price, and picture details.

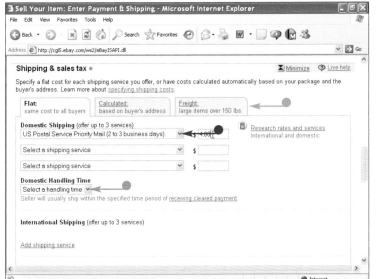

The Sell Your Item: Enter Payment & Shipping page guides you through selecting the payment methods that you want to accept.

● You can select a flat, calculated, or freight rate.

● You can select a shipping service.

● You can select a handling time.

Note: For more on shipping rates, see Task #79.

eBay Savvy!

Because buyers may be very sensitive to how much you charge for shipping, consider charging an exact amount — which involves weighing the item and looking up the shipping cost to the destination ZIP code. Exact amounts help you to avoid negative feedback from buyers who think you overcharge for shipping. If you charge for handling or packaging costs, then clearly state this in the auction description. For more information about calculating shipping costs, see Tasks #79, #81, and #87.

eBay Savvy!

When you buy on eBay, if you do not see the shipping cost specified, then you can use the Ask seller a question link on the item's listing page. For more information about the Ask seller a question feature, see Task #13.

Retrieve
SHIPPING INFORMATION

You can determine the shipping costs for an item by using the United States Postal Service, or USPS, Web site, which has a shipping calculator for both domestic and international items.

Once you know your item's weight and destination ZIP code, you can calculate postage for a postcard, letter, envelope, or package. You can then place the postage on your items and eliminate waiting in line at the post office by either handing the package to your mail carrier or placing it in a mailbox or other postal pickup location.

The USPS Web site asks you to specify the size of the package. If the length of the longest side of the package plus the distance around its thickest part equals 84 inches or less, then the USPS considers the package a regular size. If it is more than 84 inches but less than or equal to 108 inches, then the USPS considers it a large package.

You can indicate any special characteristics that your package has, and choose from different types of mail services, such as Express, Priority, or Parcel Post.

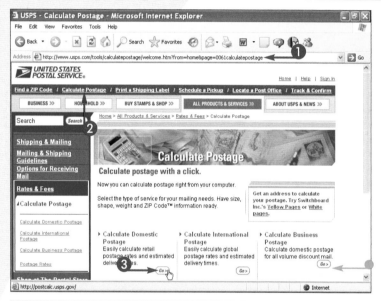

① Type **usps.com** into the Address bar of your Web browser, and press Enter.

The USPS home page opens.

② Click the Calculate Postage link.

The Calculate Postage page opens.

③ Click Go under Calculate Domestic Postage.

● You can also click Go under Calculate International or Business postage.

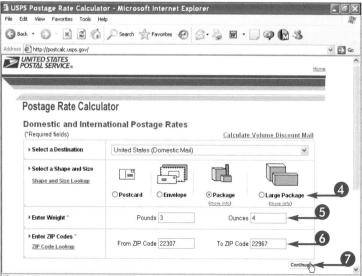

The Postal Rate Calculator page opens.

④ Click to select the shape and size of an item that you want to mail.

⑤ Type the weight of your item.

⑥ Type your ZIP code and the destination ZIP code.

⑦ Click Continue.

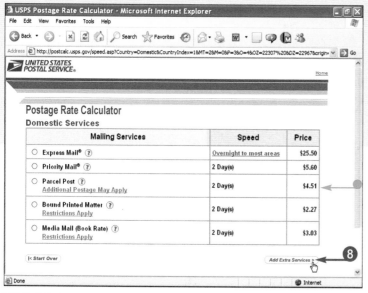

#79

DIFFICULTY LEVEL

- A table appears with shipping rates for most types of mailing services, as well as estimated delivery times.

⑧ Click Add Extra Services.

Note: *For more on the services that USPS has to offer, see Task #83.*

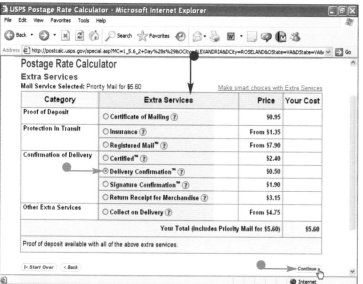

The Extra Services page opens.

- You can view the extra services and the price for each.
- If you select an Extra Service option, and click Continue, then the USPS guides you through another page to calculate the total shipping cost.

More Options!
You can also use the United Parcel Service, or UPS. You can obtain shipping and tracking information at their Web site, www.ups.com. To find shipping rates, go to www.ups.com/content/us/en/shipping/index.html and click the Calculate Time and Cost link.

eBay Savvy!
You can find links about shipping methods and costs on the AuctionBytes Web site at www.auctionbytes. com/Yellow_Pages/Postman/postman.html.

More Options!
The extra services that you can add to your package on the USPS site include certified mail, insurance, registered mail, collect on delivery — or COD — and return receipt for merchandise. Many eBay sellers use delivery confirmation so that they can prove their package was sent, in case there is a problem with the transaction.

PLACE A SHIPPING CALCULATOR
in your listing

You can save time and money and increase your customers' satisfaction by placing a shipping calculator in your auctions. This allows customers to determine their own shipping costs, and prevents e-mails from buyers about shipping fees. The calculator can also save you from making errors in estimating shipping on your own.

eBay offers a shipping calculator option in its Sell Your Item forms. eBay's shipping calculator determines United States Postal Service and United Parcel Service shipping charges based on the buyer's ZIP code within the United States. Buyers can then see

the shipping calculator in your listing in the Shipping, payment details and return policy section, under the item description.

Although eBay's shipping calculator supports most eBay auctions, it does not calculate shipping outside of the United States or for shipping services that are not shown within the calculator, such as UPS Next Day Air. eBay's shipping calculator also does not calculate the shipping costs of multiple items purchased from one seller. For information about calculating your shipping costs using the USPS Web site, see Task #79.

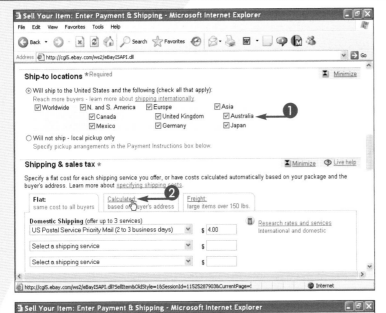

① In the Sell Your Item: Enter Payment & Shipping page, click to select the Ship-to locations option or options that you want.

② Click the Calculated link.

The Calculated tab appears, where you can calculate shipping rates.

③ Click here and select the estimated weight of the package.

④ Select the package size and domestic shipping service, and select the options that you want.

● You can click here and select a Domestic Handling Time option.

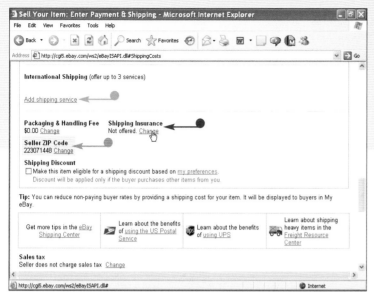

- When you scroll down, you can add a service for international shipping.

- You can select a package and handling fee and a shipping insurance option.

- Your ZIP code appears here.

5 Click Continue and fill out the remainder of the Sell Your Item form.

eBay lists your item.

- When bidders view your listing, a Calculate shipping section appears.

- Bidders can type their ZIP code and click the Calculate button to compute their shipping costs.

More Options!

You can choose from several third-party shipping calculators. AuctionInc's aiShip calculates both UPS and USPS rates, and works with all listing tools. To find out more, go to www.auctioninc.com and click Learn More! under aiShip Shipping Calculator. aiShip costs $0.10 for each auction sale, with a maximum charge of $19.50 each month. aiShip does not charge for unsold auctions or for calculator hits.

You can also use the free shipping calculator at www.beesonware.com/shippingcalculator.

Did You Know?

eBay's shipping calculator also computes insurance and taxes. Because the item's final price determines the rate, the calculator only shows the shipping insurance rate when the auction ends. For more information about eBay's shipping calculator, go to http://pages.ebay.com/help/buy/ship-calc-buyer-overview.html.

Save time and money with
FLAT RATES

You can spare yourself the trouble of looking up each item's shipping information by using flat shipping rates in your auctions. A *flat rate* is a consistent rate that is meant to be close to an item's actual shipping cost.

Although some eBay shoppers prefer exact shipping rates, many understand that flat rates can save sellers time and money — savings that a seller can pass on to buyers. If you inform prospective bidders by clearly stating in your auction description that you charge a flat shipping rate, then buyers can decide if they want to bid on your auction if they find the

shipping amount acceptable. One eBay seller has used flat rates in over 750 auctions, with no buyer complaints.

Flat-rate shipping is especially useful for sellers who list similar types of items that tend to have the same shipping cost.

However, you may not want to use flat-rate shipping for large, heavy items where a margin of error in shipping can add up to a significant amount of money. For more on large, valuable, and fragile items, see Task #87.

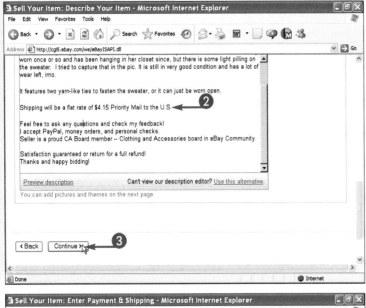

① In the eBay home page, click Sell.

eBay guides you through the process of creating a listing.

② In the Sell Your Item: Describe Your Item page, scroll down and type information about your flat rates in the item description text box.

③ Click Continue.

④ Fill out the Sell Your Item: Enter Pictures & Item Details page, and click Continue.

The Enter Payment & Shipping page opens.

⑤ Click to select your Ship-to location options.

⑥ Click the Flat tab.

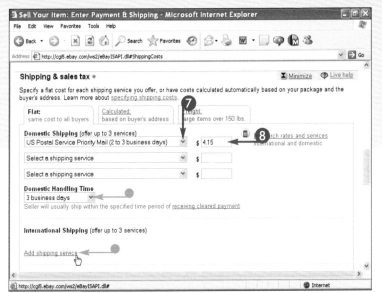

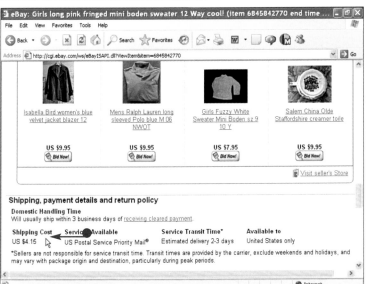

The Flat shipping rates tab appears.

⑦ Select the Domestic shipping services that you want.

⑧ Type the flat rate for your item.

● You can click here and select a domestic handling time.

● You can click here to add an international shipping service.

⑨ Click Continue.

eBay guides you through the remainder of the listing process.

● When a buyer views your listing, your flat shipping rates appear.

DIFFICULTY LEVEL

eBay Savvy!

There are different ways to determine flat rates. One seller uses the average cost of shipping the same product to three parts of the country, and then adds $1. This seller sells items with similar weights.

Another seller bases the cost of shipping on the Zone 8 ZIP codes shipping rate. They then recover postage, but not packaging costs, for buyers in Zone 8. If a buyer is in Zones 5 to 7, then the seller recovers packaging but not handling costs. If the buyer lives in Zones 1 to 4, then the seller recovers postage, all packaging materials, and a small labor charge. To help you to calculate flat rates, you can get a postal zone chart at http://postcalc.usps.gov/Zonecharts.

Print
YOUR OWN POSTAGE

You can print stamps and mailing labels from your own printer, thus eliminating long waits at the post office. You can also get free delivery confirmation and ship worldwide with Stamps.com.

To use Stamps.com, you must first sign up for the service and download the free software from the Stamps.com Web site. Stamps.com then appears as an icon on your desktop.

Stamps.com costs $15.99 each month, and you can cancel at any time. You can try the service with a four-week free trial, with $5 in free postage during the trial. You also receive a free postal supplies kit, which includes a Getting Started Guide, a sheet of NetStamps labels, a sheet of Internet postage labels, and a sheet of adhesive shipping labels.

After your trial period, you receive $20 in postage coupons, and a Stamps.com digital scale worth $50. If you do not cancel this service, then Stamps.com charges you on day 30 for using the service.

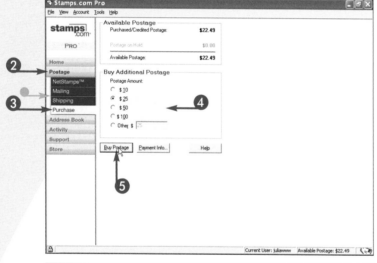

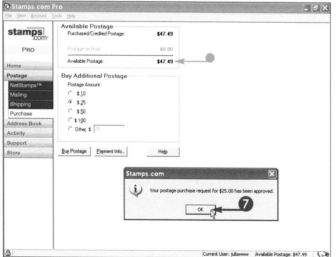

BUY POSTAGE

① On your desktop, double-click the Stamps.com icon and log in.

② In the Stamps.com home page, click Postage.

● The Postage menu appears.

③ Click Purchase.

④ Click to select a Postage Amount option.

⑤ Click Buy Postage.

⑥ Click Yes when the confirmation message appears.

A dialog box appears, telling you that your postage purchase request has been approved.

● Your new available postage balance appears.

⑦ Click OK.

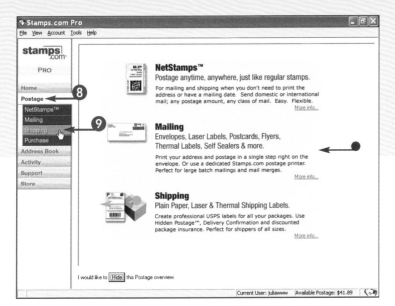

PRINT POSTAGE

8 Click Postage.

● Stamps.com explains your different postage printing options.

9 Click Shipping.

DIFFICULTY LEVEL

A page appears, displaying text boxes for shipping information.

10 Type the return and delivery addresses.

11 Select a mail piece, weight, and mailing date.

12 Click to select a mail class option.

13 Click here and select the paper for printing.

● Your total estimated cost appears.

14 Click Print.

Your postage prints.

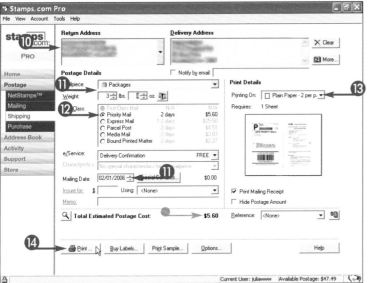

TIPS

More Options!

Stamps.com offers several pickup and drop-off options. If it is not too large, then you can give the package to your local mail carrier, or drop it into any street mailbox. If you need to add Registered Mail or USPS insurance, then you can take the package to your local post office. For an additional $12.50, you can schedule a pickup for an unlimited number of packages; this option is only available for Priority Mail, Express Mail, and Parcel Post. You can schedule a pickup online, or call 800-222-1811.

eBay Savvy!

Stamps.com offers a Hidden Postage feature for sellers, which allows them to print shipping labels without the actual postage value. Sellers find that they get fewer complaints about shipping charges this way.

PROTECT YOURSELF
with delivery confirmation and insurance

You can ensure that your packages arrive safely, and help protect yourself from dishonest bidders, by purchasing delivery confirmation and insurance. You can also request a return receipt so that the shipping service contacts you when the package arrives.

You can get delivery confirmation at a local post office for between $0.50 for Priority Mail and $0.60 for First-Class and Parcel Post.

The United States Postal Service does not charge additional fees for online delivery confirmation for Priority Mail because the USPS receives an electronic record of your transaction. However, the online

delivery confirmation service is only available to those who use online shipping labels, which are available at https://sss-web.usps.com/cns/landing.do.

The insurance fees for merchandise are $1.35 for between $0.01 and $50 worth of merchandise, and $2.30 for between $50.01 and $100 worth of merchandise. The USPS charges $2.30 plus $1.05 for each $100 or fraction thereof over $100 for between $100.01 and $5,000 worth of merchandise.

This task assumes that you have already performed the steps to retrieve the shipping information for your package, as shown in Task #79.

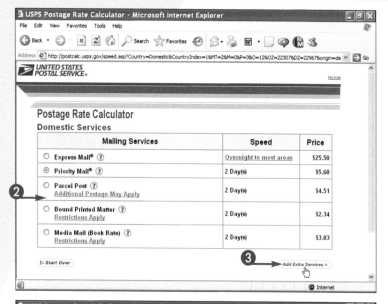

① Use the Calculate Postage link at usps.com to determine your package's shipping information.

Note: To determine your shipping information using the USPS Domestic shipping calculator, see Task #79.

② In the Postage Rate Calculator page, click to select the option that you want.

③ Click Add Extra Services.

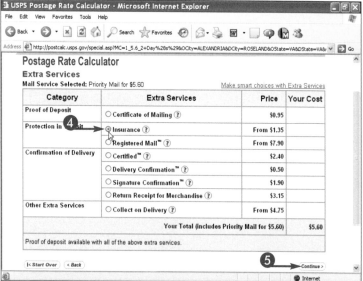

The Extra Services page opens.

④ Click to select the Insurance option.

⑤ Click Continue.

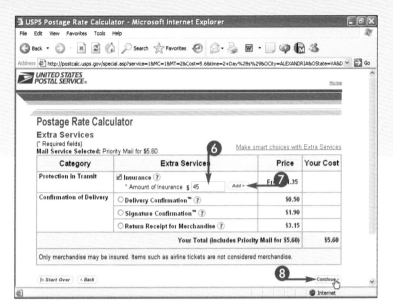

Additional options appear in the insurance section.

⑥ Type the amount for which you want to insure the item.

The maximum insurance amount is $5,000.

DIFFICULTY LEVEL

⑦ Click Add.

⑧ Click Continue.

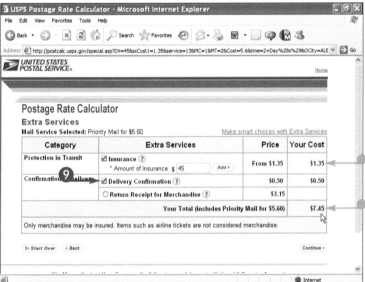

An additional Extra Services page opens.

● USPS displays your insurance cost.

⑨ Click to select the Delivery Confirmation option.

You can also select Return Receipt for Merchandise.

● USPS displays your total cost, including the cost for delivery confirmation and insurance.

TIPS

Did You Know?

You can also use delivery confirmation with extra services, such as the following: Return Receipt for Merchandise; Insured Mail; Registered Mail; Collect on Delivery, or C.O.D.; Special Handling; Merchandise Return Service — where you pay the postage for items sent back to you; Return Receipt; or Restricted Delivery — where only a specified person can receive the piece of mail. For more information, go to www.usps.com/send/waystosendmail/extraservices/deliveryconfirmationservice.htm.

Did You Know?

You can use the Delivery Confirmation option with the following: first-class packages that weigh 13 ounces or less; Priority Mail packages; Parcel Post; media mail — or book rate; bound, printed matter; or library mail. For more information, go to www.usps.com/send/waystosendmail/extraservices/deliveryconfirmationservice.htm.

Use U-PIC to
INSURE PACKAGES

You can save 60 to 80 percent on insuring packages by using Universal Parcel Insurance Coverage, or U-PIC. Depending on how many packages you send, you can save hundreds, or even thousands, of dollars each year on your insurance costs.

U-PIC is a discounted insurance service for packages that you ship with major carriers, such as the United Parcel Service, the United States Postal Service, and Federal Express. Although the carrier ships the package, it is insured by U-PIC. U-PIC has no minimum

requirements, and offers different programs for different types of shippers.

To use U-PIC, you must first fill out the Request to Provide Coverage form on the U-PIC Web site. U-PIC reviews your form and contacts you to determine which U-PIC program best suits your needs. After U-PIC approves you for coverage, they send you a policy and a supply of claim forms. Then, instead of declaring value with your carrier, you do so with U-PIC.

① Type **delta.u-pic.com/Order/ OrderWelcome.aspx** into the Address bar of your Web browser, and press Enter.

The U-PIC Order Welcome page opens.

② Click Continue.

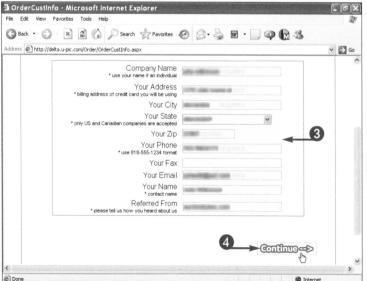

The Customer Information page opens.

③ Type your name, address, phone number, e-mail address, and other requested information.

④ Click Continue.

174

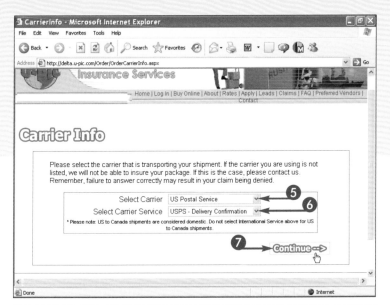

The Carrier Information page opens.

⑤ Click here and select a carrier.

⑥ Click here and select a carrier service.

⑦ Click Continue.

DIFFICULTY LEVEL

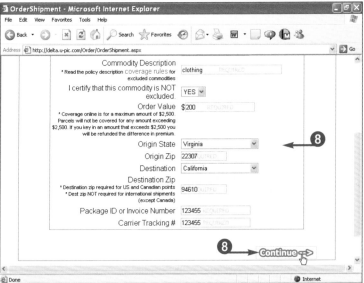

The Order Shipment page opens.

⑧ Type the requested information and click Continue.

U-PIC gives you the price to insure your package and guides you through the rest of the order process.

U-PIC finalizes your order.

TIPS

Did You Know?
On the Carrier Service page, make sure that you select which type of carrier service you want, as the services have different levels of risk, and therefore different costs.

Did You Know?
After submitting your personal information with U-PIC in the first order, you do not need to retype this information for future orders. When you type a previous order ID, along with your ZIP code for security, U-PIC automatically fills in the appropriate fields for you.

Did You Know?
If you have any questions about the U-PIC order process, then you can click the CHAT LIVE WITH SUPPORT button on the U-PIC home page. U-PIC does not process your order until it has your billing information. Until you receive an order ID and confirmation, your package is not insured.

Use eBay to purchase
PACKING SUPPLIES

Almost every type of packing supply that you need is available on eBay, and you can save a lot of time and money by purchasing them online. eBay sellers offer everything from bubble wrap and tissue paper to Tyvek mailers and packing boxes.

Because eBay is a ready-made market for shipping supplies, you can get good deals from eBay vendors who sell in bulk. You can also save money on shipping fees by purchasing multiple packing items from the same seller. Several eBay Stores specialize in

packaging supplies, and you can use the link to a seller's eBay store to search for more items from that seller. Although you do have to pay shipping fees for packing supplies that you buy on eBay, the dollar value in terms of time saved makes it worthwhile to buy the supplies online.

For more information about obtaining good deals on shipping supplies, see Task #86. For more information about buying multiple items from the same seller to save on shipping costs, see Task #16.

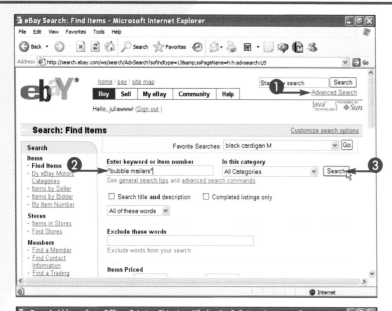

① In the eBay home page, click the Advanced Search link.

The Search: Find Items page opens.

② Type the search word or words that describe the shipping supplies that you want.

③ Click Search.

eBay lists the search results.

● You can click a link to view one of the eBay Stores that offer related items.

④ Click an item listing.

The details page opens for the listing.

The price of the item appears along with its description.

5 Click the seller's eBay Store link to search for related shipping supplies.

The seller's eBay Store page opens.

You can save money by purchasing more shipping supplies and asking the seller to combine shipping costs.

More Options!

For more information about packing and shipping supplies, and recommendations about good eBay shipping supply sellers, go to the eBay Community Discussion Board on Packaging and Shipping. From the eBay home page, click the Community button, then click Discussion Boards, and then click the Packaging & Shipping link under Community Help Boards. For more on Community Help Boards, see Chapter 10.

More Options!

Other places to find good deals on shipping supplies include www.papermart.com, www.packagingprice.com, www.uline.com, and www.viking.com. You can also check your local dollar store for attractive and inexpensive boxes. Some retail establishments, such as grocery stores, offer boxes that they no longer need for free. Check with the store management about their policy on free boxes.

Order
FREE SUPPLIES

You can get free packing and shipping supplies from the United States Postal Service, or USPS, when you order Priority Mail or more-expensive services, such as Express Mail. You can order them online, and USPS delivers them for free.

At usps.com, you can find many types of supplies, including cardboard boxes of various sizes, Tyvek mailers, postal tape, mail stickers, and labels. Some of the supplies are for special-sized items, such as long tubes that are ideal for mailing posters and some works of art.

You can also get supplies for different types of mail, such as Priority Mail, Express Mail, and Global Express Mail.

If you use Parcel Post shipping, then you cannot receive free USPS supplies, and you still need to buy postage for your packages.

You must only use the free USPS supplies for the type of mail service for which they are intended. Before you check out your free supplies, you must agree that the packaging is solely for sending the type of mail on the supply label — misuse is a violation of federal law.

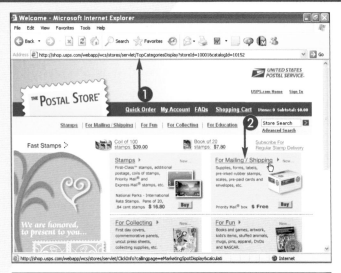

① Type **shop.usps.com** into the Address bar of your Web browser, and press Enter.

The Postal Store page opens.

② Click the For Mailing/Shipping link.

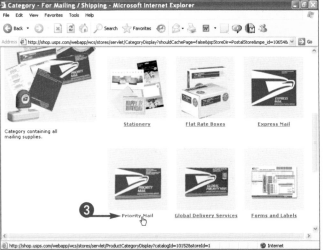

The For Mailing/Shipping page opens.

③ Click the link for the type of product you want.

You may need to scroll the screen.

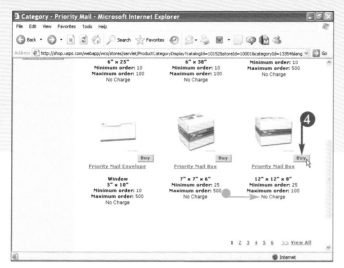

The page for that type of product opens.

● The USPS shows that there is No Charge for this product.

④ Click Buy.

86

The Shopping cart page opens.

● You can click here to Remove the item.

⑤ Click Checkout.

usps.com guides you through the rest of the checkout process, and delivers free shipping supplies to you.

TIPS

Did You Know?
Because the USPS ships supplies through Priority Mail, they may take three to five business days for delivery to domestic addresses, and three weeks to arrive at foreign addresses.

eBay Savvy!
For another free source of packing supplies, use plastic grocery bags. They are ideal, lightweight packing materials, and using them saves you from having to throw them away.

More Options!
You can also get free supplies from the United Parcel Service, or UPS, Web site. Type **www.ups.com** into your Web browser Address bar, select the option for your country, and then click the arrow icon. Click the Order Supplies link. UPS prompts you to log in. You can view the available supplies, and click the Get Now link to order them.

Send
LARGE, VALUABLE, OR FRAGILE ITEMS

In some cases, you may need to ship large, valuable, or fragile items. The packaging and shipping company Craters and Freighters specializes in these items, and offers free pickup at your location, as well as free insurance.

You can get a quote for packaging and transporting an item to anywhere in the 48 contiguous states from www.cratersandfreighters.com. You need to know the item's destination address, weight and dimensions, value, and when you want the item to arrive. You can also receive a quote for just the transportation or the packaging.

Although Craters and Freighters can be more expensive than other shipping services, they also offer advantages, such as in-home pickup, and experience in dealing with very large and valuable items. Their rates are best on items that are too big for UPS to ship.

You must register for the Craters and Freighters service before you can receive an e-quote or use their service.

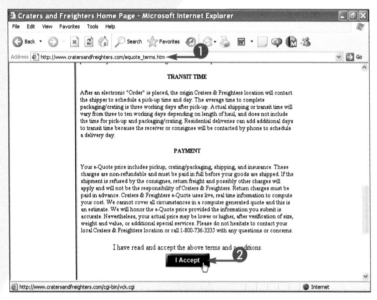

① Type **www. cratersandfreighters.com/ equote_terms.htm** into the Address bar of your Web browser, and press Enter.

A page of quote terms appears.

② Read the terms and click I Accept.

Craters and Freighters prompts you to log in.

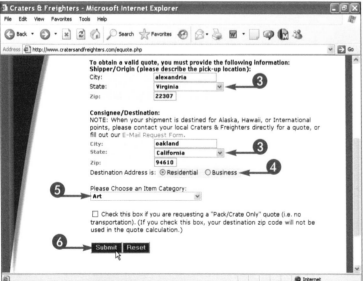

③ Type the city, state, and ZIP code of the shipment origin and destination.

④ Click to select an option for the destination address type.

⑤ Click here and select a category for the item.

⑥ Click Submit.

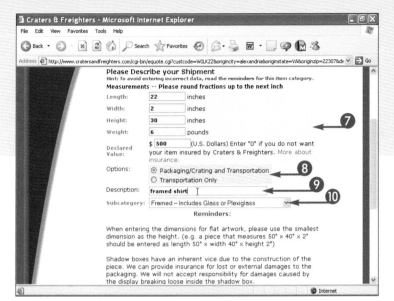

The Description section appears.

⑦ Type the dimensions, weight, and a declared value for your item.

⑧ Click to select a shipping option.

⑨ Type a description of the item.

⑩ Click here and select a subcategory.

⑪ Click Submit.

DIFFICULTY LEVEL

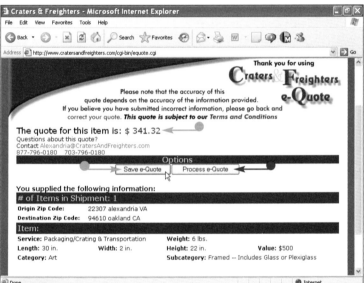

● A shipping quote appears.

● You can click Save e-Quote to save this quote.

● You can click Process e-Quote to accept the quote.

More Options!

You can also send large and heavy items through other shipping services. With UPS, you can send packages up to 90 lbs, and measuring up to 165 inches in combined length and girth. Oversize and very heavy packages may require special pricing. For more information, go to www.ups.com and register for an account.

You can get other rates and shipping options from Federal Express at www.fedex.com/us and the United States Postal Service at www.usps.com. For more information on calculating USPS rates, see Tasks #79 and #80.

More Options!

If you register your auction on the Craters and Freighters Web site, then they allow your bidders to determine their packaging and shipping costs directly from your auction listing. Go to www.cratersandfreighters.com/equote_auction_main.htm for more information.

Chapter 10

Tapping into the eBay Community Gold Mine

You can find a wealth of information and resources in the eBay community. Other auction users are not only a valuable source of information, but also of friendship and support. The eBay Discussion Boards cover a wide range of topics, so you can easily find one or more boards that interest you.

For a smaller, more-specialized community, you can join an eBay Group and share items such as photos and polls with fellow group members. You can find an eBay Group for every region of the United States, and for many other countries, as well.

You can read discussions in the boards, as well as start new topics. You can navigate the boards in several ways, such as from the oldest or the most recent post. The Boards

Search tool is an excellent way to uncover information that may otherwise be difficult to find.

If you need help immediately, then you can use eBay's Live Chat Boards, which show the responses of other eBay users right away. You can also explore the topics in eBay's Help boards. eBay community members are extremely helpful, and some member experts even compile comprehensive resources and links in their About Me pages.

You can learn new skills with eBay University's online or offline classes. You can also explore the many resources for online auction users on the Web outside of eBay. Some of these sites offer helpful, free newsletters.

Top 100

FIND A HOME
in the discussion boards

You can learn more about the types of items that you like to buy and sell as well as meet friends who share your interests by becoming a part of eBay's Discussion Boards community. The boards are full of knowledgeable eBay users from various fields of interest, who are ready to help new members.

The eBay Category-Specific Discussion Boards contain every type of item that you may want to sell or buy. You can scan the list of categories and decide which ones interest you.

Before you post to a Discussion Board for the first time, you should read the eBay Board Usage Policies, which are available in each board's welcome message. You may also want to *lurk* — read posts for a while without posting — to get accustomed to the topics that the board users discuss. For example, for some questions, the board's regular users may already have a long list of answers, or FAQs. If you are courteous, then message board users should receive you warmly.

For more information about the eBay Discussion Boards, see Tasks #89 and #91.

① In the main eBay home page, click Community.

The eBay Community page opens.

● You can click this link to go to the Chat Rooms area.

● You can click this link to go to the Answer Center.

② Click the Discussion Boards link.

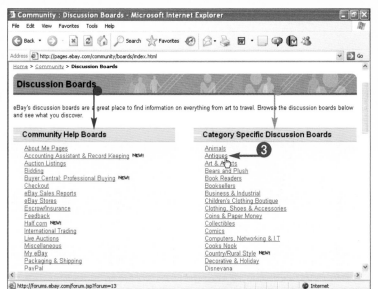

The Discussion Boards page opens.

● A list of links to Community Help Boards displays here.

● A list of links to category-specific Discussion Boards displays here.

③ Click the link of a category that interests you.

The Discussion Board page opens for that category, displaying a welcome message.

● You can click this link to read the board usage policies.

● You can click a topic to read it, and join the category's community by reading and posting messages.

TIPS

More Options!

To post a message on a Discussion Board, click Sign in at the top of the board. A new screen appears, and eBay prompts you to sign in. Once you sign in, a Post a topic link appears at the bottom of the board. Click the link to make a new post. You can also reply to an existing message by clicking the link to that message, clicking Post a reply, typing your reply in the Post a reply text box, and then clicking Post Message.

Did You Know?

eBay staff highlight discussions that are particularly helpful or fun. You can find links to these discussions on the right side of the Discussion Board screen, under the category's Community heading.

Browse the
DISCUSSION BOARDS

To find the useful information that you need on the eBay Discussion Boards — such as tips on where to find inventory, and sales techniques from fellow sellers — you must know how to navigate the boards. You can then move easily through discussions to read the posts and get the information that you want.

When you click a Discussion Board topic, the first message that appears is the one that started that topic. After that, the messages are numbered sequentially in the order that eBay users post them.

You can scroll through the messages using the Page number links at the bottom of a page of posts. You can also view a certain page by using the Go to page field that appears at the bottom of the page of posts. If there are many posts in a given topic, then you can use the link to the last page number to go to the most recently posted messages. This helps you to avoid having to read messages that are weeks or months old.

① Type **pages.ebay.com/ community/boards/index. html** into the Address bar of your Web browser, and then press Enter.

● You can also click Community in eBay's home page, and then click the Discussion Boards link.

② Click the Discussion Board that interests you.

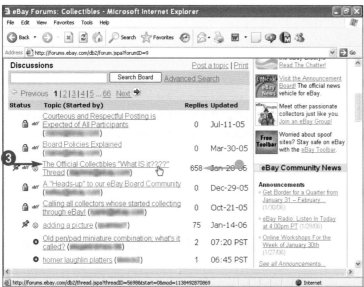

The Discussion Board page opens for the category that you selected.

A list of topics appears.

③ Click the topic that interests you.

● The number of posts in the topic appears here.

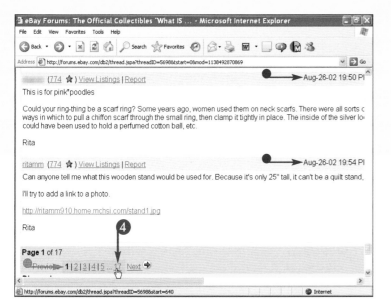

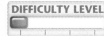
DIFFICULTY LEVEL

- The page opens for the topic that you selected, with the first messages at the top of the page, in order from the original message to most recent.

- You can scroll down to the bottom of the page to use the navigation links to quickly read the posts.

④ Click the link to the last page.

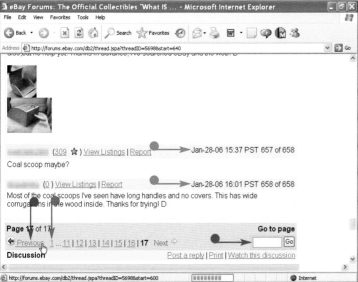

- The most recent messages appear.

- You can click Previous to see the page of messages before this page.

- You can click 1 to go back to earlier messages in the topic.

- You can type a page number here and click Go to view a particular page.

TIPS

eBay Savvy!

Some Category Discussion groups have games and contests, informally run by other board users, which are designed to attract buyers to their auctions. You can read the boards regularly to find out when the contests are run.

You can receive more information about using the Discussion Boards by accessing the eBay Board help tutorial at http://forums.ebay.com/db1/thread.jsp?forum=120&thread=65945.

More Options!

You can also search the Discussion Boards for keywords. To do so, click a Discussion Board link, and then type the word or words that you want to find in the search field at the top of the board. When you click Search Board, eBay displays links to all of the topics that match your keywords.

Get answers with
LIVE CHAT

If you have an urgent question, such as about an auction that is going to end soon, then you can receive immediate help using the Chat Boards. Chat Boards allow you to view timely advice from eBay members as soon as you type a question.

Unlike Internet chat rooms, eBay's Chat Boards do not automatically refresh your screen — you must do this manually by using the Reload button. Once you refresh, you see the most-recent messages, ranging from the last 5 minutes to the last 24 hours. The most recent chat room messages display on the top

of the page, and the chat threads disappear two weeks after the last post. You must be signed in to eBay to make a chat room post.

Once you sign in on eBay, you can choose from several chat rooms, including the following: the original chat room, The eBay Café; The AOL Café, for AOL users; the Discuss eBay's Newest Features board; and an Images/HTML Board for help with photos and images in your auctions. The eBay Q&A Board is great for general questions.

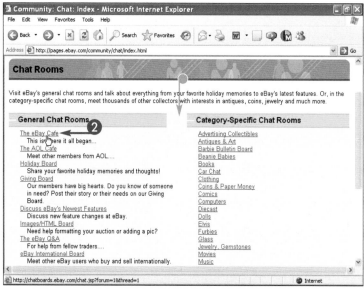

① In the eBay Community page, click the Chat Rooms link.

● The Chat Rooms page opens, displaying a General Chat Rooms list and a Category-Specific Chat Rooms list.

② Click a chat room link.

The selected chat room appears.

③ Type a message in the text box.

④ Click Save my Message!.

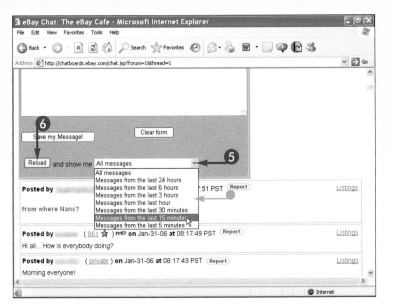

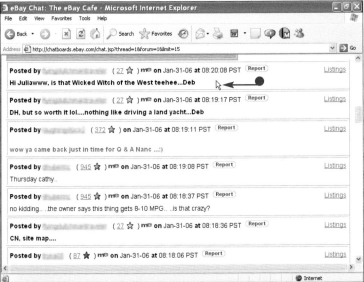

The page refreshes, and eBay sends your message to the chat room.

⑤ Click here and select a viewing option.

● The options range from the last 5 minutes to the last 24 hours.

DIFFICULTY LEVEL

⑥ Click Reload.

eBay refreshes the chat room page.

The most recent chat messages appear on the top of the page.

● You can see if anyone has replied to your chat room posting.

More Options!

eBay has many category-specific chat rooms about everything from advertising collectibles to trading cards. Category-specific chat rooms are often close communities that offer help and resources to members. For example, in the eBay Advertising Collectibles chat room, members post a welcome message with this link to helpful collectibles resources: www.signtech-rta.com/acboardlinks2.htm. This link includes other links to sites about collectible Absolut Vodka ads, a Pepsi Cola collectors club, and a cereal box archive.

Did You Know?

The time-date stamp next to a member's eBay ID at the top of their post shows when they posted their chat message. The time is in Pacific Standard Time, or PST. You can also click the Listings link to the far right of the time-date stamp to display that member's eBay auctions.

Get answers with
DISCUSSION BOARDS

You can receive answers to your eBay questions using the Community Help Boards, located in the main Boards page, to the left of the Category-Specific Discussion Boards. These Discussion boards are a great place to post questions about any subject, from eBay auction listings to shipping, because so many helpful members reply to these boards regularly.

You can also scan these boards to see if similar questions to yours have already been asked and answered. In fact, you may want to first search a specific Discussion board for the word or words about

which you have a question, because someone has probably already asked it and the answer is on the board. For information on how to search the boards, see Task #89.

The eBay Community Help Boards are in alphabetical order, starting with Auction Listings and ending with Trust & Safety (SafeHarbor).

If you are a beginner, or have a basic question, then you may want to post your question on the New to eBay board, located under General Discussion Boards, beneath the Community Help Boards.

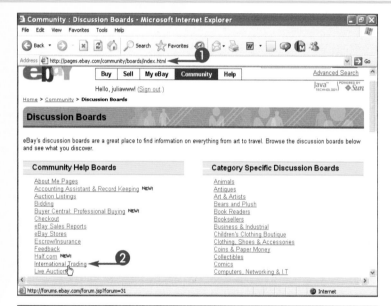

① Type **pages.ebay.com/ community/boards/index. html** into the Address bar of your Web browser, and then press Enter.

You can also click Community in the eBay home page, and then click the Discussion Boards link.

② Click a Community Help Board that is appropriate to your question.

This example uses the International Trading board link.

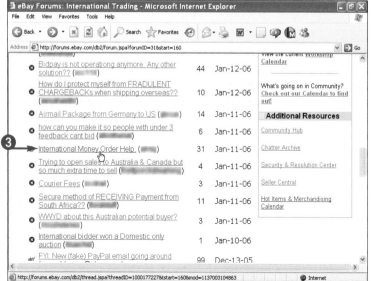

The Community Help Board page opens, with a list of topics.

③ Click an appropriate topic for your question.

You can use the navigation tools to move through the board.

Note: If an appropriate topic does not exist, then you can create one by following the steps in Task #88. For more on navigating the boards, see Task #89.

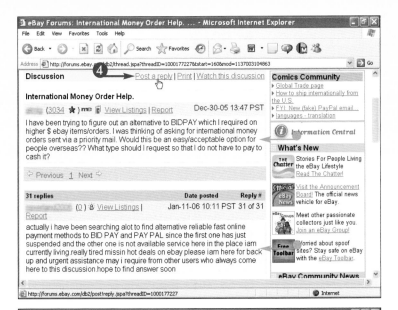

The topic appears.

- You can read the question and any answers that users have posted.

④ Click the Post a reply link.

A page opens where you can reply to the message.

⑤ Type your question or reply in the Post a reply text box.

⑥ Click Post Message.

eBay posts your message to the list of existing messages.

TIPS

eBay Savvy!

Because eBay changes its features and policies regularly, it is crucial for both sellers and buyers to keep up-to-date on these changes. You can find valuable information about changes to eBay features and policies in the eBay Community area at eBay's General Announcements Board, located at www2. ebay.com/aw/marketing.shtml. You can find updates about any technical problems that the eBay site may experience, as well as system maintenance and downtimes, at the System Announcements Board, located at www2.ebay.com/aw/announce.shtml.

Did You Know?

Several newsletters and Web sites outside of eBay report on the fast-paced auction industry and offer free information that keeps you informed about the constantly changing eBay environment. For more about outside auction communities and newsletters, see Tasks #94 and #95.

Use eBay University to
TAKE CLASSES

You can improve your eBay skills by taking a class at eBay University. eBay University offers both offline classes, which you attend in person, and online classes, which you can access from your home computer. The main eBay University page is located at http://pages.ebay.com/university/.

Online eBay University class topics include Improve your Listings with Better Descriptions and Photography, Monitor your Listings, and the Benefits of an eBay Store. Online Classes cost $19.95, and you can register for them online at http://webcast.on24.com/event/10050/launch.html.

You can sign up for offline classes at http://pages.ebay.com/university/classes.html. In the eBay University Attend Classes page, you can select from a list of cities and dates where the classes are available. Currently, eBay offers two different offline courses: Selling Basics, which includes opening a seller and PayPal account, creating listings, and setting prices; and Beyond the Basics, which covers more advanced topics, such as starting and growing an eBay business, using listing tools, and packing and shipping your inventory.

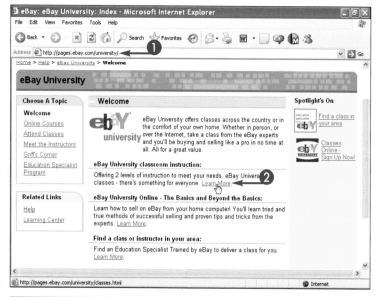

REGISTER FOR OFFLINE CLASSES

① Type **pages.ebay.com/university** into the Address bar of your Web browser, and then press Enter.

The eBay University page opens and displays the courses that it has to offer.

② Click the Learn More link for a class that interests you.

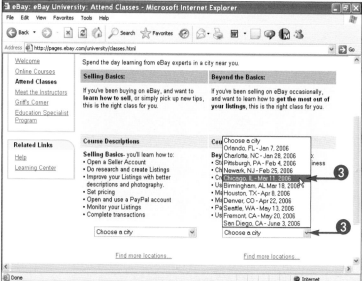

The Attend Classes page opens, displaying a description of the course that you selected.

③ Click here and select a city and date for class registration.

eBay guides you through the registration process.

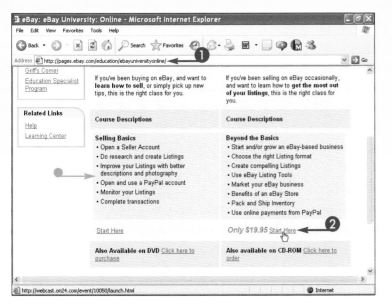

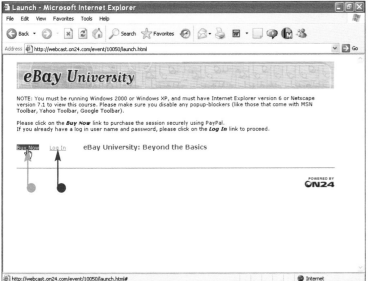

① Type **pages.ebay. com/education/ ebayuniversityonline/** into the Address bar of your Web browser, and then press Enter.

The Introducing eBay University Online! page opens.

● You can read the course descriptions.

② Choose a course and click the Start Here link.

The eBay University Registration page opens.

● You can click Buy Now to pay for the class.

● You can click Log In if you already have a login username and password.

eBay guides you through the registration process.

Did You Know?

If you have specialized knowledge, then you can host your own eBay workshop. For example, a vintage clothing merchant hosted a workshop and shared his tips for success. These tips included very specific and anecdotal examples, such as that certain plastic aprons from the 1950s sell for over $100, and that 1950s Christian Dior for Holt Renfrew dresses can sell for as much as $300 today on eBay. For more information about eBay workshops, e-mail workshopevents@ebay.com or go to http:// members.ebay.com/aboutme/workshopevents.

More Options!

You can take online classes about a wide range of eBay-related topics with eBay Workshops. eBay posts the archives of previous workshops on eBay at http://members.ebay.com/aboutme/workshopevents. Recent workshop topics include Collectibles, PayPal, Holiday Selling, and Seller's Assistant Pro Post-Sales Basics.

Network with
EBAY GROUPS

You can connect with other eBay users who share your interests or geographical location by joining an eBay Group. eBay Groups offer an excellent way to learn more about your field of interest and to get to know your fellow eBay users in a more personal community than that offered by a typical eBay Discussion Board.

People in the same eBay Group can develop their own community by using tools such as polls, photo albums, and calendars.

The eBay Groups home page allows you to view the different categories of groups that are available.

These categories include the following: Collectors Clubs, for those who share a particular collecting or selling passion such as for coins, pottery/porcelain, or stamps; Seller Groups, for different types of sellers, such as PowerSellers and Store Owners; and Regional Groups, with different groups listed by state.

You can browse the list of eBay Groups in the eBay Groups home page, located at http://groups.ebay.com. You can also search the Groups by keyword or ZIP code to find the type of group that you want to join.

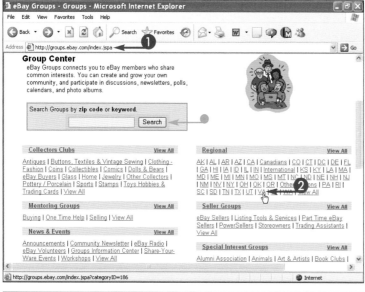

① Type **groups.ebay.com** into The Address bar of your Web browser, and then press Enter.

The eBay Group Center page opens.

● You can search the Groups by typing a ZIP code or keyword and then clicking Search.

② Click a subcategory link for a Group that interests you.

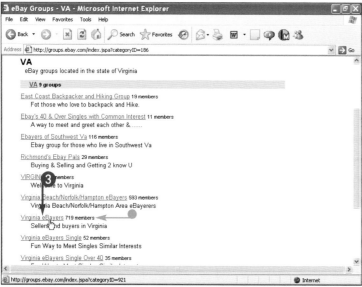

The eBay Group list appears for the category that you select.

● eBay displays the number of members that each group has.

③ Click the link for a group that interests you.

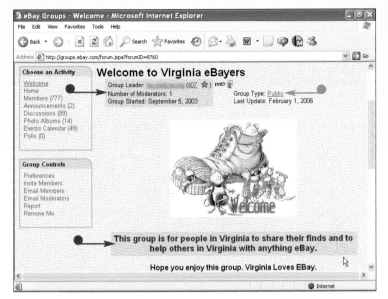

93

The eBay Groups page opens for the group that you select.

● eBay displays the Group Leader's ID and a description for the group.

● eBay displays whether the Group is public or private.

Scroll down and click Join Group at the bottom of the page.

If you have not yet logged in, then eBay prompts you to do so.

The eBay Group Discussions list appears.

● You can scroll the screen and click a discussion link to read the discussion or to post a message.

More Options!

eBay Groups can be either public or private, and are marked accordingly in the list of Groups. If you want to join a private Group, then the Group Leader can invite you to join, or you can request membership by clicking the Join Group link in that Group's page. In the screen provided, type the reason why you want to join, and click Send Request. The Group Leader contacts you if the Group grants you membership.

More Options!

For more information on participating or moderating an eBay Group, go to the eBay Groups Information Center at http://groups.ebay.com/forum.jspa?forumID=1254 and join the Group. There you can find Group Controls, such as Preferences, Invite Members, and Remove Me.

AUCTION COMMUNITIES

You can find valuable information about the sometimes-confusing array of auction tools — such as photo-hosting and listing-software services — and other auction-related topics at online communities such as AuctionBytes and the Online Traders Web Alliance, or OTWA. These sites offer information that you may not find on eBay because they discuss third-party developers as well as alternative auction sites to eBay, such as Amazon, ePier, and Yahoo.

The AuctionBytes site provides a Message Board community — where you can network and share information with other auction users — as well as

several resource tables that present information clearly. You can view the Auction Management Services at a Glance chart, which shows major auction management companies, the auction sites that they support, and their prices. You can also view a chart that compares online storefront vendors, and a table that compares various auction-site seller fees, from Amazon and eBay to Yahoo.

You must register for an account with OTWA in order to post on its boards.

For more information about message boards and networking, see Tasks #91 and #93.

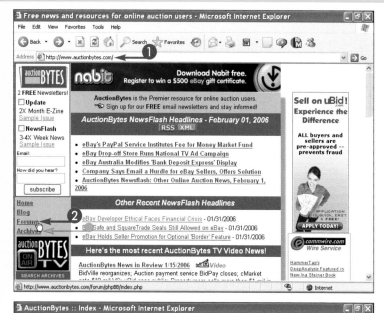

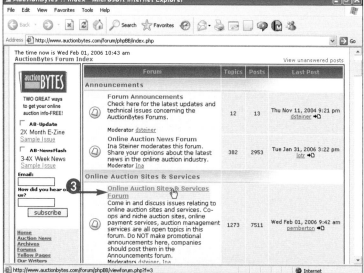

USING AUCTIONBYTES

① Type **www.auctionbytes.com** into the Address bar of your Web browser, and then press Enter.

The AuctionBytes Web site opens.

● You can click here to access archives of the AuctionBytes Update newsletters.

② Click the Forums link.

The AuctionBytes Forum Index page opens, with a list of forums.

③ Click the link of a forum that interests you.

The Forum page opens, allowing you to read and post messages.

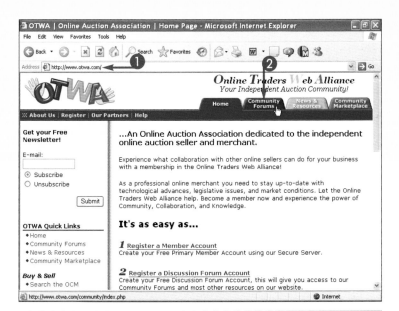

① Type **www.otwa.com** into the Address bar of your Web browser, and then press Enter.

The OTWA page opens.

② Click the Community Forums tab.

The OTWA Forums page opens.

A list of forums displays, including the Auction Sites and Services Discussion forum, the Antique and Period Furniture forum, and many more.

③ Click a Forum link.

The Forum page opens, allowing you to read and post messages, and to participate in the OTWA Community auctions.

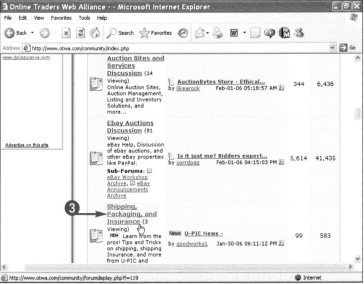

TIPS

More Options!

To post a message on the AuctionBytes boards, in the AuctionBytes home page — located at www.auctionbytes.com — click the Forums link. Select a forum and click the link. Select a topic from the list and click the topic link to open it and read the messages. Click Post Reply to respond to a message, or click the New Topic button to start a new discussion.

Success Story!

AuctionBytes has specialty collectors' forums where people share successes and tips. In one topic about collectible postcards, a user tells about selling postcards of roadside attractions from the 1950s to early 1960s for $20 to $50 each.

Stay informed with
INDUSTRY NEWSLETTERS

To keep up with the constantly changing world of online auctions, you can subscribe to some of the auction newsletters.

You can subscribe to monthly, weekly, or daily newsletters, depending on the frequency that you prefer. Auction newsletters include advice from collectibles experts, packing and shipping tips, and new features on eBay and other auction sites. Many of the newsletters focus on maximizing your profits and selling tips.

Some monthly newsletters include: The Auction Seller's Resource, at www.auction-sellers-resource.com; Auction

Gold, at www.auctionknowhow.com/AG; Cool eBay Tools at www.coolebaytools.com; and Creative eBay Selling, at www.silentsalesmachine.com.

Some weekly newsletters include AuctionBytes, at www.auctionbytes.com, and The Auction Guild's TAGnotes, at www.auctionguild.com.

For more information about online auction communities, see Task #94.

Although this example uses AuctionBytes, you can also use the steps in this task for other newsletters.

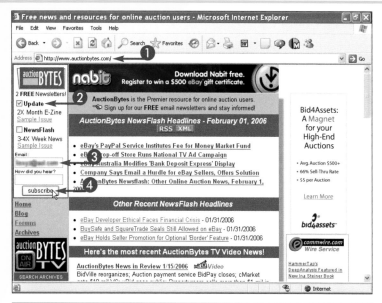

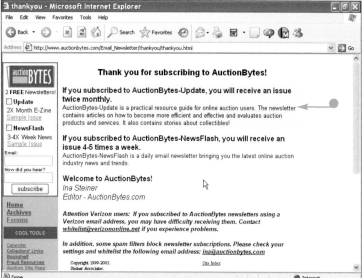

SUBSCRIBE TO A NEWSLETTER

① Type the newsletter URL into the Address bar of your Web browser, and then press Enter.

This example shows the AuctionBytes newsletters, available from the AuctionBytes home page at www.auctionbytes.com.

② In the newsletter Web site, select the options for the newsletter that you want.

③ Type your e-mail address.

④ Click subscribe.

● The Web site informs you that your subscription is active for the newsletter that you selected.

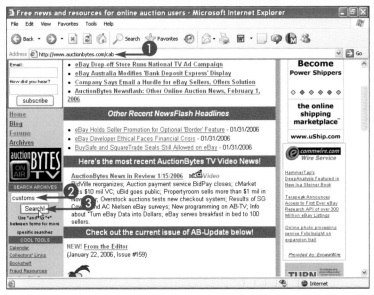

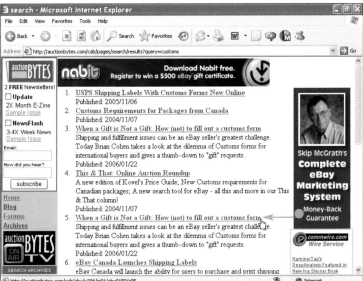

① Type **www. auctionbytes.com** into the Address bar of your Web browser, and then press Enter.

In this example, the newsletter is AuctionBytes.

The AuctionBytes Web site opens.

② Type your word or words into the Search text box.

③ Click Search.

The search results list appears.

● You can click an article link to read more about the topic.

TIPS

Did You Know?

eBay also has its own monthly general community newsletter, called The Chatter, which is available at http://pages.ebay.com/community/chatter. The Chatter includes hints, articles about notable eBay members, and profiles of eBay staff. The newsletter also offers interviews with representatives of popular collectible manufacturers, such as Precious Moments figurines and Fenton Art Glass. You can read past issues of The Chatter by clicking the Chatter Archive link, which is available at the lower-left side of the main Chatter page. For information about eBay's Category-Specific newsletters, which are available for some eBay categories, see Task #57.

More Options!

You can search the Internet for more auction-related newsletters. Try conducting a search using the Google search engine, at www.google.com, or the Yahoo directory, at http://dir.yahoo.com/ Business_and_Economy/Shopping_and_Services/ Auctions/Industry_Information.

Chapter 11

Taking Your eBay Business to the Next Level

To compete with the best sellers, you need the data and tools that enable you to present your items professionally. It helps to use the latest technology and stay on top of trends. For example, the Really Simple Syndication feature in eBay Stores offers a great opportunity for you as a seller, as does optimizing your auctions and eBay Store for search engines.

Other tools that can give you an edge include adding audio to your auctions — the sound of a human voice adds a personal touch that can translate into more sales — and colorful, professional auction templates, such as ListTrendy's.

It is crucial to find out information about your buyers, such as where they are located and how they find your listing, which you can do

with services such as Sellathon's ViewTracker. Andale's What's Hot research can save you from making costly mistakes when buying products that do not have enough buyer demand. Tools such as Terapeak's research service allow you to learn more about your competition in a given category or subcategory, such as the prices and number of bids that the top sellers receive.

When you do business in volume, seller tools that allow you to create, edit, and manage listings and pictures in bulk — such as eBay's Blackthorne — can greatly increase your efficiency. Services such as Marketblast also help to keep your records organized so that you can take on more customers. You can also automate other routine tasks such as leaving feedback and relisting.

Top 100

Determine how bidders
FIND YOUR LISTING

You can track how eBayers find your listing by using Sellathon's ViewTracker tool. For example, you can determine the search words that are most effective for your auction titles, which can improve your auctions' visibility.

You can view how eBayers navigate to your auction, such as by searching or browsing, which can help you to determine the relative importance of your item's Category placement and the words that you use in your item title and description.

You can also discover how many visitors and "watches" your item has, the visitors' location, and other information. This data can help you to make better sales and marketing decisions. For example, knowledge about the location of your visitors can help you to decide whether to offer international shipping.

ViewTracker gives you tracking code that you can easily copy and paste into your auction description when you list or revise your item. You do not need experience with HTML. You can then view tracking data about your listings on the Sellathon Web site.

To use these services, you must first register at www.sellathon.com.

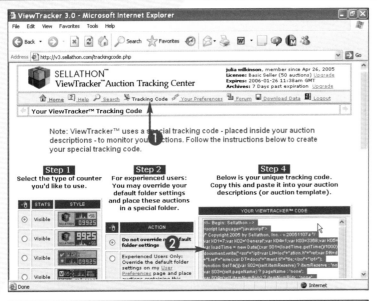

ADD VIEWTRACKER CODE TO YOUR LISTING

Login to your Sellathon account at www.sellathon.com.

① In the ViewTracker home page, click the Tracking Code link.

The Your ViewTracker Tracking Code page opens.

② Click here and press Ctrl+A to select the code, then Ctrl+C to copy it.

③ In the Revise Your Item page for the eBay listing you want to track, click Title & Description.

You can also add the tracking code during the listing process.

④ Click the Enter your own HTML tab.

⑤ Click here, and at the end of your item description, press Ctrl+V.

● The Sellathon code appears in your item description.

⑥ Click Save Changes.

eBay guides you through the rest of the revision process, and Sellathon tracks your auction.

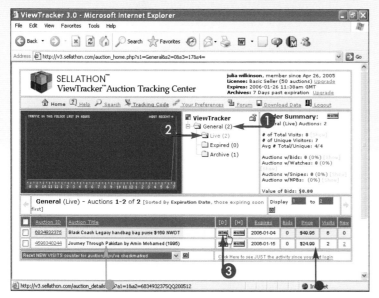

1 In the main Sellathon home page, click the General folder.

2 Click the Live folder.

● A list of your live auctions appears.

● You can view the number of bids, current price, number of visits, and number of new visits for your auction.

3 Click DETAIL.

The Details page opens.

● You can view the method of arrival for each visit.

● You can view the search terms.

● You can view how many people watch your auction.

4 Choose a visitor and click here.

● You can view the eBayer's location.

You gain valuable information about your auction viewers.

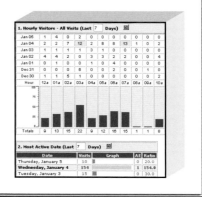

More Options!

You can view more data, such as the busiest hours of the day and night, the most active dates and days of the week, and a comparative analysis of your auction to all live auctions. In a list of Sellathon Live or Expired auctions, click the HI-LITES button next to the auction title that you want to research. A page of charts appears.

PLACE AUDIO
in your auctions

You can increase your profits and better communicate with your customers by adding sound to your auctions with a service such as SellersVoice. According to SellersVoice, you can increase profits anywhere from 20 to 300 percent using this simple tool.

When you add a voice to your auction, you add a personal touch and appeal to your potential buyer's emotions.

SellersVoice is simple to use. You simply call the phone number provided on the site and record your message. You then log in to the site at www.SellersVoice.com, and your new recording appears.

You can choose to add your audio to your eBay auction or to your Web site. You can even create an AudioPostcard.

You can choose to have your audio play automatically when your auction page opens, or to play only when a visitor chooses.

To perform this task, you must first sign up for a SellersVoice account. SellersVoice offers a three-week trial for only $1. After that, you can subscribe to SellersVoice for $29.00 each month, which includes an unlimited number of different messages and auctions each month.

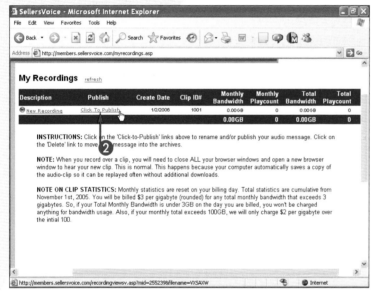

① Call the telephone number provided to record your audio message, and then log in to SellersVoice.

The My Recordings page opens.

② Click this link.

The Select a Publishing Method page opens.

③ Click the Add your Audio to your eBay Auction link.

● You can also click the Add your audio to Other Websites link or the Create an AudioPostcard link.

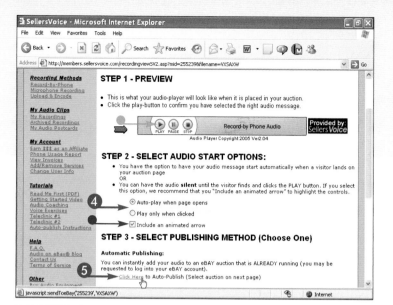

The Steps page opens.

- You can click PLAY to listen to your audio message.

④ Click to select an audio start option.

- You can select the option to include an animated arrow.

⑤ Click this link to Auto-Publish.

eBay asks you to agree to its terms and conditions.

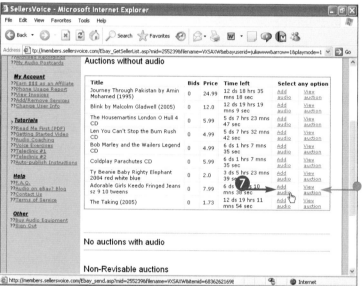

⑥ Click Agree and then click Continue.

A page opens, displaying a list of your auctions.

⑦ Select an auction and click the Add audio link.

- You can click a link here to view an auction.

Did You Know?

Your auction's viewers can click the Pause or Stop buttons if they do not want to listen to the audio message. They can also start the audio again by clicking the Play button. These buttons appear below your item description.

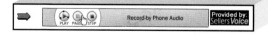

ANALYZE YOUR COMPETITION
with Terapeak

You can discover key sales statistics about your competition for a particular item or category on eBay by using Terapeak's marketplace research service, which is available at www.terapeak.com.

You can view the top sellers for any item, their rank, and their sales market share. You can also view the number of items sold, successful listings, total listings, success rate, and bids. For an item or category, you can also view the total sales, average price, number of total listings, number of total bids, and success rate statistics. This can help you to determine what kind of sales volume you can expect if you follow the best practices for that category. For example, data such as an average price can also help you to decide if an item may be profitable for you to sell.

To view the seller data, you must first sign up for Terapeak's Research Complete plan, which costs $16.95 each month. This plan includes data for three months of closed eBay listings, smart search filters, data about top sellers, a hot products list, and more.

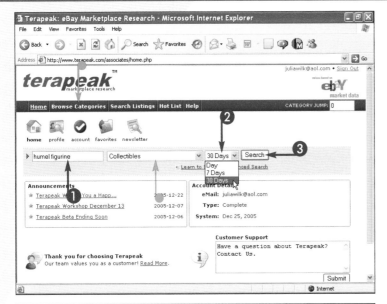

① In the Terapeak main page, type the item that you want to research in the text box.

● You can click here and select a category option.

② Click here and select a time period.

③ Click Search.

● You can also click the Browse Categories link.

Terapeak tells you that it is searching.

The Search Results page opens.

● You can view the start price, end price, number of bids, number of items sold, and end time for each listing.

④ Click End Price.

Terapeak sorts the list from the highest to lowest end price.

⑤ Click sellers.

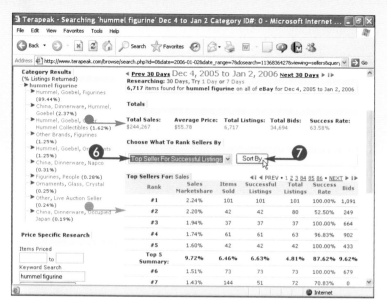

The Top Sellers page opens.

● You can view the top sellers and their statistics.

● You can view the average price, total number of listings, success rate, and other information.

6 Click here and select an option.

7 Click Sort By.

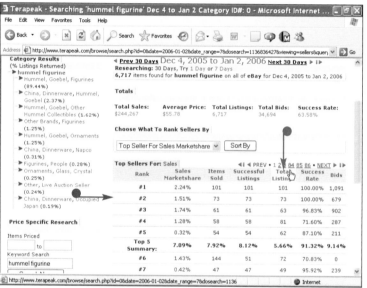

Terapeak sorts the list by the option that you selected.

● You can view the top sellers for that option.

● You can click a column heading to sort by another option.

You learn key statistics about successful sellers of your type of item.

TIP

Did You Know?

You can view which subcategories within a given category have high, low, or in-between sales by using Terapeak's color-coded list. In the Terapeak home page, simply click Browse Categories, and then click a category of your choice. Selected categories show a colored box to their left, indicating High to Low sales. Subcategories within a given category also show these color-coded boxes.

Increase your sales with
WANT IT NOW

You can discover what eBay buyers want and increase your sales by using eBay's Want It Now feature.

Want It Now is an area on eBay where buyers can post messages about items that they want, and sellers can respond to those posts with a link to an auction that they think the buyer may want. The types of items that buyers post here are usually hard-to-find items that buyers cannot find in the current auctions on the eBay site.

You can browse the categories on Want It Now and get ideas for items to sell, or you can type the name of a specific item and view any matching requests.

You can either respond to a Want It Now post with a link to one of your current auctions, or you can choose to sell your item from the link in the Want It Now post; eBay automatically responds to that post for you with a link to your new auction. There is no cost for using Want It Now.

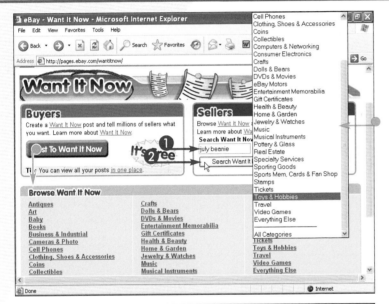

① In the main Want It Now page at http://pages.ebay.com/wantitnow, type the name of an item that you want to sell here.

● You can also click here and select a category.

● You can also click Browse Want It Now.

② Click Search Want It Now.

● If there are Want It Now posts that match your criteria, then they appear here.

● You can see if any sellers have posted a response.

③ Click the post to read it and see if you have what the eBayer wants.

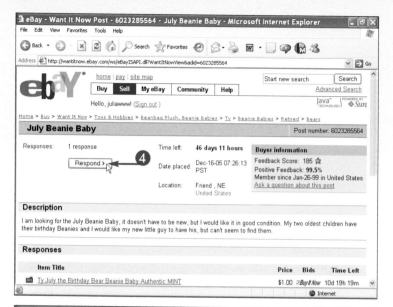

The post opens.

④ Click Respond.

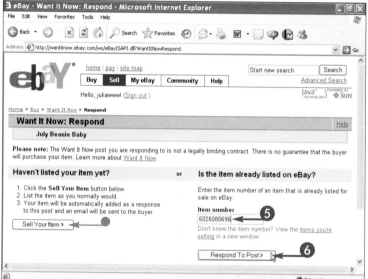

The Want It Now: Respond page opens.

⑤ Type the item number of the item that you want to offer.

⑥ Click Respond to Post.

● If you have not already listed your item, then you can click Sell Your Item, and eBay automatically adds your item as a response to the post.

eBay tells you that you have responded to a Want It Now post.

The eBayer can decide whether to bid on your item.

TIP

More Options!

You can also post to Want It Now as a buyer. In the main Want It Now page, simply click the Post to Want It Now button. The Create a Post page opens. Type a title and a short description. Select a category; if you want, you can add a picture by clicking the Browse button. Click the Post to Want It Now button.

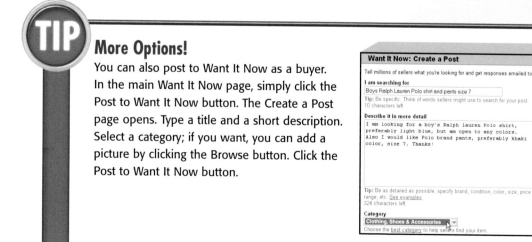

Optimize your listings for
SEARCH ENGINES

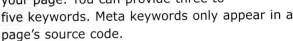

#100

DIFFICULTY LEVEL

You can add a header, meta description, and meta keywords to your eBay listings to increase the chances that search engines will display them in their results pages. A good placement in search engines can result in more people viewing your listings, and more bids. You can also submit your About Me page and eBay Store to search engines, because they contain substantive content and link to your auctions.

A meta description is 20 to 30 words that describe what the listing is about, and that search engines display below the page title in search results. Meta keywords are words that are relevant to your listing

that allow search engines to know which keywords to associate with your page. You can provide three to five keywords. Meta keywords only appear in a page's source code.

You do not need to manually submit your individual eBay listings to search engines; in fact, if you submit all of your specific listings, then the search engines may view them as spam.

For more information about search engines, see eBay's tutorial at http://pages.ebay.com/education/seo%2Dintroduction/#Meta.

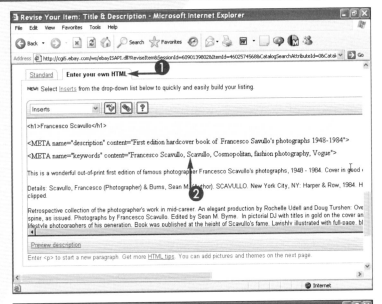

OPTIMIZE YOUR LISTING FOR SEARCH ENGINES

① In the Sell your Item: Describe Your Item page, click the Enter your own HTML tab.

② Type a header, meta description, and meta keywords tag.

③ Click Continue and finish the listing.

You have optimized your item for search engines.

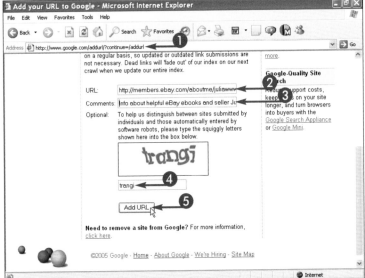

SUBMIT YOUR ABOUT ME PAGE TO GOOGLE

① Type **www.google.com/addurl/?continue=/addurl** in your Web browser.

② Type your URL.

③ Type your comments.

④ Type the letters that display in the box.

⑤ Click Add URL.

Your Web browser submits your page to Google.

Attract more buyers with
LISTINGS FEEDS/RSS

You can use Really Simple Syndication technology, or RSS, to inform your buyers about your listings. With an eBay Store, you can set up a listings "feed" to which people can subscribe and get regularly updated information about your latest product offerings. This can lead to more bids on your items.

When you set up a feed with eBay's Manage My Store feature, an RSS button appears on the lower-left side of your Store, and people can use that button to subscribe to your feed.

Your buyers can view your listings feeds with a free RSS reader or aggregator, such as bloglines, at www.bloglines.com. RSS readers allow people to subscribe to online content such as blogs, news, and your Store listings feed.

You can also select an option to make your Store listings available to third-party search engines and comparison sites such as Shopping.com.

To use the RSS/Listings feed, you must first have an eBay Store. For more information on creating an eBay Store, see Task #65.

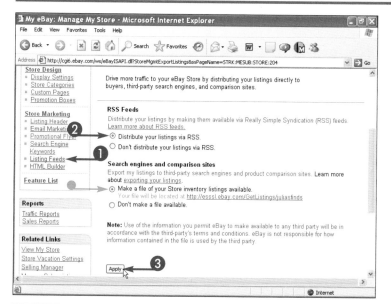

① In the Manage My Store main page, click the Listings Feeds link.

The Listings Feeds page opens.

② Click to select the Distribute your listings via RSS option.

● You can click here to make a file of your Store listings available.

③ Click Apply.

eBay distributes your listings through RSS.

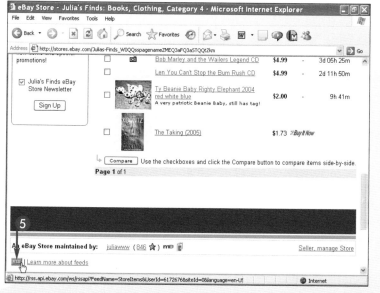

④ Click the Store icon at the top of the page.

Your eBay Store main page opens.

You may need to scroll down the page.

⑤ At the lower left, click RSS.

You now subscribe to the feed.

You can view your Store feed using an RSS news reader.

Create fast, fun auction templates with
LISTTRENDY

You can quickly and easily create auction templates with fun, colorful graphics using ListTrendy. Professional graphics can help to make your bidders confident that you are a serious seller.

ListTrendy allows you to select from a variety of graphic themes, such as sports, toys, or clothing. You can also choose from many different designs with different color schemes, and add your own graphic to a listing. ListTrendy hosts your images, and allows you to add up to 400 images for each listing.

ListTrendy makes it easy to create graphics because it numbers the steps on the bottom of the creation screen. You can add content and a short description, which appears in your eBay listing. You can even add music to your listing.

ListTrendy offers a one-month free trial. After that, ListTrendy charges are based on the number of listings that you post each month, starting from $2.50 for 10 listings, up to $250.00 for 1,000 listings.

To create templates using ListTrendy, you must download the software at ListTrendy.com.

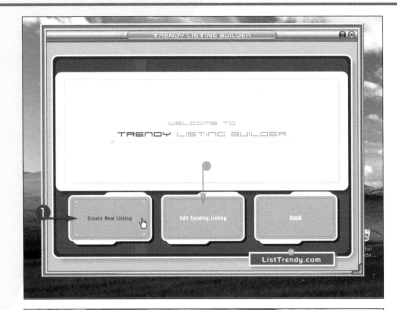

Launch ListTrendy from your desktop.

The Welcome to ListTrendy screen opens.

① Click Create New Listing.

● You can also click here to edit an existing listing.

The Trendy Listing Builder window opens.

② Click browse.

③ Select a folder and click OK.

④ Type a name for your new listing.

⑤ Click Create Listing.

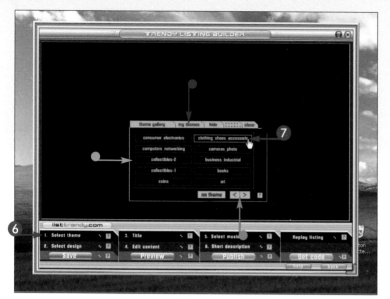

The design window opens.

6 Click Select theme.

● The theme gallery opens.

● You can upload your own graphic by clicking here.

● You can click here to scroll through the sets of themes.

7 Click a theme.

#102

The theme appears.

8 Click Save.

9 Click Select design.

10 Click a design to select it.

ListTrendy guides you through the rest of the process.

11 Click Save.

12 Click Publish.

ListTrendy creates your template.

Did You Know?

To use your template, in the main ListTrendy window, click the Get code button. A Notepad window appears, displaying the code. Press Ctrl+A to select and then Ctrl+-C to copy the code. In the eBay Describe Your Item

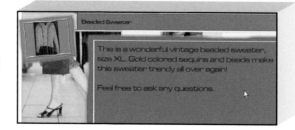

page, click the Enter your own HTML tab, and press Ctrl+V to paste your code into the text window. Complete your listing as usual. The design appears in your auction.

MONITOR BUYER DEMAND
with Andale research

You can research which items sell well on eBay, and save time and money by avoiding products that do not, with Andale's What's Hot research service. Andale's service can help you to decide which items to sell in the future and how your current listings should sell.

The main What's Hot on eBay page shows the recent top-selling items across all of eBay. You can either search for a specific item, or browse the eBay categories to find best-selling products.

When you search for a specific item, Andale shows you a list of top products, how many are listed, their

selling prices, and other information. You can narrow the results by category or average sale price.

You can also view a list of specific items that sold, their completed auction titles, price, and number of bids, so that you can determine the best way to present a similar item.

Andale's What's Hot service costs $3.95 each month. To use the service, you must first have an Andale account. For more information on researching eBay auctions, see Task #59.

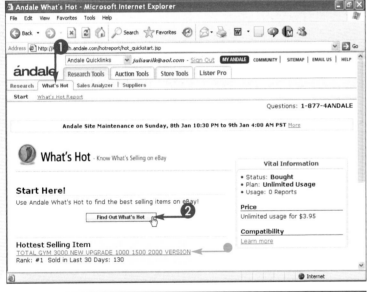

① In the main Andale Research Tools page, click What's Hot.

● You can view the hottest-selling item in the last 30 days.

② Click Find Out What's Hot.

The What's Hot on eBay page opens.

● You can see a list of hot products in all categories.

● You can browse categories for best-selling products.

③ Type the name of a product that you want to research.

④ Click Search.

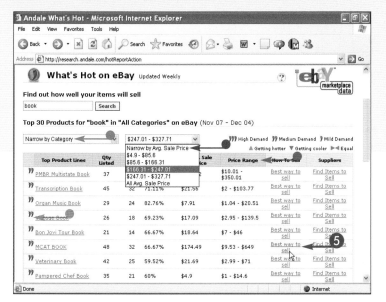

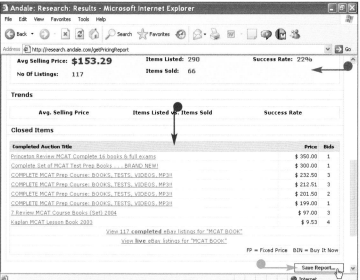

The What's Hot on eBay: Top Products page opens.

#103

● You can view which items have mild to high demand.

● You can narrow your search by category.

● You can narrow your search by average sale price.

● You can view the quantity listed, quantity sold, percent sold items, average sale price, and price range.

⑤ Click the Best way to sell link for an item.

The Price Summary page opens.

● You can view the average selling price and other information.

● You can view titles, price, and bids of a completed auction.

● You can click here to save a report.

TIP

Did You Know?

You can view a chart of an item's popularity over time. In the list of Andale's What's Hot search results, click an item title. A page opens, displaying details for that item, with charts that display how hot the item is over time, in 30-day increments. It also displays the average sale price and volume in 30-day increments.

Hotness over time

Hotness in 30 day increments

Price and Volume over time

Average Sale Price in 30 day increments

CREATE AND EDIT IN BULK
with Blackthorne

You can create multiple listings offline and submit them using Blackthorne, eBay's listing tool. Blackthorne allows you to manage all of the aspects of your listing process and photo thumbnails from one centralized area.

Formerly called Seller's Assistant, Blackthorne allows you to create part or all of your listings in stages. You can create as much of your listing as is convenient and save the rest until later. For example, you may want to upload your photos one day, and create text and submit auctions to eBay on another day. You

can view the status of your ongoing listings in the Blackthorne main page.

You can easily insert your own photos in your auctions; for certain items you can choose pre-filled information and stock photos.

Blackthorne offers two plans, Basic and Pro. Basic costs $9.99 each month, and both plans offer a free 30-day trial.

You must first sign up for Blackthorne at http://pages. ebay.com/blackthorne and then download and install the software. These examples use Blackthorne Basic.

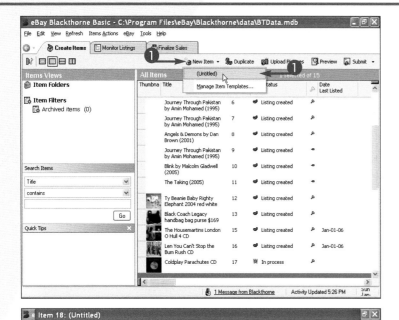

1 In the main Blackthorne Create Items page, click New Item and select (Untitled) option.

The New Item screen opens.

2 Type a title.

3 Type a description.

● You can select a theme here.

● You can select a template for your ad.

4 Click here and select a category.

5 Click here and select a picture from your hard drive.

6 Type a starting price.

● You can select a shipping option.

7 Click OK.

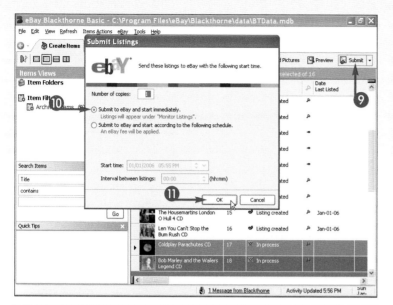

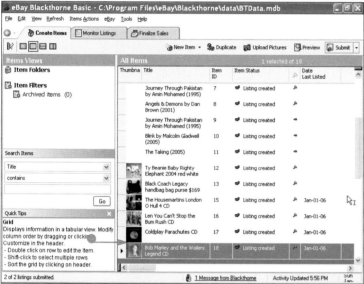

Blackthorne shows your item in the All Items list.

⑧ Create additional listings for any additional items.

You can Shift-click to select multiple items.

⑨ Click Submit.

The Submit Listings dialog box appears.

⑩ Click to select an option.

⑪ Click OK.

● Blackthorne displays the listings that you created.

You can submit multiple items to eBay at once.

TIP

More Options!

You can create a template that automatically inserts certain text in all of your listings, such as information about your return policies. In the New Item page, select the Enhanced option under Ad Template, and then click the Edit button. The Ad Template Studio opens. Type the text that you want to appear in multiple auctions or every auction, and then click OK.

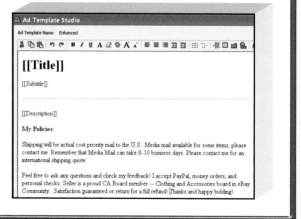

MANAGE PICTURES AND INVENTORY
with Blackthorne

You can edit multiple photographs at once and manage your product inventory more efficiently using Blackthorne Pro. Blackthorne Pro's Picture Studio optimizes your photos for eBay listings, creating better-quality photos that can boost your sales.

The Picture Studio can automatically compress and size your photographs when you load them. You can also rotate, and adjust the brightness, contrast, and scaling of multiple images at once.

You can record item quantities and specify a low inventory level number, so that you know when you need to order more products. Blackthorne also allows

you to track items' storage locations, so that you can easily find them when you need them. You can also keep track of consignments and link a consignor's information to a particular listing.

To use Blackthorne Pro, you must first have a Blackthorne account. The service, which is geared toward higher-volume sellers, costs $24.99 each month and includes other features such as free listing designer templates and support for multiple user IDs. Blackthorne offers a free 30-day trial. For information on Blackthorne Basic, see Task #104.

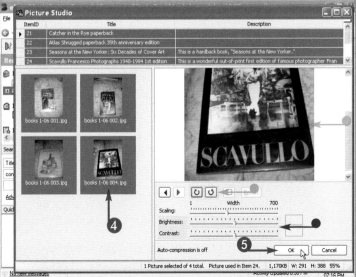

CREATE AND EDIT MULTIPLE PHOTOS

1 From the Create Items page, use your mouse to select all of the items whose pictures you want to edit.

2 Click Items Actions.

3 Click Edit Pictures.

The Picture Studio opens.

4 Click a photo.

● The photo appears.

● You can click here to rotate the photo.

● You can click and drag the sliders to adjust brightness and contrast.

5 Click OK.

Picture Studio optimizes your photos.

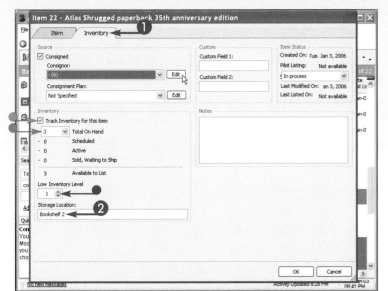

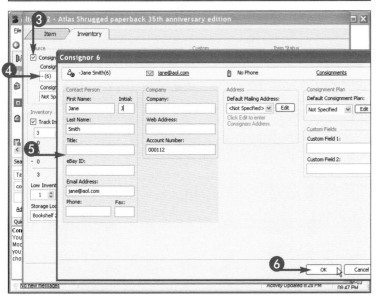

DIFFICULTY LEVEL

① From an Item page, click the Inventory tab.

● You can select the Track Inventory for this item option.

● You can click here and select a Total on Hand amount.

● You can specify a low inventory level.

② Type a location.

③ Click to select the Consigned option.

④ Click here and select New Consignor.

The New Consignor page opens.

⑤ You can type a consignor name, e-mail address, and other information.

⑥ Click OK.

⑦ Click OK in the Item page.

You can now track your inventory.

TIP

More Options!

You can monitor listings with Blackthorne Pro. In the main Blackthorne page, simply click the Monitor Listings tab. You can view the time left in the auction, the number of watchers, the number of bids, the current high bid, and other information. Blackthorne also offers tabs to finalize sales, view buyers, view and add suppliers, and view and add consignors.

FIND SUPPLIERS
with Andale

You can find suppliers for the types of products that you want to sell using Andale's Suppliers feature. Andale has a large network of manufacturers, wholesalers, and other merchants who offer many kinds of products, and this feature can save you time in locating them.

When you create a profile to specify which products you are looking for, Andale Suppliers matches you with sellers in the network. If you prefer, you can choose to only view suppliers near your location. You can also use Andale Suppliers as a Seller to find people who want to buy your merchandise.

You can choose one of two ways to generate leads: you can either make your profile available to all members of the network, or you can include a link on your eBay ads.

Andale Suppliers is free to join for Andale members with an account. An Unlimited Contacts plan is available for $3.95 each month.

For more information on how to monitor buyer demand with Andale, see Task #103.

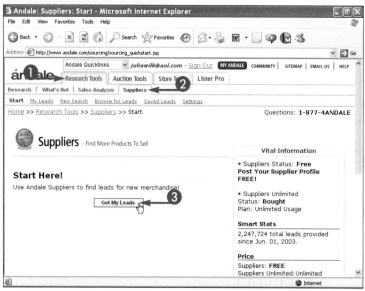

1 In the Andale main page, click the Research Tools tab.

2 Click Suppliers.

The Suppliers page opens.

3 Click Get My Leads.

The Setup Your Suppliers Profile page opens.

4 Click to select an About Me option.

5 Type your contact information.

● You can select the option to only view Suppliers members that are near your location.

6 Click Continue to Standard Form.

● You can also click Pre-fill Categories to have Andale preselect options for you.

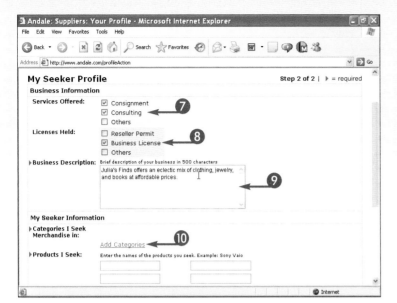

The My Seeker Profile page opens.

⑦ Click to select the Services Offered options that you want.

⑧ Click to select a Licenses Held option.

⑨ Type a business description.

⑩ Click the Add Categories link.

 # 106

DIFFICULTY LEVEL

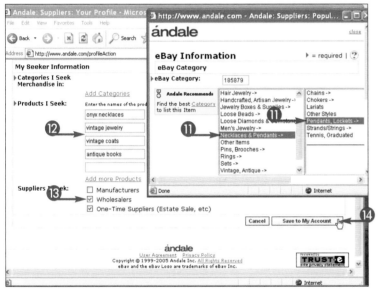

The eBay Information window opens.

⑪ Select an eBay top-level category, and then a subcategory, and click Save.

⑫ Type the names of products for which you are looking.

⑬ Click to select the types of suppliers that you want.

⑭ Click Save to My Account.

Andale matches you with suppliers as they become available.

TIPS

eBay Savvy!

A good resource to find wholesale suppliers is www.gowholesale.com. You can browse through a large selection of wholesale categories, including Drop Ship, Closeouts, and Refurbished, as well as product types such as computers, electronics, and clothing. You can also search for products, view the top searches today, participate in the forum, and view a selection of featured lots.

More Options!

You can track your leads on the Andale Web site. In the Suppliers page, click the My Leads link on the lower right. A list of your leads appears. You can also choose to receive e-mails with new leads. In the Suppliers page, click Settings, then click Email Settings, and select the "Send a weekly e-mail with my new leads" option.

AUTOMATICALLY EXTEND your auction

107

You can automatically relist your unsold and ended auctions on eBay using jayandmarie's Relister, which is available at http://ethicaltools.com. This is a useful and timesaving tool for sellers who sell multiple quantities of the same or similar items, and need to relist frequently.

You can choose to relist your items for 1, 3, 5, 7, or 10 days. You can also choose to set the listing duration for all of your items at once. Remember that if you select the 10-day listing duration, then eBay charges additional fees.

If you want to relist all of your items at once, then you can do so quickly with the Select All link. You can also use the Clear All link to delete all listings.

DIFFICULTY LEVEL

If you have a large number of ended listings and need help to find the ones that you want to relist, then you can use the Search Ended Listings feature.

Relister is available for a free trial, and costs $5.00 each month after that. To use Relister, you must first have an Ethical tools account.

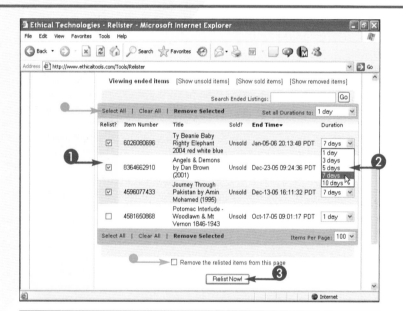

① In the Relister main screen, click to select the auctions that you want to relist.

② Click here and select a duration for each listing.

● You can select an auction and then click Remove Selected to remove the auction.

● You can click here to select all of the listings.

③ Click Relist Now!.

jayandmarie's Relister tells you that your listings have been scheduled to relist now.

● You can click here to relist more items.

Leave feedback
AUTOMATICALLY

You can leave feedback automatically with AuctionMate's feedback feature, in order to save time and increase the chances that you receive feedback. It is very important for eBayers to leave feedback, and it encourages your buyers to leave feedback for you as well. However, sellers are sometimes so busy with the other aspects of their business that they forget this critical task.

AuctionMate's feedback feature allows you to leave feedback automatically when you mark an item as paid or shipped. You can also choose not to leave automatic feedback. You can define up to five

feedback lines, and you can choose which line you want to use.

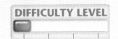

DIFFICULTY LEVEL

AuctionMate offers a free two-week trial period. After that, pricing plans start from $14.95 each month for 100MB of image-hosting space, to $99.95 each month for 1GB of image-hosting space.

To use AuctionMate's feedback tool, you must first have an AuctionMate account, which is available at www.auctionmate.com.

For information on feedback, see Task #39.

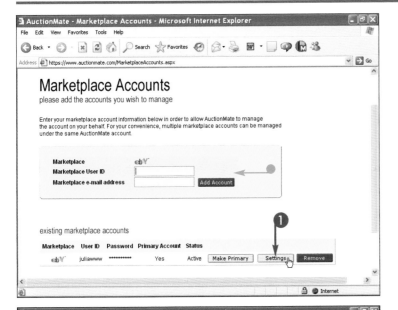

From AuctionMate's main page, click the Settings tab.

The Marketplace Accounts page opens.

You may need to scroll down the page.

● You can add an additional account.

① Click Settings.

The Customize Settings page opens.

You may need to scroll down the page.

② Type your feedback.

③ Click here and select a Feedback Line to Use option.

④ Click here and select a Leave Positive Feedback When option.

⑤ Click Save.

You now leave feedback automatically.

Manage consignments with
MARKETBLAST

You can keep track of your consignments and inventory with the Marketblast tool. Marketblast is an eBay seller management software that allows you to handle multiple tasks, from creating listings to contacting and following up with customers.

You can view your entire inventory from one screen in Marketblast, and also sort your inventory by options such as Vendor, Consignment, and Out of Stock. Marketblast can also send you a reminder when your inventory gets to a certain low number that you designate.

Marketblast enables you to create a record for each item in your inventory, which you can link to a consignment record, if necessary. When you add a new consignment record, it automatically appears in a Contacts list, so that you can easily add new consignments from your regular customers.

To use Marketblast's consignment management tool, you must first have a Marketblast account, which is available at www.marketblast.com. The cost is $99.00 each year, and a free demo is available.

For information on managing inventory with eBay's Blackthorne tool, see Task #105.

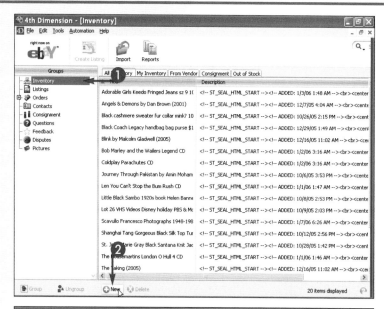

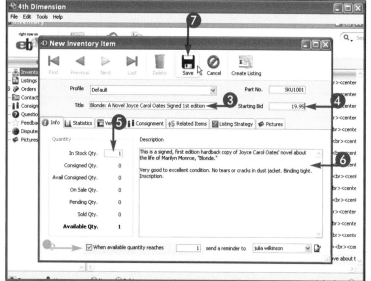

ADD AN ITEM TO YOUR INVENTORY

① From Marketblast's main page, click Inventory.

The Inventory page opens.

② Click New.

You may need to scroll down the page.

The New Inventory Item window opens.

③ Type a title.

④ Type a starting bid.

⑤ Type an in-stock quantity.

⑥ Type a description.

● You can set a low-inventory reminder.

⑦ Click Save.

The item appears in the Inventory list.

① In the main Inventory page, click an item.

The Edit Inventory window opens.

② Click the Consignment tab.

The Consignment page opens.

③ Click New.

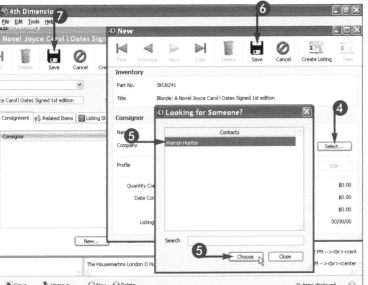

The New Consignor window opens.

④ Click Select.

Note: If you did not yet add the contact, then click Yes, and follow the prompts.

Your Contacts list appears.

⑤ Select a contact and click Choose.

⑥ Click Save.

⑦ Click Save.

You can now track your consignment.

Did You Know?

Marketblast allows you to use Flickr.com as a storage area for your images. Flickr offers up to 20MB each month for free, 2GB each month for $24.95 annually, or $47.99 for two years. You can also use your own FTP site for image storage. Marketblast can automatically upload your images to Flickr.com or whatever image server you choose, and automatically creates your image URL. It can even protect your images with custom watermarks.

Caution!

When you add an item to inventory, do not edit the Part No. field. Your inventory title does not need to be the same as the listing title, but to avoid confusion, you may want to keep them the same.

Chapter 6

Getting Better Deals with Advanced Buyer Tools

To make savvy buying decisions, it helps to use all of the tools at your disposal to navigate the millions of items that are for sale on eBay and other auction sites. These tools help you to compare products' features, and also to compare deals both within and outside of eBay.

If you often shop on eBay, then it may be difficult to keep track of all of the items on which you bid. A program like Nabit can help you to monitor your watch list items without having to repeatedly log in to My eBay.

You can easily view all of the items that are available to you, not just within eBay's regular auctions, but also within the growing collection of eBay Stores. You can use timeBLASTER to search both places at once, as well as to quickly view photo albums of the items offline, so that you do not miss out on any items.

You may want to shop outside of eBay as well. AuctionSHARK enables you to search across many auction sites, including eBay. The comparison search engine Shopping.com also allows you to easily compare features and prices of similar products.

You can read other eBay users' opinions about various products in the Reviews & Guides section, and if you write a review or guide, you can attract buyers to your own listings.

If you want to purchase an expensive item, then PayPal Buyer Credit allows you to spread out your payments over time, as well as offers purchase protection.

Top 100

MONITOR AUCTIONS
continuously from your desktop

You can view items on your eBay watch list quickly and easily from your desktop with the Nabit tool. Nabit eliminates the need to continually log in to My eBay. Also, because it automatically refreshes your watch list items and rotates their images in a slideshow format, you are less likely to forget to bid in time on the items that you want.

Nabit allows you to easily place a bid, Buy It Now, or view the entire item listing. You can also search eBay directly from the Nabit window.

You can track dozens of items at once, and you can also sort your items by the Watching, Bidding, All, or Ended categories. The "Watching" list shows auctions in order from those that end soonest. You can view the "Ending" column to see how much time is left in the auction, so that you know which items to bid on first.

You can download and install the Nabit software from the Web site, www.getnabit.com. Before you use the program for the first time, you must sign into Nabit with your eBay user id password.

PLACE A BID ON AN ITEM FROM NABIT

❶ In the Nabit main page, click Place Bid.

Note: *You must have at least one item on your watch list.*

● You can type words here and click the search button to search eBay from the Nabit window.

● You can click here to view the item listing.

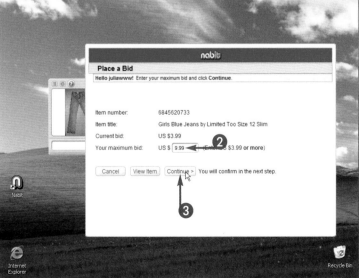

The Nabit Place a Bid screen appears in your Web browser.

Nabit prompts you to log in, if you have not already done so.

❷ Type your bid amount.

❸ Click Continue.

Nabit prompts you to Review and Confirm Bid.

You can place a bid on an item before the auction ends.

1 In the Nabit main page, click here.

DIFFICULTY LEVEL

The Nabit watch list window appears.

● You can view the current price.

● You can view how much time is left until the auction ends, or if the auction has ended.

2 Click here and select the option by which you want to sort your list.

In this example, the sort option is Watching.

Nabit sorts the list.

TIPS

Did You Know?
You can adjust the speed with which the Nabit images rotate. Click the small white circle on the bottom of the speedmeter button, and drag it to the right to increase the speed, or to the left to decrease it. You may want to use a higher speed if you have many items on your list, and a slower speed for fewer items.

More Options!
You can add items manually to your Nabit watch list. To do so, simply type the item number that you want into the text box to the left of the plus sign in the Watch List menu, and then click the plus sign button. The item appears in your Nabit Watching list.

SEARCH BOTH EBAY STORES AND AUCTION LISTINGS
at once

You can search eBay Stores listings and regular eBay auction listings simultaneously by using the latest timeBLASTER for eBay tool. Currently, if you do a search on eBay.com, eBay Stores listings are not included in the search results unless there are fewer than 20 regular auction results. Because many eBay buyers do not run a separate search in the eBay Stores section, they may miss items that they want. With timeBLASTER for eBay 6.0, you can find items

from both locations quickly and easily, and are less likely to miss finding Store items.

The timeBLASTER allows you to create searches and save the results to offline photo albums, so that you can quickly view the results. If you prefer, you can also choose to search only auctions or Store items.

When you set up the software, timeBLASTER asks for your eBay User ID and password.

For more information on timeBLASTER, see Task #10.

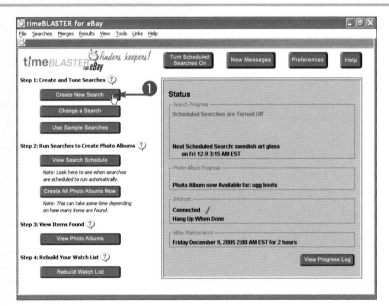

① In the timeBLASTER main page, click Create New Search.

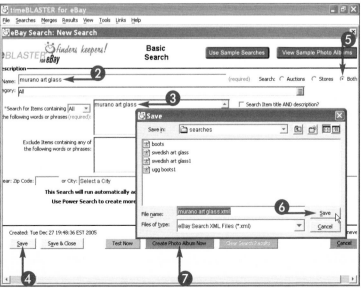

A search description window appears.

② Type a name for your search.

③ Type the items for which you are searching.

④ Click Save.

⑤ Click the Both option.

⑥ In the dialog box that appears, click Save.

⑦ Click Create Photo Album Now.

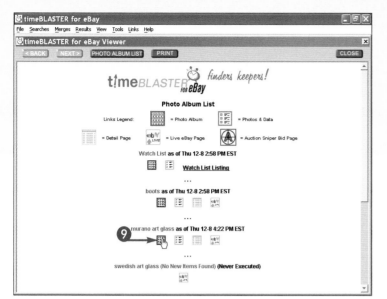

The timeBLASTER main page reappears, showing the status of the newly created search.

⑧ Click the View Photo Albums button.

The Photo Album list appears.

⑨ Click the icon of the Photo Album that you want to view.

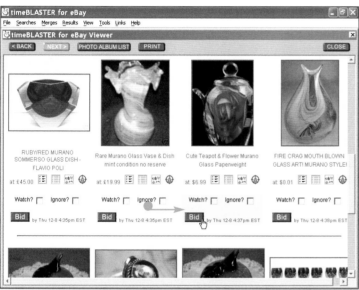

The Photo Album appears, allowing you to view photos and titles of multiple items on one page, as well as both Stores and regular auction items.

● You can click to select the Watch? or Ignore? options to either watch or ignore an item, and click the Bid button to bid on an item.

TIPS

More Options!

The timeBLASTER Test Now feature allows you to view Auction and Store search results in two separate Web browser windows. In the New Search/Search Description window, simply click the Test Now button. Two Web browser windows appear, and each window specifies in the upper-left corner whether the listings are Store or Auction results.

Did You Know?

The timeBLASTER for eBay Photo Album images reside on your computer, not on eBay, so you can view them quickly. You can also view images of all the items in your search with timeBLASTER, whether they are in the eBay Gallery or not. You can click on an image to instantly see the full-sized image provided by the seller.

SEARCH MULTIPLE AUCTION SITES
at once

You can search across multiple auction sites simultaneously by using the AuctionSHARK site, at www.auctionshark.com. This saves you time because you do not need to visit the auction sites separately. You can also compare prices from the different sites so that you can find the best deal.

In addition to eBay, AuctionSHARK allows you to search sites such as Yahoo.com, amazon.com, and Overstock.com. You can select any combination of auction sites to search, or search all of the sites. You can also choose to view the results from all of the auction sites at the same time, or to sort the results by site. For example, you can view the results from Yahoo.com in a separate list. You can also view key information such as the time left in an auction, the current bid price, or whether there is a reserve or Buy Now feature, all from the search results list.

To narrow down your search, you can use specific search words; you can also type words to exclude to further narrow down your results.

① In the main AuctionSHARK page, click Advanced Search.

② Type your search words here.

● You can type any words that you want to exclude here.

● You can select or deselect sites here.

③ Click Go.

AuctionSHARK displays a screen that tells you it is searching.

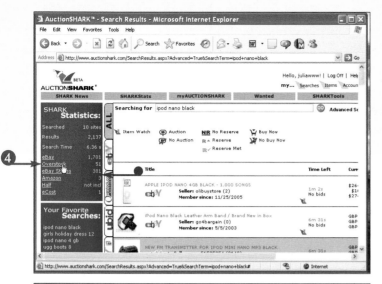

The results page appears with a list of matching items.

● AuctionSHARK displays the number of results that it finds on each site.

④ Click the site that you want to view.

This example selects Overstock.com.

112

DIFFICULTY LEVEL

The results appear for the site that you selected.

⑤ Click a listing of your choice.

You can get more information about the item.

You can place a bid on or buy the item.

TIPS

More Options!

You can create AuctionSHARK watch lists. To place an item on your watch list, click the Add to Item Watch icon (🛒) in the listing that you want to watch. Your Item Watch list appears. You can also click the "my... Items" link at the top right of the page to access your Item Watch list, or click the myAUCTIONSHARK tab at the top of the page.

Did You Know?

You can use information such as an item model number to perform a fast and efficient search. For example, when an AuctionSHARK user wanted an AC adapter for their new laptop, they typed in the laptop model number, found one quickly, and saved $20.

Get exposure and information with
EBAY REVIEWS AND GUIDES

You can get information and opinions about products from other eBay users and make better buying decisions with eBay Reviews and Guides.

Located at http://reviews.ebay.com, or by clicking the Reviews & Guides link in the main menu, reviews cover key products such as digital cameras, MP3 players, and video game systems. You can browse the reviews by category, or search directly for a specific product. Guides are short pieces of content that can be about almost any subject. Currently, eBay has guides on many topics, such as eBay shipping and Red Sox jerseys.

You can sort the search results in various ways, such as by date or most helpful.

You can also write a review or a guide, which can gain you valuable exposure and direct traffic to your listings. For example, eBay users can access your listings from a box on your guide that links to your items for sale and to your eBay Store.

If you write a review or guide about the types of products that you sell, then people who read it are more likely to view your auctions.

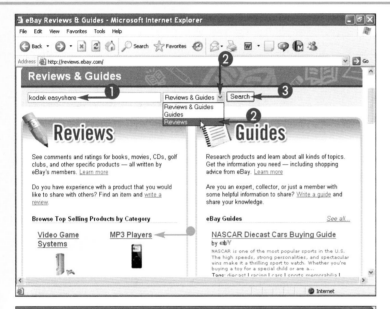

VIEW A REVIEW

1 In the main Reviews & Guides page, type the product name that you want to read about.

2 Click here and select Reviews.

3 Click Search.

● You can also browse product reviews by category.

The reviews list appears.

● You can sort the list by popularity, rating, or number of reviews.

4 Click a review.

The review appears for you to read.

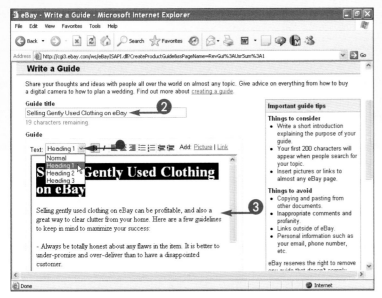

113

DIFFICULTY LEVEL

WRITE A GUIDE

1. In the main Reviews & Guides page, click the Write a guide link.

   eBay prompts you to sign in.

   The Write a Guide page appears.

2. Type your Guide title.

● You can click here and select a Heading text type.

3. Type the text of your guide.

   You may need to scroll the screen.

4. Type the text of your tags here.

5. Click Save & Continue.

   eBay prompts you to select a category for your guide.

6. Click the Submit Guide button.

   A new page appears, and eBay displays an onscreen message that you have submitted your guide.

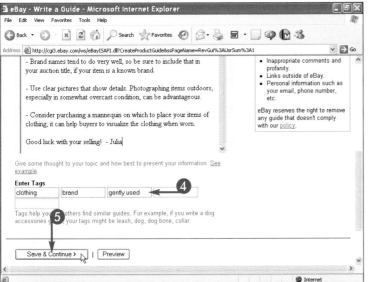

TIPS

eBay Savvy!

If you sell items on eBay, then you can get valuable exposure for your auctions when you write a review, because other members can view your auctions by accessing your reviews page. From your review, in the Member Information box in the upper right, an eBay member clicks the Store view or List view link beneath the "View items for sale by this member" heading. They can then view your regular auction or Store listings. They can also click the me icon (🖼) to go to your About Me page. From there, they can view your current listings as well as read about you and view your feedback.

Did You Know?

Search engines pick up content from the eBay Reviews & Guides page; if you write a review, then people may find your auctions from search Web sites such as Google.com. For example, if you type "artisan glass beads" into Google, then an eBay guide appears first in the search results list.

COMPARE PRICES AND PRODUCT RATINGS

with Shopping.com

You can compare products by price and ratings with Shopping.com. Shopping.com searches across many different merchant Web sites and presents you with the data that you need to make effective buying decisions.

Shopping.com allows you to select two or more items to compare side-by-side, so that you can view their ratings, price ranges, and availability right next to each other. You can also easily access the products' reviews—from Epinions.com—from the search results.

Once you choose a specific product, you can then view prices from a variety of online stores. Shopping.com displays a list of prices, which you can sort from high to low or low to high. You can view the merchants' ratings and read store reviews as well.

You can easily access the store of your choice through one button.

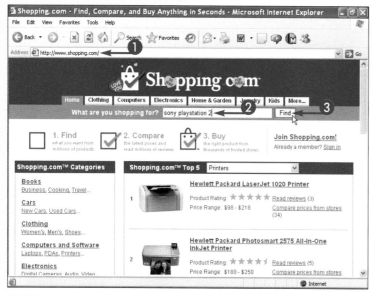

① Type **shopping.com** into the Address bar of your Web browser, and then press Enter.

The Shopping.com page appears.

② Type the name of the product that you want.

③ Click Find.

The search results list appears.

● You can view the price range for each product and how many stores carry it.

④ Click to select the products that you want to compare.

⑤ Click Compare Products.

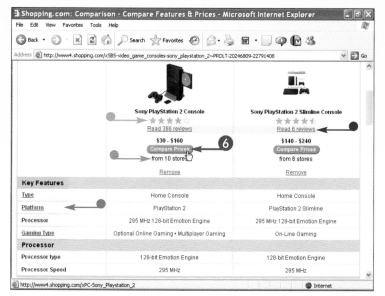

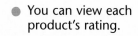

Shopping.com displays the products side-by-side.

- You can view each product's rating.

- You can view how many reviews Shopping.com has for each product.

- You can view how many stores carry each item.

- You can compare the product features.

⑥ Click Compare Prices for the product that you want.

Shopping.com displays the stores that carry the item and the price that each store offers.

- You can sort the list from low to high or high to low.

- You can click Buy It to purchase the item.

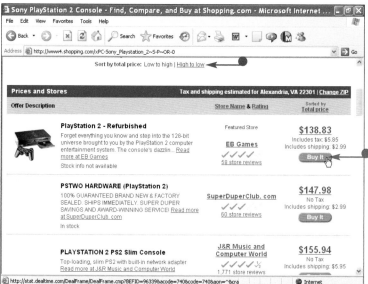

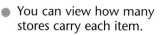

TIPS

More Options!

If you see an item that you like but do not want to buy it right away, then you can place the item on your saved list. To add an item to your saved list, click the Save it option below the item in the search results list. To view all of the items that you have saved, click "See your saved list," which appears near the top right of the Shopping.com page, under the search text box, once you have saved at least one item. You can also access the "See your saved list" link by clicking "1. Find" in the Shopping.com home page.

Did You Know?

Do you want to know what the top searches are on Shopping.com, and which products are hot? You can find out what the top 20 searches are, which products are most in demand, the top gaining searches, and more in the Shopping.com Consumer Demand Index, at www4.shopping.com/cdi.

Manage your payments with
PAYPAL BUYER CREDIT

You can increase your buying power and manage your payments over time with PayPal Buyer Credit. This allows you to buy more expensive items and spread out your payments the way you choose. Items that you buy with PayPal Buyer Credit also enjoy buyer protection from PayPal, and you are not liable for purchases made with your credit line that you did not authorize.

To obtain PayPal Buyer Credit, you must first have a PayPal account. You can then apply for buyer credit from the main page of PayPal.com. Once PayPal

approves you, PayPal automatically adds the line of credit to your PayPal account.

Many eBay buyers prefer to pay for items with PayPal, because the PayPal payment service is integrated into the eBay site. When you pay with PayPal, eBay prompts you to pay for items after you win them, which reduces the chance that you will forget to pay for the item on time.

For more information about PayPal, see Tasks #33, #34, and #35.

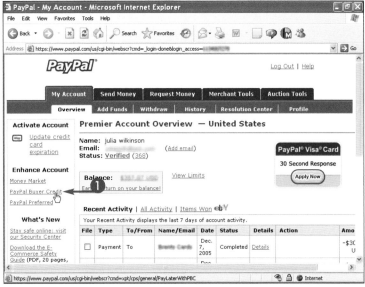

① In the PayPal main screen, at www.paypal.com, click the PayPal Buyer Credit link.

Note: *You need to log in to the PayPal site, if you have not already done so.*

The PayPal Buyer Credit page appears.

● You can view information about PayPal Buyer Credit.

② Click Apply Now.

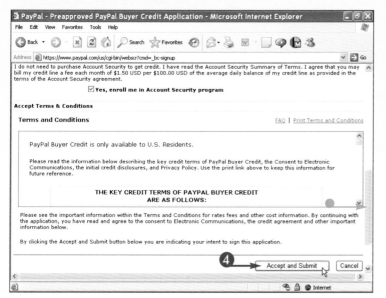

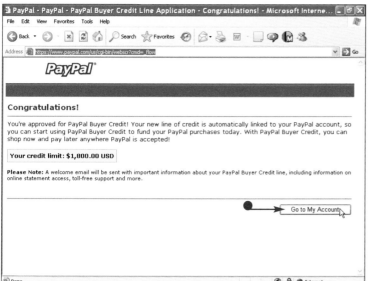

The PayPal application page appears.

● You may need to scroll the screen to see the whole application.

③ Fill out the application.

④ Click Accept and Submit.

A new page appears, informing you that you are approved, and that you can now use PayPal Buyer Credit.

● You can click Go to My Account to go to your account page.

Did You Know?

As a buyer, you do not have to pay to use PayPal; sellers pay all of the fees for PayPal transactions. PayPal's standard fee for sellers in the U.S. is 2.9 percent plus $0.30 per transaction. As a seller, if you earn at least $3,000 a month through PayPal, then you are eligible to apply for Merchant status, which reduces the percent that you pay on each transaction; rates can be as low as 1.9 percent.

eBay Savvy!

You can tell if a buyer offers PayPal as a payment option from a list of eBay search results. In the search results list, simply look for the column titled PayPal. If the PayPal icon appears in this column next to the item title, then the item's seller accepts PayPal.

Creating an Off-eBay Presence

As you grow your business, you may want to create a presence off eBay so that you can sell in multiple channels and control your marketing.

An eBay ProStore allows you to easily build an e-commerce Web site with no knowledge of HTML. Your Store has its own URL, and you can customize the Store with your own logo and welcome text, as well as choose from a variety of color schemes for its design. You can import items from eBay or your eBay Store into your ProStore, and also list items on eBay from your ProStore.

One selling channel that is especially easy to use is Half.com. Owned by eBay, Half.com is a great place to sell items that have an ISBN or UPC number, such as books and videos. You can easily list an item by entering its ISBN or UPC number, and in most cases, Half.com can

provide a stock photograph for your listing. As a result, you do not need to provide a digital image, which saves you time.

Another option that you have is to create a Store using Vendio's Store Wizard, which allows you to sell items on eBay as well as other online marketplaces such as amazon.com and yahoo.com.

Once you have your own Web presence, you can drive targeted traffic to your products by using promotional tools such as Google AdWords. You can choose multiple keywords or phrases for your ad campaign, and when people perform a Google search using these keywords, they can view your ad. You pay only when users click your ad. You can also run site-targeted ads on Web sites in the Google Network.

Top 100

Create an off-eBay presence with
EBAY'S PROSTORES

You can create an off-eBay Web site where you can extend your brand, sell your products, and gain new customers. You can also run marketing campaigns that are not subject to the restrictions of eBay auctions or Stores.

eBay's ProStores Store Setup Wizard allows you to easily create your Store with no previous knowledge of HTML. You can choose a Store theme, or color scheme, from 26 available palettes.

Your ProStore has its own URL and home page, and you can create custom welcome text, or an About Us page, that greets your customers. You can also include

a Customer Service message, as well as text about Store policies in the About Us page. You can even add a custom logo to your ProStore.

ProStores offers a free one-month trial subscription. You can choose from four different store levels — Express, Business, Advanced, or Enterprise — with monthly subscription fees of $6.95, $29.95, $74.95, and $249.95, respectively. Transaction fees are 1.5 percent for an Express Store, and 0.5 percent for all other Stores.

You must first register for a ProStore at www.prostores.com.

① In the ProStores Store Administration: Store Manager page, click the Store Setup Wizard link.

The Build your online store in 3 easy steps page opens.

● You can click this link to view the Site Wizard checklist.

② Click get started.

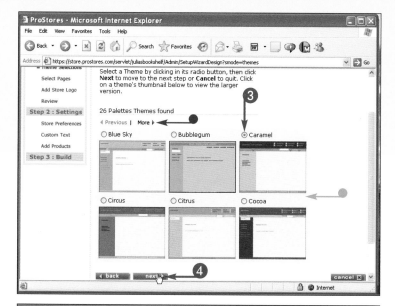

The Theme Selections page opens.

● You can view sample themes.

● You can click More to view more themes.

③ Click to select a theme.

④ Click next.

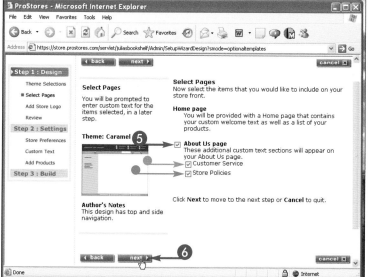

The Select Pages page opens.

⑤ Click to select the About Us page option.

● You can click to select the option to add Customer Service text.

● You can click to select the option to add Store Policies text.

⑥ Click next.

ProStores guides you through the rest of the setup process to create your off-eBay Store.

TIPS

More Options!

You can import items from eBay or your eBay Store into your ProStore. For an Express ProStore, login to your ProStores account and click Product Manager. Click the eBay Listings link. The eBay Listings Manager page opens. Click the setup link. Click the Click here to login as an existing seller or register as a new seller and obtain a token link. eBay guides you through the rest of the process. You can also list items on eBay from your ProStore. For more information on both importing and listing eBay items using your ProStore, click Support & Resources from the Control Panel of your ProStore account.

Did You Know?

Your customers can access your ProStore by using its URL. Your customers can view your logo, welcome text, and product list from your Store home page, and click links to checkout, view their cart, and view your About Us page. For more information on what you can do with your Store, see www.prostores.com/prostores-whyopen.shtml and click the interactive tour link.

Boost your off-eBay sales with
GOOGLE ADWORDS

You can get new customers for your eBay Store, ProStore, or other e-commerce Web site using Google's online ads program, AdWords. Google Adwords allows you to drive specifically targeted traffic to your Store or Web site by choosing keywords, which are words and phrases that are related to your product, to trigger the ads.

You can create one or more ad campaigns, each with its own Ad Group. You can choose either a *keyword-targeted* or *site-targeted* campaign. Keyword-targeted ads appear when users search with your chosen keyword. Site-targeted ads appear when users visit any Google Network site — including Google partners such as Ask.com, Gmail, and Shopping.com — with content that matches your keywords.

The frequency and placement of your ad on the Web browser page is determined by factors such as how many keywords you specify and your daily budget.

To use Google AdWords, you must first create a Google account. Google charges $5 to set up an AdWords account, and you must present a credit card.

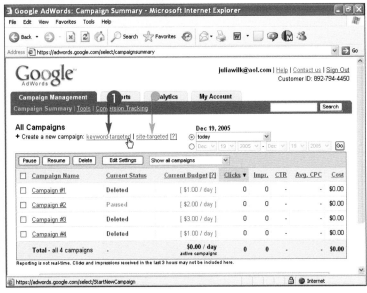

① In the Campaign Management main page, click the keyword-targeted link.

● You can also choose a site-targeted campaign.

The New Campaign Setup page opens.

② Type a campaign name.

③ Type an Ad Group name.

④ Select a customer language option.

⑤ Scroll down and select a customer location option.

⑥ Click Continue.

The Target customers by country or territory page opens.

⑦ Select the countries or territories that you want to target, and click Add.

⑧ Click Continue.

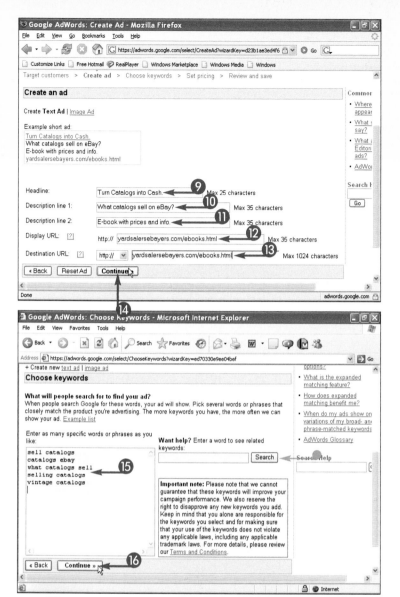

The Create an ad page opens.

⑨ Type a headline.

⑩ Type a description of your product or service.

⑪ Type a second description.

⑫ Type your display URL.

⑬ Type your destination URL.

⑭ Click Continue.

⌗117

The Choose keywords page opens.

● You can type related keywords here and click Search to view them.

⑮ Type the keywords for your ad.

⑯ Click Continue.

Google guides you through the rest of the process and places your ads.

Did You Know?

You can control how much you spend; your daily budget can be anywhere from 1 cent ($0.01) to however much you are comfortable spending. You can choose a maximum *cost-per-click,* or CPC, from $0.01 to $100. If your chosen keyword has a minimum, your maximum cost-per-click must be at least that much to show in the Google search results. You pay only when someone clicks your keyword-targeted AdWords ads, or for impressions on your site-targeted AdWords ads. Site-targeted ads require a minimum CPM — cost per thousand — price of $0.25 for each 1,000 impressions.

Caution!

Make sure that you set a daily budget that you can afford. You can check your campaign and ad effectiveness by clicking the Reports tab in the main Campaign Management page to view which ads are the most effective. You can then delete keywords that do not result in enough click-throughs.

Expand your sales to
HALF.COM

You can sell items such as new and used books, movies, CDs, games, and game systems quickly and easily with eBay's alternative marketplace, Half.com.

You do not need to upload a photo of your item to sell on Half.com, because Half.com provides stock photographs of most items, which makes the listing process very simple. Also, because you can choose from a list of pre-set item condition options, you only need to type a short description of your item, along with an optional longer description.

Selling on Half.com is easy; all you need to do is enter the ISBN or UPC number of your item, and Half.com fills in much of the information for you from a database. Half.com even prompts you with a suggested sales price, and information about how much your item last sold for on the site, so that you can easily determine a price.

To sell on Half.com, you must either have an existing eBay account, or sign up separately for a Half.com seller account.

In the Half.com main page at www.half.ebay.com, click Sell Your Stuff.

The Sell your items on Half.com page opens.

1 Type the ISBN, UPC, or Manufacturer Part Number.

2 Click Continue.

● You can also select a category such as Books, Movies/DVDs, or Music.

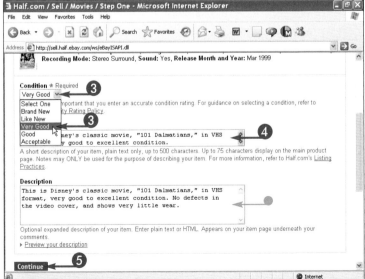

The Sell Your Item: Describe your item page opens.

3 Click here and select a Condition option.

4 Type a short description of the item.

● You can type an optional description.

5 Click Continue.

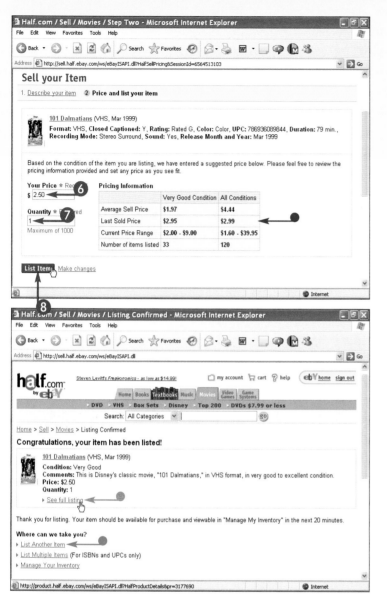

The Price and list your item page opens.

6 Type a price for your item.

Half.com prompts you with a suggested price.

● You can view the average selling price, last sold price, current price range, and the number of the same items that are currently listed.

7 Type a quantity for your item.

8 Click List Item.

Half.com tells you your item has been listed.

● You can click the See full listing link to view the entire listing.

● If you want to list another item, then you can click the List Another Item link.

TIPS

Did You Know?

The ISBN or UPC number is usually located above or below the barcode on an item. Books have an ISBN number, which sometimes ends in an x; you need to type the x with the rest of the number. You should type the UPC number for all items other than books. Although some movies, CDs, and other non-book products include an ISBN as well as a UPC number, you should not type the ISBN number to sell the item. Be sure to include any smaller numbers that may appear to the right or left of the UPC's main barcode numbers.

eBay Savvy!

You can list multiple items at once. From the main Half.com Sell your items page, simply click the Multiple Item Listing page link.

Create your own store with
VENDIO

You can sell directly from a customized Store that works with many automated selling features by using Vendio, a third-party auction service provider. Vendio's interface allows you to sell items directly from a Web site, as well as through eBay and other online selling sites, such as amazon.com and yahoo.com, or any combination thereof. Vendio also sends daily information about all of the available Store items to Froogle.com, Google's shopping engine.

Vendio Store prices start with the Bronze Plan at $4.95 each month, plus 1 percent of the items' final

values. However, the maximum final value fee that you pay for each item sold is $4.95. For example, if you sell an item for $1,000, then you pay a fee of $4.95, rather than $10, which is 1 percent of $1,000.

The Vendio Store Gold Plan costs $14.95 each month, plus $0.10 for each sold item. For each pricing plan, you can list an unlimited number of items.

To set up a store, you first need to register at www.vendio.com. For more information about Stores, see Tasks #65 and #116.

In the Welcome to Vendio's Store! page, click Launch Store Wizard.

The Vendio Store Wizard page appears.

① Click Begin.

When Vendio prompts you, type your name, address, and e-mail, and then click Next.

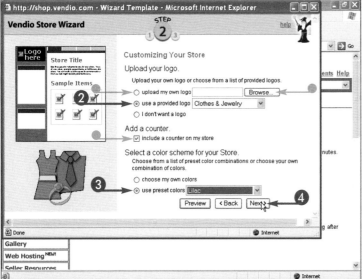

The Customizing Your Store page appears.

② Click to select an upload option for your logo.

● You can select this option and click Browse to locate and upload your own logo.

● You can specify whether you want a counter.

③ Select a color scheme option and then choose a color.

④ Click Next.

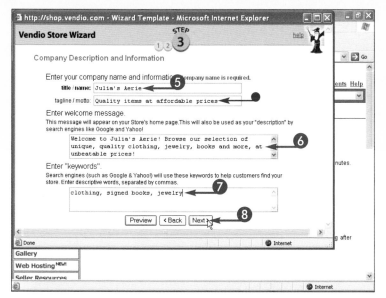

The Company Description and Information page appears.

⑤ Type a Store name.

● You can type a store tagline.

⑥ Type a store welcome message.

⑦ Type keywords for search engines.

⑧ Click Next.

119

DIFFICULTY LEVEL

The Vendio Store Wizard guides you through the rest of the signup process.

Vendio creates your Store.

TIPS

More Options!

To list items on eBay from your Vendio Store, you must sign up for Vendio's Sales Manager. Sales Manager speeds up your listing process by saving your shipping, payment, and marketplace preferences, allowing your buyers to calculate their shipping fees, and managing many post-sale tasks. To sign up, go to www.vendio. com/tours/sm/index.html, and click FREE TRIAL. The cost ranges from $12.95 each month plus a $0.20 listing fee and 1 percent final value fee, to $39.95 each month plus a $0.10 listing fee. Vendio also offers a pay-as-you-go plan for $.10 for each listing plus 1 percent final value fee.

More Options!

Vendio also offers a tool called Customer Manager that helps you to manage customer e-mails. For more information, see www.vendio.com/my/cm/promo_cm.html.

Create a
CUSTOMER MAILING LIST

You can create a mailing list for your eBay Store to boost your sales and to keep your buyers informed about your merchandise.

You can create up to five mailing lists for different products or promotions. For example, you can create one newsletter about CDs, another about books, and a third newsletter about Store sales.

eBay allows you a certain number of free monthly e-mails. The number depends on your Store subscription level. If you have a Basic Store, then you are allowed 100 free e-mails; a Featured Store

is allowed 1,000 free e-mails; and an Anchor Store is allowed 4,000 free e-mails. If you exceed your quota, then you pay $0.01 for each extra e-mail.

You can view how many subscribers you have and the lists of your subscribers through the "Total Subscribers" link in the Email Marketing page, available in the left-hand navigation area in the main Manage My Store page.

To create a customer mailing list, you must first have an eBay Store. For more information on creating an eBay Store, see Task #65.

① In the main Manage My Store page for your eBay Store, click Email Marketing.

The Email Marketing page opens.

② Click Create Mailing List.

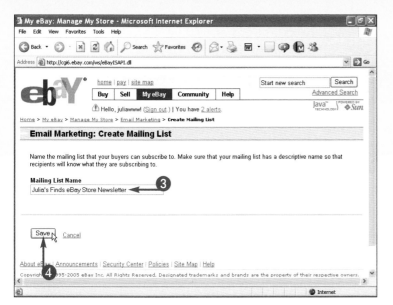

The Email Marketing: Create Mailing List page opens.

③ Type a Mailing List Name here.

④ Click Save.

DIFFICULTY LEVEL

● The Email Marketing: Mailing Lists page reappears and displays your Mailing List name.

● You can click here to create e-mails to send to your list.

● You can click here to view your subscriber list.

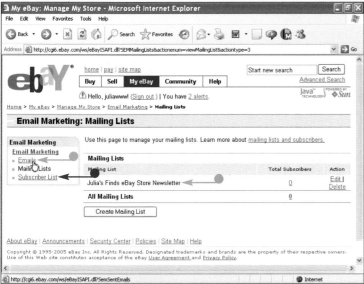

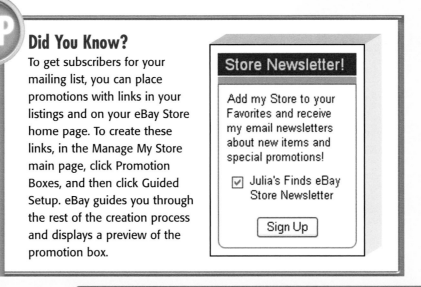

Did You Know?

To get subscribers for your mailing list, you can place promotions with links in your listings and on your eBay Store home page. To create these links, in the Manage My Store main page, click Promotion Boxes, and then click Guided Setup. eBay guides you through the rest of the creation process and displays a preview of the promotion box.

Store Newsletter!

Add my Store to your Favorites and receive my email newsletters about new items and special promotions!

☑ Julia's Finds eBay Store Newsletter

Sign Up

Index

Index

desktop, 40–41, 228–229
Discuss eBay's Newest Features, chat room, 188
Discussion Board page, category listings, 185
discussion boards
    category scanning, 184–187
    Community Help Boards, 190–191
    eBay staff highlights, 185
    Feedback, 85
    games/contests, 187
    General Announcements Board, 191
    keyword search, 187
    lurking before posting, 184
    message posting, 185
    navigation techniques, 186–187
    packing supply resource, 177
    searches, 190–191
    topic display, 186–187
Dutch (multiple item) auction, 60–61, 94

E

eBay
    buyer protection limits, 81
    Help Center, 25
    insertion fee brackets, 96
    international sites, 39
    Prohibited and Restricted Items list, 90
    seller tips, 113
    Seller's Edge articles, 113
    site map navigation, 24–25
    top-level exposure techniques, 146–147
    Turbo Lister, 114–117
    VeRO (Verified Rights Owner) program, 88–89
eBay Advertising Collectibles, chat room, 189
eBay Café, chat room, 188
eBay Community page, 142–143, 184–189
eBay Enhanced Picture Services, slideshows, 124–125
eBay Giving Works page, bidding process, 66–67
eBay Glossary, Contact Us link, 25
eBay Groups, joining, 194–195
eBay Motors, bid process, 62–63
eBay Policies page, Prohibited and Restricted Items list, 90
eBay ProStore, 242–243
eBay Q&A Board, chat room, 188
eBay Real Estate, bid process, 64–65
eBay Reviews and Guides, buyer tool, 234–235
eBay Store
    account setup, 132–133
    Anchor Stores, 133
    Basic Store, 133
    cross-promotion techniques, 134–137
    customer mailing lists, 250–251
    description information, 133
    Featured Stores, 133
    ID-verified requirement, 132
    item management, 134–135
    logos, 133
    Merchandising Manager, 136–137
    packing supply resource, 176–177
    PayPal account requirement, 132
    promotions, 133
    RSS (Really Simple Syndication) feeds, 211
    searches, 230–231
    themes, 132
    vacation settings, 135
eBay Toolbar, buying alerts, 40–41
eBay University, auction classes, 192–193
eBay workshops, hosting, 193
eBay's Marketplace Research, fees, 17
e-commerce, 242–249
Editor toolbar, HTML editing, 130–131
electronic transfers, PayPal, 74–77
e-mail
    Auction Sniper, 55
    eBay workshops, 193
    My Favorite Search, 18–19
    RSS (Really Simple Syndication) feeds, 211
    seller questions, 30–31
    Vendio's Customer Manager, 249
    watch list reminders, 29
e-mail addresses, 11, 73
Email Marketing page, customer mailing lists, 250–251
Enter Pictures & Item Details page, terms of sale, 163
Enterprise, eBay ProStore level, 242
Epinions.com, product comparisons, 236
escrow services, 63, 78–79
escrow.com, account setup, 78–79
eSnipe, sniping service, 55
Even if not the high bidder, Items by Bidder page parameter, 10
Exclude these words, Advanced Search parameters, 6
Express, eBay ProStore level, 242
EZsniper, sniping service, 55

F

Favorite Seller, My eBay addition, 37
favorites, seller/store, 19
Featured Auction listing, guidelines, 150–151
Featured Plus! auctions, guidelines, 150–151
Featured Stores, fees, 133
Federal Express, shipping service, 47, 181
feedback
    automatic feedback services, 223
    goodwill enhancement, 84–85
    Home Page Featured auction requirements, 151
    member comments, 32–33
    negative feedback removal, 83, 85
    retaliatory avoidance, 81
    second-chance offers, 103
Feedback discussion board, feedback discussions, 85
Feedback Forum, positive feedback benefits, 84–85
fees
    Anchor Stores, 133
    Andale Gallery, 154
    Andale Suppliers, 220
    Andale's What's Hot service, 214
    AuctionMate feedback services, 223
    Blackthorne, 216
    Blackthorne Pro, 218
    bold/highlight enhancements, 148, 149
    Buy It Now auction, 92
    campaign ads, 140
    CPC (cost-per-click), 245
    customer mailing lists, 250
    delivery confirmation, 172
    eBay home page link, 147

Index

Index

Index